Providing for
the Poor

 New Historical PERSPECTIVES

New Historical Perspectives is a book series for early career scholars within the UK and the Republic of Ireland. Books in the series are overseen by an expert editorial board to ensure the highest standards of peer-reviewed scholarship. Commissioning and editing is undertaken by the Royal Historical Society, and the series is published under the imprint of the Institute of Historical Research by the University of London Press.

The series is supported by the Economic History Society and the Past and Present Society.

Series co-editors: Professor Elizabeth Hurren (University of Leicester) and Professor Heather Shore (Manchester Metropolitan University)

Founding co-editors: Simon Newman (University of Glasgow) and Penny Summerfield (University of Manchester)

New Historical Perspectives Editorial Board

Professor Charlotte Alston	Northumbria University
Professor David Andress	University of Portsmouth
Dr Christopher Bahl	Durham University
Dr Milinda Banerjee	University of St Andrews
Dr Robert Barnes	York St John University
Dr Karin Bowie	University of Glasgow
Professor Catherine Clarke	Institute of Historical Research, University of London
Professor Neil Fleming	University of Worcester
Professor Ian Forrest	University of Oxford
Dr Emma Gallon	University of London Press
Professor Leigh Gardner	London School of Economics
Dr Sarah Longhair	University of Lincoln
Dr Charlotte Wildman	University of Manchester
Dr Nick Witham	University College London

Providing for the Poor

The Old Poor Law,
1750–1834

Edited by
Peter Collinge and Louise Falcini

LONDON
ROYAL HISTORICAL SOCIETY
INSTITUTE OF HISTORICAL RESEARCH
UNIVERSITY OF LONDON PRESS

Published by
UNIVERSITY OF LONDON PRESS
SCHOOL OF ADVANCED STUDY
INSTITUTE OF HISTORICAL RESEARCH
Senate House, Malet Street, London WC1E 7HY

© The authors 2022

The authors have asserted their right under the Copyright, Designs and Patents Act 1988 to be identified as the authors of this work.

This book is published under a Creative Commons Attribution-NonCommercial-NoDerivatives 4.0 International (CC BY-NC-ND 4.0) licence. More information regarding CC licences is available at https://creativecommons.org/licenses.

Copyright and permissions for the reuse of many of the images included in this publication differ from the above. Copyright and permissions information is provided alongside each image.

Available to download free or to purchase the hard copy edition at https://www.sas.ac.uk/publications.

ISBNs
978-1-914477-11-9 (paperback edition)
978-1-914477-10-2 (hardback edition)
978-1-914477-12-6 (.epub edition)
978-1-914477-13-3 (.mobi edition)
978-1-914477-14-0 (.pdf edition)

DOI 10.14296/npin8958

Cover image: Detail from Thomas Rowlandson, *A Select Vestry* (1806), The Elisha Whittelsey Collection, Acc. No: 59.533.959, Metropolitan Museum of Art, New York.

Contents

List of illustrations	vii
List of tables	viii
List of abbreviations	ix
Acknowledgements	xi
Notes on contributors	xiii
Preface: The Small Bills and Petty Finance project *Peter Collinge and Louise Falcini*	xv
Introduction: The Old Poor Law *Peter Collinge and Louise Falcini*	1

I. Paupers and vagrants

1.	Accounting for illegitimacy: parish politics and the poor *Louise Falcini*	25
	Interlude 1: Thomas Woolgar, the mystery man *Jean Irvin*	50
2.	Clothing the poor *Elizabeth Spencer*	53
	Interlude 2: Elizabeth Overing, sent to Bedlam *Elizabeth Hughes*	80
3.	Vagrancy, poor relief and the parish *Tim Hitchcock*	83
	Interlude 3: Elizabeth Malbon (*c.*1743–1801) *Dianne Shenton*	103

II. Providers and enablers and their critics

4.	Women, business and the Old Poor Law *Peter Collinge*	107
	Interlude 4: The Wilkinsons and the Griffin Inn, Penrith *Margaret Dean*	133

5. The overseers' assistant: taking a parish salary, 1800–1834 137
   Alannah Tomkins

   Interlude 5: The parochial career of James Finlinson (1783–1847) 164
   William Bundred

6. Who cares? Mismanagement, neglect and suffering in the
   final decades of the Old Poor Laws 167
   Samantha A. Shave

   Interlude 6: Abel Rooker (1787–1867), surgeon 194
   Janet Kisz

III. Public histories

7. Public histories and collaborative working 199
   Louise Falcini and Peter Collinge

   Conclusion 219
   Alannah Tomkins

   Index 227

List of illustrations

2.1	Detail of a bill for material supplied by Joshua Harrison, 1776	63
2.2	Margaret Fenton's bill for making gowns, frocks and stays, 26 April [1823]	71
2.3	Coarse linen stays, 1760–80	74
3.1	Settlement data recorded by Henry Adams, 1777–86	95
3.2	The origin of vagrants, 1777–86: moderated by population	95
3.3	Sussex vagrants, 1820–3.	99
3.4	Distribution of vagrants by county, 1820–3	99
3.5	Distribution of vagrants, 1777–86 and 1820–3	100
3.6	Expenditure per vagrant by county, 1820–3	100
3.7	Extract of an overseers' voucher for Wednesbury, Staffordshire, showing ale for E. Malbourn's funeral, 1801	104
4.1	Pre-printed bill for expenses at the Griffin Inn, Penrith, submitted to the overseers of Threlkeld, c.1800	133
5.1	Advertisement for an Assistant Overseer, Greystoke, 1835	149
5.2	Advertisement for a Master and Mistress of St Mary's Workhouse, Carlisle, 1785	149
6.1	John Rutter's observations of two poorhouses in Shaftesbury, 1819	180
6.2	Payment to Abel Rooker for half a year's contract for Darlaston Workhouse, Staffordshire, 1822	195

List of tables

0.1	Numbers in receipt of outdoor relief in Wednesbury, 1770–96	14
1.1	East Hoathly's biannual poor rate, 1757–69	40
2.1	Fabrics and prices across 240 overseers' vouchers, Cumberland, 1770–1837	61
2.2	Fabrics and prices across 65 overseers' vouchers, Wigton, Cumberland, 1770–8	63
2.3	Fabrics and prices across 164 overseers' vouchers, Staffordshire, 1769–1831	64
2.4	Fabrics and prices across 90 overseers' vouchers, Wednesbury, Staffordshire, 1778–1801	65
3.1	Demographic distribution of vagrants removed via Middlesex, 1777–86	93
4.1	Cost of poor relief in Brampton and Lichfield, 1803	111
4.2	Business owners in Brampton and Lichfield in Pigot's *National Commercial Directory for 1828–9*	112
5.1	Assistant overseers appointed to selected parishes in Cumbria, Staffordshire and Sussex after 1800	155

List of abbreviations

CAS   Cumbria Archive Service
DCRO   Durham County Record Office
DHC   Dorset History Centre
ESRO   East Sussex Record Office
SRO   Staffordshire Record Office
TNA   The National Archives
VCH   *Victoria County History*

Acknowledgements

The production of *Providing for the Poor* has been made possible through the support and interest shown by many colleagues, friends and organizations. It emerged out of the research conducted during the project 'Small Bills and Petty Finance: Co-creating the History of the Old Poor Law'. At the pilot stage in Staffordshire, this was funded by Keele University's Impact Acceleration Fund and the Jack Leighton Trust. The expansion of the project to include the counties of Cumbria and East Sussex was made possible through generous funding from the Arts and Humanities Research Council.

Archivists and search-room staff in record offices and libraries in Brighton, Carlisle, Kendal and Stafford gave generously of their time and assistance and granted permission to reproduce images from items in their collections. Particular thanks go to Matthew Blake in Staffordshire; to Robert Baxter, Louise Smith, Michael Stephens, Sarah Wood and Andrew Wright in Cumbria; and to Elizabeth Hughes and Christopher Whittick, who supported and enabled the project in East Sussex.

Several of the chapters began life as conference and study day presentations in Amsterdam, Derby, Edinburgh, Keele, Leiden, Oxford, Vancouver, York and Zurich and benefited from the questions and discussions they generated. Thanks are due to Joe Harley and Peter Jones who, along with Elizabeth Spencer, collaborated in our project workshops and augmented our sense of what it is possible to achieve with overseers' vouchers.

Thanks are also due to the anonymous reviewers for their constructive comments. Steven King produced a detailed report on the draft of *Providing for the Poor* and, along with Heather Shore, ran a workshop for the editors of the volume. Their timely advice has been invaluable.

We are grateful to our publishers, the Royal Historical Society and the University of London Press.

Ben Jackson of Sussex Humanities Lab provided valuable research and technical development for the 'Small Bills' data capture platform and associated mobile phone app, while Kelcey Swain of Larchwood Research created the project website.

The 'Small Bills' project and this book have benefited enormously from the dedication, enthusiasm and research skills of the volunteers:
- in Cumbria: Anita Bamforth, Beth Banks, Ellie Berry, Chris Brady,

William Bundred, Angie Davidson, Margaret Dean, Elaine Hicks, Pauline Huston, Hazel Jefferson, Joe McDarby, Bob Nicholl, Alison Nicholson, Keith Osborne, Jill Saunders, Claire Smith and Claire Wilson.
- in East Sussex: Mary Barnett, Susan Carnochan, Gina Cuthbertson, Kay Dixon, Linda Grange, Hilary Holt, Elizabeth Hughes, Jean Irvin, Jane Long, Christine Morris, Margaret Rowe, Sandra South, Veronica Stevenson, Joan Turner and Anne White.
- in Staffordshire: Denise Allman, Brian Cooper, John Hughes, Janet Kisz, Josh Newton, Sandra Probert, Rose Sawyers, Norman Moir, Dianne Shenton and Jackie Williams.

Peter Collinge and Louise Falcini

Notes on contributors

Peter Collinge is a researcher and writer. He worked as a postdoctoral researcher on the AHRC-funded project 'Small Bills and Petty Finance: Co-creating the History of the Old Poor Law'. He was awarded his PhD on businesswomen in Georgian Derbyshire from Keele University in 2015. He teaches at Keele University. His research interests span public history; the Old Poor Law; businesses and their networks; and health, leisure and tourism in the long eighteenth century. His published work includes articles in *Business History, Epoch, The Journal for Eighteenth-Century Studies, Midland History and Northern History.*

Louise Falcini is a Research Fellow at the University of Sussex and a member of the Sussex Humanities Lab. Her research focuses on the poor and marginalized in the long eighteenth century. She completed her AHRC-funded PhD at the University of Reading in 2018, examining cleanliness and the poor in eighteenth-century London. She has subsequently published on vagrancy and migration, including a large collaborative dataset. Her broader research interests include the technologies and infrastructure of co-production and how these can be made simple, cheap and accessible.

Tim Hitchcock is Professor of Digital History at the University of Sussex, and from 2014 to 2021 served as co-director, and latterly director, of the Sussex Humanities Lab. He has published widely on the histories of poverty, gender and sexuality, focusing primarily on eighteenth-century London. With Professor Robert Shoemaker and others, he has also created a series of websites that give direct public access to primary sources evidencing the history of Britain and underpinning the evolution of a 'new history from below'. These sites include The Proceedings of the Old Bailey <https://www.oldbaileyonline.org>; London Lives, 1690 to 1800 <https://www.londonlives.org>; Locating London's Past <https://www.locatinglondon.org>; Connected Histories <https://www.connectedhistories.org>; and Digital Panopticon: The Global Impact of London Punishments, 1780–1925 <https://www.digitalpanopticon.org>.

Samantha A. Shave is Senior Lecturer in Social Policy at the University of Lincoln. Their research is concerned with the development and impact of poor relief policies and practices under the Old and New Poor Law. Their published work includes a monograph, *Pauper Policies: Poor Law Practice in England, 1780–1850* (Manchester, 2017), and journal papers in *Rural History*, *The Historical Journal*, *Continuity and Change* and *The Agricultural History Review*. Samantha is a regular expert consultant for popular radio, TV and print media and, in 2018, a guest on BBC Radio 4's *In Our Time* on the Poor Laws.

Elizabeth Spencer is Lecturer in Eighteenth Century and Public History at the University of York. She was awarded her WRoCAH-funded PhD from the University of York in 2018 with a thesis that explored the description of women's clothing across the long eighteenth century, and has since published on the topic. Her article '"None but Abigails appeared in white aprons": the apron as an elite garment in eighteenth-century England' was awarded the Textile History prize for 2018. Elizabeth's current research focuses on women and accounting in England between 1680 and 1830, and she has broader research interests in gender, consumption and material culture across the early modern period.

Alannah Tomkins is Professor of Social History at Keele University. Her research has focused on the history of the English Poor Law and the social history of medicine, her most recent book being *Medical Misadventure in an Age of Professionalisation, 1780–1890* (Manchester, 2017). She was the principal investigator on the AHRC-funded project 'Small Bills and Petty Finance'. Her forthcoming work is related to the history of nursing before 1820.

The Interludes in *Providing for the Poor* have been produced by volunteer researchers on the AHRC-funded project 'Small Bills and Petty Finance': William Bundred and Margaret Dean in Cumbria; Elizabeth Hughes and Jean Irvin in East Sussex; and Janet Kisz and Dianne Shenton in Staffordshire.

Preface: The Small Bills and Petty Finance project
Peter Collinge and Louise Falcini

In June 1784 Joseph Wilson, overseer of the poor for the parish of Skelton, Cumberland, drew up 'A Bill of Expences and Trouble Concerning Jane Sewel Child & Father'.[1] It included the cost of a journey to Penrith, about seven miles from Skelton; another journey made by Wilson and John Turner to Matterdale; and five shillings paid to a midwife.[2] The total bill amounted to 16s 6d. After the birth, Jane Sewell and her new-born child were denied further relief. Sewell then approached magistrate William Wilson to intervene.[3] She complained that, despite her being very poor and unable to provide for herself and her child, the parish had repeatedly declined relief. In response, Wilson issued a summons instructing Skelton's overseers to appear before him at Mrs Roper's Sun Inn, Penrith, to explain their decision.[4] Having heard the case, Wilson ordered relief. Surviving overseers' vouchers, the bills and receipts generated as part of the administration of the Old Poor Law show that over the next four years Jane Sewell received regular relief for her child's maintenance. The receipt of money was acknowledged by Sewell's father.[5] There is then a silence in the records until 1793 when, after the birth of her fourth illegitimate child, a warrant was issued. This instructed Jane Sewell and John Nicholson, the putative father, to appear before magistrates William Wilson and Edmund Law at Isaac Wilkinson's inn, Penrith, for examination.[6]

---

[1] 'Sewel' appears as 'Sewell' in other documents. Cumbria Archive Service (CAS), PR10/V/10/11, Expenses and trouble concerning Jane Sewel child & father, 3 June 1784; PR10/76, Skelton, Warrants, 30 July 1793; PR 10/81, Skelton, Overseers' accounts, 1734–1817; M. Dean, 'Jane Sewell (1759–1823) Parish of Skelton, Cumberland', The Poor Law (2019) <https://thepoorlaw.org/jane-sewell-1759-1823-parish-of-skelton-cumberland> [accessed 13 Apr. 2021].

[2] It also included unspecified expenses amounting to 3s 6d and payment of 2s 6d 'to a woman'.

[3] Steven King notes that 'petitions by paupers to magistrates represent the end of a long, parochially based decision-making process'. S. King, 'Poor relief and English economic development reappraised', *The Economic History Review*, l (1997), 360–8, at 363.

[4] CAS, PR10/74, Skelton, Warrant for refusal to pay on bastardy orders, 28 Sept. 1784.

[5] For example, CAS, PR10/V/12/35, 18 May 1786.

[6] CAS, PR10/76, Skelton, Warrants, 30 July 1793.

In the struggle for welfare between individuals, localized politicking and the wider economics of the parish, Sewell's story is a familiar one. It identifies a range of people each of whom, for different reasons, had an interest in the Old Poor Law: Sewell herself; Nicholson; Sewell's father; the overseer, Joseph Wilson; John Turner; the innkeepers, Mrs Roper and Isaac Wilkinson; and the magistrates, Wilson and Law. As the receipt of 19*s* 6*d* each quarter gave Sewell (albeit limited) spending power, it is likely that there were others in the locality, such as retailers, who also took an interest in the case.[7] Parish relief would allow Sewell to settle in part or in full any outstanding debts she may have accrued or to pay for food, lodgings, fuel and children's clothing as she saw fit.

The partial biography of Jane Sewell draws attention to overseers' vouchers as a new evidential pathway for research into the Old Poor Law and into the wider operation and administration of parish welfare during the latter part of the long eighteenth century. It also raises methodological issues relating to overseers' vouchers, namely their presence, absence or unevenness in the historic record. As discussed in the Introduction, such issues could have arisen from the ways in which information was recorded in the vouchers or transferred between documents at the time, or by later retention and archival policies. In this volume, issues of presence, absence or unevenness issues are combined with thematic topics regarding parish welfare. These include the agency of the poor, illegitimacy, the role of parochial administrators and wider authorities, and the involvement of goods and service providers. Each is examined from different, yet interconnected, standpoints. Elizabeth Spencer, Peter Collinge and Alannah Tomkins use the rich detail of the vouchers to explore new perspectives on the provision of relief for the poor. Tim Hitchcock, Louise Falcini and Samantha Shave either use the vouchers as embarkation points for new thinking about the Old Poor Law or consider how researchers might approach future work on welfare more broadly defined. Collectively, the contributors ask: Who was responsible for the poor and in what capacity? What was the extent, nature and duration of the relief given? And who, other than the poor, benefited from or participated in the process and with what agency?

Research into the bills and receipts generated in the process of administering the Old Poor Law was made possible by a project funded by the Arts and Humanities Research Council, 'Small Bills and Petty Finance: Co-creating the History of the Old Poor Law'.[8] This collaboration involved the universities of Keele and Sussex, over forty volunteer researchers, and the staff of the county

---

[7] No vouchers are extant to show how Sewell spent her relief money.
[8] AHRC grant number AH/R003246/1.

record offices of Cumbria, East Sussex and Staffordshire. Although bills and receipts form one of the cornerstones in histories of consumption, they tend to be limited to specific sections of the literature, including the wealthy and their purchases.[9] Indeed, although they are an important historical resource, before the 'Small Bills' project began in 2018 overseers' vouchers appeared only tangentially in the historiography of the poor law. Their absence is not hard to account for. At best, their survival is patchy. Even so, their sheer volume is problematic for individual researchers. Both issues are discussed further in the Introduction. Moreover, the vast number of transactions they document and the inconsistent ways in which their contents were recorded present significant methodological challenges. Over the course of four years, however, the collaborative nature of this project, utilizing the commitment, skills and local knowledge of volunteer researchers – explored in Chapter 7, 'Public histories and collaborative working' – provided the means by which this information was gathered. By capturing, coding and analysing the information contained in thousands of overseers' vouchers from thirty parishes and townships across three counties, the 'Small Bills' project has generated a significant new dataset.[10] Consisting of some 41,500 lines, it reflects the goods and services supplied to the poor and enables research on the Old Poor Law to go beyond existing scholarship on pauper letters and inventories, parish practices and policies.[11]

Providing for those unable to support themselves created complex relationships that crossed boundaries of gender, class and age. Through the lens of overseers' vouchers, the actions of both parish officials and the parish poor become more visible, as do the roles of tradespeople and service providers, their assistants, clerks, apprentices and family. The vouchers thus help to fill the silences in parochial account books or to give context to the many transactions they record. They help to clarify what Steven King termed the 'ambiguities around poor law expenditure', and make possible a

---

[9] For example, J. Stobart, '"So agreeable and suitable a place": the character, use and provisioning of a late eighteenth-century suburban villa', *Journal for Eighteenth-Century Studies*, xxxix (2016), 89–102.

[10] See the project website, The Poor Law: Small Bills and Petty Finance 1700 to 1834 <www.thepoorlaw.org>.

[11] S. King and P. Jones, *Navigating the Old English Poor Law: The Kirkby Lonsdale Letters, 1809–1836* (Oxford, 2020); J. Harley, *Norfolk Pauper Inventories, c.1690–1834* (Oxford, 2020); T. Sokoll, 'Writing for relief: rhetoric in English pauper letters, 1800–1834', in *Being Poor in Modern Europe: Historical Perspectives, 1800–1940*, ed. A. Gestrich, S. King and R. Lutz (Oxford, 2006), pp. 91–111; S. Ottaway, *The Decline of Life: Old Age in Eighteenth Century-England* (Cambridge, 2004); S. A. Shave, *Pauper Policies: Poor Law Practice in England, 1780–1850* (Manchester, 2017).

more granular analysis of the microeconomics of the parish.[12] The vouchers, however, are by no means comprehensive and do not provide a universal answer to the uncertainties of parish finance, especially in relation to vagrancy. Yet, as shown in the case of Jane Sewell, they do expose processes and tensions that stand behind the recording of expenditure in overseers' accounts. Providing new insights into the economics of poverty and of the parish, such processes and tensions are linked through financial reciprocity, obligation, parochial responsibility and overlapping networks.

The conundrum of determining what constitutes a representative sample of different socio-economic communities is well known, and for historical research into materials like vouchers can never be fully resolved.[13] Each county selected for the 'Small Bills' project – Cumbria (incorporating the historic counties of Cumberland, Westmorland, parts of Lancashire 'North of the Sands' and parts of the West Riding of Yorkshire), Staffordshire and East Sussex (half of the historic county of Sussex) – however, benefits from the survival of a good range of vouchers from a variety of settlement types. Vouchers are particularly numerous for East Sussex's parishes. Both the nature of the vouchers and the individual settlements from which they have been drawn are explored further in the Introduction. The project counties fall on either side of the broad north-west–Midlands–south-east axis identified in Steven King's analysis of regional poor relief, itself built on the older economic history division between highland and lowland. While acknowledging what could amount to significant differences within local areas, overall this suggests the existence of a relatively generous provision in the south-east (based on an established wider definition of entitlement) and stricter conditions in the north-west.[14] A decline in relative wages and an associated fall in demand for women's labour, particularly in the rural south-east and rising wages in the north-west, however, mean that these differences in entitlements measure the way in which the poor law worked rather than living standards.[15] Indeed, by the 1790s, 'eight out of the eleven highest-wage counties were in the north and midlands and only three were in the south-east'.[16] This underlines the economic hardships of the early nineteenth century suffered in the largely rural areas of the southern counties despite a more 'generous' relief system.

---

[12] S. King, *Poverty and Welfare in England, 1700–1850* (Manchester, 2000), p. 87.

[13] King, *Poverty and Welfare*, pp. 7–8.

[14] King, *Poverty and Welfare*, pp. 257, 261–5.

[15] F. W. Botham and E. H. Hunt, 'Wages in Britain during the Industrial Revolution', *The Economic History Review*, xl (1987), 380–99, at 396.

[16] Botham and Hunt, 'Wages in Britain during the Industrial Revolution', 397.

Geographic separation of the counties enables the identification of commonalities and distinctiveness in the approach officials took towards the poor in their parishes. As Samantha Shave has demonstrated – and as Tomkins elaborates further in relation to assistant overseers in this volume – through publications, visits and correspondence, those responsible for administering the poor law in geographically distant parishes sought advice, shared examples of good practice and were prepared to travel in order to secure positions.[17] For Staffordshire and Cumberland Collinge provides evidence of similar trading practices among businesswomen, while Spencer's analysis of textiles and prices identifies both similarities and differences between the two counties. The Interludes in this volume, together with other pieces to be found on the project website, provide insights into the quotidian lives of the men and women in the settlements studied in the course of the 'Small Bills' project. The quantitative and qualitative evidence gathered during the project thus extends and broadens regional, subregional and local understandings of welfare provision.[18]

Each of the project counties contains a variety of settlement and landscape types in an attempt to capture the experience of the majority of the population at the turn of the eighteenth century. Indeed, in 1834 Cumberland was noted as one of seven counties deemed 'typical' of England overall.[19] According to the *Abstract of Answers and Returns Relative to the Expence and Maintenance of the Poor*, Cumberland contained 215 parishes, of which fifty-five maintained some or all of their poor in workhouses; Westmorland, 108 parishes and seven workhouses; and Staffordshire, 246 parishes and seventy-three workhouses. Sussex contained 308 parishes and 155 workhouses.[20] Within these counties, settlements with surviving vouchers encompass hamlets, villages, townships, market towns, a cathedral city and industrializing areas. Each location was characterized by some or all of the following: the established church, a school, a dissenting chapel, at least one public house, improved transport links, fairs, markets and small-scale textile production. Urban improvement – paving, lighting, newly built houses and public buildings – was also evident. Each also had

---

[17] Shave, *Pauper Policies*, pp. 150–65.

[18] S. King, 'Reconstructing lives: the poor, the poor law and welfare in Calverley, 1650–1820', *Social History*, xxii (1997), 318–38, at p. 319; C. S. Hallas, 'Poverty and pragmatism in the northern uplands of England: the North Yorkshire Pennines, *c.*1770–1900', *Social History*, xxv (2000), 67–84, at 68.

[19] S. Williams, *Poverty, Gender and Life-Cycle under the English Poor Law, 1760–1834* (London, 2011), p. 21.

[20] *Abstract of Answers and Returns relative to the Expence and Maintenance of the Poor* (Parl. Papers 1803–4 [C. 175], xiii), pp. 84, 476, 532, 556.

a number of retail craft producers – blacksmiths, butchers, carpenters, cobblers, grocers and petty dealers, hatters, tailors and dressmakers – the people whose business activity and contact with the Poor Law generated overseers' vouchers. These features, however, did not necessarily guarantee any alignments in styles of Poor Law management.

Combining both academic pieces and shorter texts authored by volunteer researchers, *Providing for the Poor* focuses on paupers and on providers and enablers of welfare to show evidence of the 'complex web of negotiations between and within central and local welfare authorities, and between welfare providers and recipients'.[21] It examines the Old Poor Law as a mechanism for supporting local economies, problems at the margins of parish welfare, pauper entitlement, behaviour and agency, and the responses of parish officials and of those beyond the immediate Poor Law system. Individual chapters open up new lines of enquiry, contribute to existing debate on Poor Law implementation or reflect on the broader issues of power at the heart of the Old Poor Law. While overseers' vouchers form the basis of the chapters on textiles, businesswomen and assistant overseers, the chapters on illegitimacy, vagrancy and welfare reform consider aspects that are largely absent from the vouchers. The chapter on public history and the Interludes recognize the immense contribution made by archival volunteer researchers to the 'Small Bills' project. Each Interlude, linked to one or more of the substantive chapters, uses vouchers as starting points for partial biographies of people who came into contact with the Old Poor Law. Collectively, they illustrate that those who either generated the vouchers or benefited from what they contained matter in Poor Law history.

Part I focuses on the poor and their interactions with the parish. Conflicts at the intersection between paupers' rights and responsibilities, the law and parochial authority in a small rural parish in East Sussex lie at the heart of Louise Falcini's chapter on 'Accounting for illegitimacy'. Taking a micro-historical approach, it argues that the interests of ratepayers could be challenged by the agency of paupers in their 'negotiations' surrounding illegitimacy. In 'Clothing the poor' Elizabeth Spencer draws on over 400 vouchers from Cumbria and Staffordshire focusing on textiles, haberdashery and prices. She demonstrates how regular repeat purchases and the services of the local needle trades to make, mend or replace garments provide insights into the relationship between paupers, their clothing, parishes and local economies. Tim Hitchcock's 'Vagrancy, poor relief and the parish' explores the role of vagrancy as a form of punishment, as a regulator of migration and as an arbiter of settlement under the Old Poor Law. The approximately

---

[21] Shave, *Pauper Policies*, p. 6.

14,000 people detailed by the vagrant contractor for Middlesex in the 1780s reveals a picture of mobile humanity moving constantly across a complex landscape of seasonal work, of military deployment and demobilization; and of step-wise urban migration from village to regional centre to London. This evidence is contrasted with parliamentary returns of vagrants punished in houses of correction in the 1820s to reveal the role of the system in controlling both migration and more localized forms of disorder.[22]

In Part II, 'Providers and Enablers and their Critics', Peter Collinge's 'Women, business and the Old Poor Law' shifts the focus from women as recipients of poor relief to women as suppliers and providers. It emphasizes how women conducted business, identifies the level of engagement they had with parish authorities and the wider community, and provides a greater appreciation of the Poor Law system as a consumer of goods and services in local economies. In 'The Overseers' assistant' Alannah Tomkins asks who these men were. By considering the occupational backgrounds, social standing and life chances of men who secured these posts, this chapter sees the assistant overseer as a representative of changing relief policies. While the offer of paid parish roles required vestries to consider their own interests, their concerns were sometimes overwritten by a desire to give an income to men who might otherwise have suffered financial problems. Parish 'pay' takes on a new meaning if assistant overseers were being offered a defence against immiseration. Samantha Shave's 'Who cares? Mismanagement, neglect and suffering in the final decades of the Old Poor Laws' analyses and contextualizes two pamphlets. These questioned the 'morality' of the relief system, and documented the suffering of the poor and the extent to which their authors wanted to provoke scandal. In considering whether the 'welfare process' has been conceived too narrowly and whether historians could consider a greater range of individuals as important and influential in the negotiations over poor relief, the chapter reflects many of the themes of this volume.

Part III, on public histories and collaborative working, situates the volume both in the context of recent work on crowdsourcing and on the co-creation of resources and in the wider historiography of public history. It examines the processes, practicalities and wider implications of collaborative working by drawing on the collective experiences of archival staff, academics and the communities of volunteers connected with the 'Small Bills' project. The last chapter brings together the broad themes of the volume, looking at the paupers, providers and enablers of the Old Poor Law together with

---

[22] The returns provide details of all those punished in a house of correction as a vagrant between 1820 and 1823.

those who sought to criticize it. The economics of the parish are firmly embedded across the historical chapters, although each uses a markedly different perspective, from financial incentives, local expenditure and business acumen to financial mismanagement and personal bankruptcy.

Providing for the Poor stresses the 'centrality of poor relief and its administration in local communities', and reflects the widening scope of research into the management of relief and the poor under the Old Poor Law and the significant roles of co-creation and collaborative history in such investigations.[23] From micro-histories to larger-scale analyses, it provides new perspectives and methodological approaches, and opens up new research possibilities in histories of the Old Poor Law.

---

[23] P. M. Solar, 'Poor relief and English economic development: a renewed plea for comparative history', The *Economic History Review*, c (1997), 369–74, at 2, 6–8.

Introduction: The Old Poor Law

Peter Collinge and Louise Falcini

The origins of the Old Poor Law lay in the restrictive statutes of the later medieval period, which sought to regulate the lives of both the itinerant poor – unsettled beggars and vagabonds – and the 'impotent poor' – the aged or frail. By the late sixteenth century, each parish in England and Wales was legally obliged to appoint an overseer of the poor and to provide relief for their aged, sick or infirm parishioners. They were also empowered to provide some form of local employment for able-bodied men without work. The parish financed this relief through the collection of a local tax levied on the notional rental value of all domestic buildings, set annually and collected by the overseer. These basic provisions were amended to enable parishes to distinguish 'their' poor from the wider pool of potential claimants. From 1662, the Settlement Act permitted parishes to remove anyone likely to seek parochial relief to their place of 'legal settlement'. In 1691 a further Act specified several ways in which a new settlement could be acquired by either birth, marriage, apprenticeship or employment for longer than a year. Applying for relief without a legal settlement could lead to forced removal.[1] Over the course of the eighteenth century, this system of settlement and removal evolved and became ever more complex, resulting in both growing administrative costs and new patterns of relief. By the early nineteenth century, it was common (but not guaranteed) for 'out-parish relief' to be given.[2] This allowed people to claim relief from their parish of legal settlement while continuing to live elsewhere. The management of out-parish relief generated the archive of pauper letters that has informed much of the recent historical scholarship on the Old Poor Law.[3] The complex character of 'settlement', however it was managed,

---

[1] T. Sokoll, 'Writing for relief: rhetoric in English pauper letters, 1800–1834', in *Being Poor in Modern Europe: Historical Perspectives, 1800–1940*, ed. A. Gestrich, S. King and R. Lutz (Oxford, 2006), pp. 91–111, at pp. 94–5; S. King, *Poverty and Welfare in England, 1700–1850* (Manchester, 2000), p. 22.

[2] King, *Poverty and Welfare*, p. 23; D. Eastwood, 'Rethinking the debates on the Poor Law in early nineteenth-century England', *Utilitas*, vi (1994), 97–116, at 105.

[3] S. King and P. Jones, *Navigating the Old English Poor Law: The Kirkby Lonsdale Letters,*

P. Collinge and L. Falcini, 'Introduction: The Old Poor Law' in *Providing for the Poor: The Old Poor Law, 1750–1834*, ed. P. Collinge and L. Falcini (London, 2022), pp. 1–22. License: CC BY-NC-ND 4.0.

reinforced an intense localism and profoundly shaped the lives of the poor. The system led ineluctably to bitter disputes over settlement between parishes, evidenced in Louise Falcini's chapter on illegitimacy (Chapter 1); while many paupers found their lives turned upside down. Arguably, the laws of settlement had their greatest impact on women who took their husbands' place of settlement on marriage. In widowhood, women like Elizabeth Malbon might find themselves removed to a parish they had never visited.[4] Equally, single women found difficulty in securing parochial assistance, particularly when it concerned matters of settlement.[5] Legitimate children took the settlement of their parents but illegitimate children were assigned settlement in the parish in which they had been born. From 1744, an infant born to an unmarried mother identified as a 'vagrant' took their mother's place of settlement.[6] All of this occasioned a great deal of Machiavellian politicking within and between parishes as the officers jostled to avoid taking financial responsibility. The management and implementation of settlement in relation to the mobile, itinerant poor is taken up in Tim Hitchcock's chapter on vagrancy (Chapter 3). In Chapter 1, Falcini addresses the financial 'negotiations' between paupers, parishes and the law in a small rural parish.

A permissive legal framework that allowed parishes and townships to determine their own strategies for managing the poor could have profound consequences for the circulation of cash in local economies and the operation of the Old Poor Law as an economic system. Parishes switched between schemes or adopted mix-and-match policies according to circumstance, the availability of resources, and the abilities, zeal or indifference of those appointed to oversee their implementation. Outdoor relief, consisting largely of regular cash payments known as pensions or rent paid directly to property owners, was offered throughout the period. In some places, paupers paid their rent, and fed and clothed themselves and their dependent children from a parish pension. In such instances, evident in the case of Jane Sewell, overseers' vouchers might record the distribution of money but not how it was spent. In others, overseers

---

1809–1836 (Oxford, 2020); S. King, *Writing the Lives of the English Poor, 1750s–1830s*, i, *States, People and the History of Social Change* (Montreal, 2019); Sokoll, 'Writing for relief'.

[4] See Interlude 3 (D. Shenton, 'Elizabeth Malbon (*c.*1743–1801)') in this volume.

[5] A. M. Froide, *Never Married: Singlewomen in Early Modern England* (Oxford, 2005), pp. 34–5; B. Hill, *Women Alone: Spinsters in England, 1660–1850* (New Haven, 2001) pp. 101–2; C. Steedman, *History and the Law: A Love Story* (Cambridge, 2020), pp. 130–61. Women could gain settlement through repeated annual hirings as servants: C. Steedman, *Labours Lost: Domestic Service and the Making of Modern England* (Cambridge, 2009), p. 106.

[6] 17 Geo II c 5, Vagrancy Act, 1744.

supplied discretionary, 'casual' relief in the form of fuel, food and drink, medical services, clothing and footwear, and funeral expenses. For most of the period the Old Poor Law was in operation, these varied disbursements were organized by overseers and authorized by vestries who also determined which goods and service providers were utilized. By the early nineteenth century, the increasingly onerous burden of poor-relief administration led some parishes to appoint salaried assistant overseers. This underresearched group of local administrators who shaped and were shaped by their experiences of poverty are the subject of Alannah Tomkins's chapter (Chapter 5). As the systems adopted locally were complex and varied, so too were the 'negotiations' pursued by paupers and parishes. Frequently, these were direct and reflected the relative agency of the actors involved. Scandal and elite advocacy, however, could also come into play, affecting the behaviour of local administrators and paupers. Samantha Shave takes up this theme in Chapter 6 by questioning the role of religion and parish clergy at times of extreme stress on the welfare system when shocking cases of neglect were brought to wider attention. When and where it was deemed necessary, magistrates mediated disagreements between the poor and the vestry, administered the law and provided oversight of the system.[7]

In addition to relieving the poor 'outdoors' in their own homes, 'indoor' relief in workhouses gradually rose to prominence, justified as supposedly more efficient or just punitive. Poorhouses or workhouses provided accommodation for the needy with the intention of setting the 'able' poor to work. From the 1690s, a dozen Corporations of the Poor, established by Act of Parliament, created large workhouses designed to cater for whole cities. Smaller parochial workhouses began to emerge in the 1710s and, following the passage of the Workhouse Test Act in 1723, became relatively common. The same Act also allowed parishes to deny relief to paupers who refused to enter workhouses and permitted parishes to 'farm' out their poor under contract to private workhouses or establishments run by a neighbouring parish. It also allowed small parishes to join with others to create shared workhouses.[8] Farming paupers out tended to be relatively expensive, but for some parishes it remained a 'viable alternative' because it was a more time- and cost-effective way of applying a 'workhouse test' than constructing and maintaining their own premises. Farming was particularly prevalent in Cumberland. Indeed, Steven King notes the 'tendency for communities in the north and west of England to turn to "farming" for longer and rather more frequently as a way

---

[7] S. King, 'Poor relief and English economic development reappraised', *The Economic History Review*, l (1997), 360–8, at 363.

[8] King, *Poverty and Welfare*, pp. 18–27.

of controlling their poor relief bills than communities in the south'.[9] This had an impact on patterns of parish spending and consequently on the overseers' vouchers generated as a result.

The institutional landscape changed again with the passage of Gilbert's Act in 1782. This enabled multiple parishes to form 'Gilbert Unions' that could construct workhouses for the 'vulnerable' poor with the aim of creating institutions substantially different from the workhouses of the preceding fifty years.[10] One such union, established in 1811 at Kirkby Lonsdale, Westmorland, included seventeen townships: eight in Westmorland, seven in Lancashire and two in Yorkshire.[11] In West Sussex, some seven Gilbert unions and several single parish incorporations were established. These unions were less popular in East Sussex than elsewhere in the county, though Samantha Shave has argued that Gilbert's Act did influence practice, even when it was not applied directly.[12] Despite positive intentions, however, enabling acts simply added further components to an already complex web of overlapping, and at times competing, legislation. For some, they compounded existing views that the Poor Law was 'chaotic and inefficient'.[13]

Most workhouses provided accommodation for between twenty and fifty people.[14] The able-bodied were expected to contribute to their own maintenance by road mending, small-scale manufacture, cooking, cleaning, picking oakum, breaking stones or working the land.[15] The extravagant hopes that the poor would become self-sustaining, however, were rarely realized. In 1787, 'Being old people, weak and feeble', the work undertaken by inmates at Longtown, Cumberland, came 'to very little'.[16] In St Mary's

---

[9] King, *Poverty and Welfare*, p. 185.

[10] S. Shave, *Pauper Policies: Poor Law Practice in England, 1780–1850* (Manchester, 2017), pp. 4, 37–8, 57–9.

[11] W. Parson and W. White, *History, Directory and Gazetteer of Cumberland and Westmorland* (Leeds, 1829), pp. 688–9; <www.cumbriacountyhistory.org.uk/township/kirkby-lonsdale> [accessed 25 June 2021].

[12] Shave, *Pauper Policies*, pp. 257–8.

[13] M. Daunton, *Progress and Poverty: An Economic and Social History of Britain, 1700–1850* (Oxford, 1995), p. 451.

[14] J. Boulton and J. Black, 'Paupers and their experience of a London workhouse: St Martin-in-the Fields, 1725–1824', in *Residential Institutions in Britain, 1725–1970: Inmates and Environments*, ed. J. Hamlett, L. Hoskins and R. Preston (London, 2015), pp. 79–91, at pp. 79–80.

[15] P. Collinge, '"He shall have care of the garden, its cultivation and produce": workhouse gardens and gardening c.1780–1835', *Journal for Eighteenth-Century Studies*, lxiv (2021), 21–39.

[16] CAS, SPUL/4/1, Report on poorhouses at Longtown, Bewcastle, Horsgill, Farlam and Kingmoor, 1787.

workhouse, Lichfield, paupers manufactured blankets, while in the tiny parish of East Hoathly small sums of money were spent on providing flax for the pensioned poor to spin (albeit not in an institutional setting).[17] The moral appeal of work in exchange for relief was deep-seated and long-lasting and, as in East Hoathly, stretched beyond the walls of workhouses. The reality, however, was that the expense necessary to maintain such work very seldom made the economics of these schemes profitable, despite claims from local manufacturers that they undercut businesses or distorted markets.[18]

The latter part of the long eighteenth century saw increasing pressure on poor relief in both economic and political terms.[19] A combination of population growth, war with France (with its associated enlistment and demobilization), a trade depression, rising under- and unemployment, agricultural enclosure, poor harvests and price inflation all combined to increase the amount spent nationally on poor relief.[20] In the early 1780s poor relief in England and Wales amounted to £2 million per annum but by 1818 it had risen to £8 million. Measured per capita, expenditure rose from four shillings per pauper in 1776 to thirteen shillings in 1818.[21] Recent work by Brodie Wadell has identified the significant rise in the rate of growth in expenditure on poor relief, with spikes in 1781–2 and 'several years in the 1790s'.[22] This general increase, evident in all three project counties, also increased the circulation of money in local economies. In 1803 Cumberland spent £27,604 on relieving the poor, averaging 5s ¾d per head of the population (117,230 in 1801).[23] By 1821, when the population had risen to 156,124, poor relief had reached £56,637, averaging 7s 3d per head.[24] County averages could conceal wildly divergent parochial experiences. In Hayton,

[17] *The Victoria History of the County of Staffordshire* (London, 1990), xiv. 89; see East Sussex Record Office (ESRO), PAR378/31/3/16/33, and PAR378/31/3/21/29, East Hoathly, Overseers' vouchers, 1779 and 1785.

[18] Boulton and Black, 'Paupers and their experience of a London workhouse', p. 82; J. S. Taylor, 'The unreformed workhouse 1776–1834', in *Comparative Developments in Social Welfare*, ed. E. W. Martin (London, 1972), pp. 57–84, at p. 69.

[19] King, *Poverty and Welfare*, pp. 26, 143.

[20] Shave, *Pauper Policies*, p. 2.

[21] Shave, *Pauper Policies*, p. 5.

[22] B. Waddell, 'The rise of the parish welfare state in England, c.1600–1800', *Past & Present*, ccliii (2021), 151–94.

[23] *Abstract of Answers and Returns relative to the Expence and Maintenance of the Poor* (Parl. Papers 1803–4 [C. 175], xiii), p. 476. Unless stated otherwise, all figures are to the nearest pound.

[24] *Report from the Select Committee on Poor Rate Returns* (Parl. Papers 1822), Supplemental Appendix, 1819–22, pp. 18, 25.

near Brampton, the population increased by 58 per cent – from 1,015 to 1,604 – between 1801 and 1831, while the £211 expended on relief in 1803 had risen to £465 by 1828, an increase of 120 per cent.[25] A similar picture can be found in Staffordshire where the cost of poor relief increased from 7s 5d per head of the population to 8s 10½d.[26] Abbots Bromley's population increased by 23 per cent but its spending on poor relief increased by 49 per cent.[27] Likewise, annual spending on the poor in East Hoathly, Sussex, rose from 18s 10d per head of population in 1803 to approximately £1 2s 1½d in 1821.[28]

Rising costs were not without consequences. Real and perceived extravagance on the part of vestries and rising parish debts (despite increases in the poor rate and rising real wages in the Midlands and the north) ensured that the issue of poor relief was never off local or national agendas.[29] Harvest failures in the mid-1790s and wide-scale food riots among the poor

---

[25] Hayton's population figures can be found at <https://www.cumbriacountyhistory.org.uk/township/hayton> [accessed 25 June 2021]. *Abstract ... Expence and Maintenance of the Poor*, p. 78; CAS, PR102/122, Overseers' accounts and papers, 1790–1843.

[26] Based on a population of 239,153 in 1803: *Abstract ... Expence and Maintenance of the Poor*, p. 476. The figure for 1821 is based on the lower population figure (341,040) quoted in the body of the report. The figure reported in the summary is 345,895, which would give an annual cost of poor relief of 8s 9d per head of the population: *Report from the Select Committee on Poor Rate Returns* (Parl. Papers 1822), *Supplemental Appendix*, 1819–22, pp. 18, 25.

[27] Abbots Bromley's population rose from 1,318 in 1801 to 1,621 by 1831: *VCH Staffordshire* (London, 1908) i,. 325. The £536 spent on relief in 1803 rose to £800 by 1833: *Abstract ... Expence and Maintenance of the Poor*, p. 470; Staffordshire Record Office (SRO), D1209/6/2, Abbots Bromley, Overseers' accounts, ledger of expenditure and receipts, 1827–43; *VCH Staffordshire*, i. 325.

[28] Naomi Tadmor identifies a 'near six-fold rise in parish expenditure' on disbursements in East Hoathly between 1712 and 1772: N. Tadmor, 'Where was Mrs Turner? Governance and gender in an eighteenth-century village', in *Remaking English Society: Social Relations and Social Change in Early Modern England*, ed. S. Hindle, A. Shepard and J. Walter (Woodbridge, 2013), pp. 89–112. The annual sum spent on poor relief in East Hoathly in 1803 was £371 15s 4d: *Abstract ... Expence and Maintenance of the Poor*, p. 528. The annual sum spent on poor relief in East Hoathly in 1821 was £564 9s and the annual cost per head of population in the county of Sussex was £1 3s 3½d in 1821: *Report from the Select Committee on Poor Rate Returns*, pp. 178, 532.

[29] F. W. Botham and E. H. Hunt, 'Wages in Britain during the Industrial Revolution', *The Economic History Review*, xl (1987), 380–99, at 394–7; R. Sweet, *The English Town, 1680–1840: Government, Society and Culture* (Harlow, 1999), p. 103; P. Langford, *A Polite and Commercial People: England 1727–1783* (Oxford, 1989), pp. 151–4; D. R. Green, 'Icons of the new system: workhouse construction and relief practices in London under the Old and New Poor Law', *The London Journal* xxiv (2009), 264–284.

(if not necessarily paupers) resulted in a hardening of attitudes.[30] While the approach of individual parishes and townships remained diverse and the 'crisis' was not felt uniformly across the country, all parishes reconsidered what level of support was appropriate for their poor. Pockets of deprivation, where restricted resources could stretch only so far, existed in areas often characterized by 'generous' provision, while examples of individual and collective generosity can be found in areas of more limited provision.[31] Even so, manifestations of crisis were most apparent in the south and east. The results were a rise in protests, an increase in the amounts expended on the casual poor, the implementation of stricter relief regimes and shocking examples of neglect.[32] Amid an atmosphere of 'weakening of support for the old poor law' and a 'crisis in the management of poverty', the poor were 'increasingly problematized and stigmatized'.[33]

In the southern counties of England, one consequence of landowners reducing agricultural wages was to force parishes to increase their poor-relief contributions to individual labourers. Supplementing agricultural wages, it was argued, favoured farmers, depressed labourers' incomes, distorted labour markets and was not always welcome.[34] Moreover, there was widespread criticism that the burden of the poor rates fell disproportionately on the smaller ratepayers and failed to take adequate assessments of stock-in-trade. Substantial land and business owners and those trading in luxury goods, it was argued, were not shouldering a sufficient share of the tax burden.[35] In 1822–3 in Cumberland, for example, the total poor rate amounted to £58,540. Of this, £43,503 was levied on land, £12,625 on houses, £1,518 on manorial profits and only £894 on mills and factories.[36] In Bolton, Lancashire,

---

[30] Green, 'Icons of the new system', 269–70; L. Smith, 'Lunatic asylum in the workhouse: St Peter's Hospital, Bristol, 1698–1861', *Medical History*, lxi (2017), 225–45, at 227; Eastwood, 'Rethinking the debates on the Poor Law', 105; Taylor, 'Unreformed workhouse', pp. 64, 67.

[31] S. Williams, *Poverty, Gender and Life-Cycle under the English Poor Law, 1760–1834* (Woodbridge, 2011), pp. 5–6; King, *Poverty and Welfare*, pp. 142, 188–9.

[32] Williams, *Poverty, Gender and Life-Cycle*, pp. 5, 9, 143; C. J. Griffin, *The Politics of Hunger: Protest, Poverty and Policy in England, c.1750–c.1840* (Manchester, 2020).

[33] Williams, *Poverty, Gender and Life-Cycle*, pp. 8, 92.

[34] C. J. Griffin, 'Parish farms: a policy response to unemployment in rural southern England, c.1815–1835', *Agricultural History Review*, lviii (2011), 176–98, at 177–83.

[35] R. Dryburgh, '"Individual, illegal and unjust purposes": overseers, incentives, and the Old Poor Law in Bolton, 1820–1837', Oxford Economic and Social History Working Papers 50, University of Oxford, Department of Economics (2003), pp. 20–2 <https://www.nuff.ox.ac.uk/Economics/History/Paper50/50dryburgh%281%29.pdf?msclkid=c128fae9a6b511ec951acf776327afb6> [accessed 18 Mar. 2022].

[36] Parson and White, *Directory Cumberland*, p. 31.

politically motivated individuals claimed that Poor Law administrators favoured family and business networks when allocating funds. Large textile firms acting as property owners benefited at the expense of shopkeepers, householders and owners of small properties when the vestry paid the rents of textile workers.[37] In the project counties, a comparison of businesses listed in trade directories with those recorded in overseers' vouchers reveals the reliance placed by parishes on a relatively small number of goods and service providers.[38] It is not surprising, therefore, that in overarching narratives of mismanagement those responsible for parochial relief were believed to be out to 'gratify themselves and their Favourites' at the expense of the deserving poor.[39]

Until the late eighteenth century when poor relief 'became ever more central and essential', resorting to parish relief was often undertaken as part of the 'economy of makeshifts' involving trade credit, pawning, occasional theft, borrowing from family and friends, and appeals to charities and friendly societies.[40] In Cumberland, contemporaries recognized that the poor rate would have been much higher 'if its evils were not alleviated by the munificent posthumous charities that have been bequeathed'.[41] While they 'lessened the strain on the formal poor relief system', however, charities and friendly societies routinely refused relief to those in receipt of parish welfare (as occurred in Keswick).[42] In part, this was because pressure on them was growing: in Staffordshire, Lichfield's Mendicity Society offered temporary shelter to vagrants (accounting for some absences in overseers' vouchers) but found that by 1827 expenditure exceeded income.[43] Likewise,

[37] Dryburgh, '"Individual, illegal and unjust purposes"', pp. 19–22.

[38] See Chapter 4 (P. Collinge, 'Women, business and the Old Poor Law') in this volume.

[39] Thomas Gilbert, quoted in S. Shave, 'The welfare of the vulnerable in the late eighteenth and early nineteenth Centuries: Gilbert's Act of 1782', *History in Focus*, xiv (2008) <https://archives.history.ac.uk/history-in-focus/welfare/articles/shaves.html> [accessed 14 Apr. 2020].

[40] Williams, *Poverty, Gender and Life-Cycle*, pp. 7, 19; O. Hufton, *The Poor of Eighteenth-Century France, 1750–1789* (Oxford, 1974); J. Innes, 'The "mixed economy of welfare" in early modern England: assessments of the options from Hale to Malthus (c.1683–1803)', in *Charity, Self-Interest and Welfare in the English Past*, ed. M. Daunton (London, 1996), pp. 104–34; S. King and A. Tomkins (eds), *The Poor in England, 1700–1850: An Economy of Makeshifts* (Manchester, 2003), p. 1; J. Broad, 'Parish economies of welfare, 1650–1834', *The Historical Journal*, xlii (1999), 985–1006, at 985–6.

[41] Parson and White, *Directory Cumberland*, p. 31.

[42] C. S. Hallas, 'Poverty and pragmatism in the northern uplands of England: the North Yorkshire Pennines, c.1770–1900', *Social History*, xxv (2000), 67–84, at 73. Thanks to Keith Osborne for the Keswick reference: Carlisle Library, Jackson Collection, L93, Keswick Friendly Society, 1776.

[43] *VCH Staffordshire*, xiv. 91. From 1828, St Mary's parish contributed an annual

most parishes declined applications from people already in receipt of relief from other quarters. Conversely, vestries might countenance using charitable income to reduce the poor rate; in mid-eighteenth-century Greystoke those in receipt of poor relief could also receive money from land rents.[44] Parochial income derived from charitable bequests, however, varied significantly between counties. In the period 1786–8, parishes in Cumberland benefited from £251 in interest from invested money, while those in Staffordshire gained £1,083 and in Sussex £1,247.[45] In addition, the money was distributed unevenly between parishes. In Sussex, a county with significant income from financial endowments, East Hoathly received the interest on just £100, which amounted to £4 per year to distribute to the poor.[46]

The operation of the Poor Law between 1750 and 1834 was by no means consistent. Across this period and throughout their longer history, a bewildering array of legislation, much of it enabling rather than compulsory, ensured that local practice would vary considerably.[47] Steven King characterized some Midland counties, including Staffordshire, as having a 'strong unity of Poor Law experience', whereas he found that north-western counties, including Cumberland, displayed a 'ramshackle and inadequate collection of welfare strategies' of 'complex local diversity'.[48] Determining precisely who was and was not considered deserving of assistance within these overlapping frameworks was as discretionary as the nature, extent and duration of relief given.[49] As was evident in the case of Jane Sewell, parish welfare was essentially a balancing act between the 'discretionary disbursements' made to the poor based on their sense of 'wide-ranging entitlements', the ratepayers who funded poor relief and the decisions of

---

subscription of five pounds: SRO, LD20/6/7, Subscription to the Mendicity Society, 16 Sept. 1833.

[44] W. White, *History, Gazetteer, and Directory of the County of Staffordshire, and the City and County of Lichfield* (Sheffield, 1834), pp. 94–103; J. F. Ede, *History of Wednesbury* (Wednesbury, 1962), p. 159; CAS, PR5/43, Greystoke, Poor account book, 1740–1812.

[45] *Abstract of Returns of Charitable Donations for the benefit of poor persons, made by the ministers and churchwardens of the several parishes and townships of England and Wales* (Parl. Papers 1816) [relating to 1786–8]. Annual product of invested money.

[46] This legacy was given by Samuel Atkins in 1742. By the 1760s it had been subsumed into the general parish fund: D. Vaisey (ed.), *The Diary of Thomas Turner, 1754–1765* (East Hoathly, 1994), pp. 326–7.

[47] S. King, *Poverty and Welfare*, pp. 18–47; Williams, *Poverty, Gender and Life-Cycle*; Shave, *Pauper Policies*, pp. 1–6, 57–149.

[48] King, *Poverty and Welfare*, pp. 263, 266.

[49] Shave, *Pauper Policies*, p. 3.

parochial administrators, tempered on occasion by magistrates.[50] Under the direction of vestries, it was the overseers and later their assistants who authorized payments for goods and services supplied as part of a much larger process by which each parish sought to relieve, direct, control or punish the poor as they saw fit. Excluding those classed as aged or infirm, it was rare for poor relief to be given on a permanent basis, ensuring that the underlying negotiations involved would be ongoing.[51] In recent micro-historical studies, this intermittent relief across the life cycle has been documented in a variety of parishes.[52] Both Henry French and Steven King identify the 1790s until the 1830s as a period when 'able-bodied' young men and women were receiving relief more frequently. These trends are particularly difficult to document using the vouchers, however, partly because parish pensions were often less reliably identified in vouchers and partly, because of the absence of significant runs of vouchers across relevant time periods.[53]

Parish administration in the Small Bills counties

Apart from more formal and extensive roundsman schemes, the variety of organizational forms, structures and welfare frameworks in existence under the later Old Poor Law are illustrated by the parishes and townships included in the 'Small Bills' project. They correspond to David Eastwood's view that 'Vestries ... would farm the poor one year ... make more regular use of workhouse incarceration in ... another, and perhaps finally seek salvation in a labour rate scheme'.[54] King noted too the variety of action taken towards the poor; it was 'rare for parishes and townships to follow a single definitive poor law policy'.[55] Whether relief provision was indoor or outdoor, casual or permanent, or in- or out-parish, the entire overlapping system, subject to much variation, depended on the levying and collection

---

[50] Williams, *Poverty, Gender and Life-Cycle*, p. 79; Eastwood, 'Rethinking the debates on the Poor Law', 103, 106.

[51] Broad, 'Parish economies of welfare', 986.

[52] H. French, 'How dependent were the "dependent poor"? Poor relief and the life-course in Terling, Essex, 1762–1834', *Continuity and Change*, xxx (2015), 193–222; S. King, 'Reconstructing lives: the poor, the Poor Law and welfare in Calverley, 1650–1820', *Social History*, xxii (1997), 318–38. See also S. A. Shave, 'The dependent poor? (Re)constructing the lives of individuals "on the parish" in rural Dorset, 1800–1832', *Rural History*, xx (2009), 67–97; Williams, *Poverty, Gender and Life-Cycle*, pp. 101–30.

[53] The longest run of overseers' vouchers in the 'Small Bills' project appears in the Sussex parish of East Hoathly; however, the vouchers for the critical period, *c.*1790–1820, are absent. Further analysis is ongoing.

[54] Eastwood, 'Rethinking the debates on the Poor Law', 105.

[55] King, *Poverty and Welfare*, p. 143.

of a local tax or poor rate. The redistribution of money this entailed was not as straightforward as taking only from the wealthy and giving solely to the poor because purchasing power derived from poor-rate income might be distributed to provision either households or workhouses. Moreover, as discussed in Peter Collinge's chapter on businesswomen and commercial environments, it is evident that parish decisions about how, where and on whom money was to be spent could have a notable impact on local businesses. Consideration of a sample of parishes included in the 'Small Bills' project illustrates this administrative diversity.

East Hoathly in East Sussex lies nine miles north-east of the county town of Lewes in a landscape dominated by the hills of the High Weald and the South Downs. The parish encompassed 2,000 acres of woodland and mixed agricultural land divided into small, tenanted farms, scattered hamlets and a small village. By 1801 the whole of the parish contained only fifty-six domestic dwellings occupied by seventy-six families. Between 1801 and 1841, the population of the parish rose from 395 to 607 and the number of dwellings increased accordingly, but the parish attracted relatively few migrants. In 1841 only thirty-one out of the 607 inhabitants were recorded as having been born outside of the county.[56] As well as the church, the parish supported at least two public houses, a general dealer and a school with a handful of private pupils. The overseers' vouchers make it clear, however, that several craftspeople and traders operated locally, augmented by one or two petty officials. While East Hoathly was an unremarkable rural parish in many ways, it is notable for two things that helped determine its inclusion here. First, there is a significant run of overseers' vouchers between 1742 and 1834, making it the largest parish collection in the sample. Second, it was the home of Thomas Turner (1729–93), shopkeeper and prolific diarist.[57] Turner was twenty-one when he first came to the parish in 1750 to run a small general shop. He threw himself into parish life and administration. He briefly kept the local school and later became a churchwarden, overseer of the poor and surveyor. He also assisted the local tax collector and advised many of his neighbours. The survival of Turner's diary offered an opportunity to compare overseers' vouchers with a narrative source and prompted the choice of East Hoathly from among a large number of East Sussex locations with surviving receipts.

Like many small rural parishes, East Hoathly cared for its poor in the community. In the mid eighteenth century regular pensions were paid to

---

[56] *Abstract of Answers and Returns under the Population Act, 3 & 4 Vic. C. 99* (Parl. Papers 1841), p. 322.

[57] D. Vaisey, 'Turner, Thomas (1729–1793)', *Oxford Dictionary of National Biography* <https://doi.org/10.1093/ref:odnb/48266> [accessed 14 Aug. 2018].

approximately six to eight individuals, mainly elderly or otherwise infirm paupers. Food, clothing, footwear and fuel were distributed among the pensioners and the many marginal families that required occasional assistance. The parish also paid rents, provided medical assistance, maintained several illegitimate children and made occasional payments to the itinerant poor. In the year ending Easter 1776, East Hoathly expended £150 of the local rate on the poor. By Easter 1803, this had increased to almost £372. Of this, £358 was spent on relieving the poor and a further £13 on the removal of paupers, overseers' expenses and legal costs. In 1803 the parish was permanently caring for twenty-two adults, two children under five and a further thirteen children. There does not seem to have been a wage subsidy scheme in East Hoathly but charitable donations to the poor included some meagre gifts of bread and beer and occasionally money at Christmas.[58]

In northern England, amid the mountains, fells and lakes of Cumberland, much of the land was given over to the grazing of sheep and cattle. Arable crops including barley, oats, wheat, peas and beans were grown on enclosed land.[59] The largest centres of population in 1801 were the county town of Carlisle (10,221), the ports of Whitehaven (8,742) and Workington (5,716) and the market town of Cockermouth (2,865). Cumberland's predominantly agricultural economy, supplemented by textile production, provided most of the employment for the labouring poor but industry was expanding from its domestic base. Frederick Morton Eden noted that spinning was the general employment in the 1790s for women in labouring families.[60] Domestic spinning, however, was slowly giving way to the industrial manufacture of cotton and linen. Quarrying and mining were also growing in significance.[61] Many of the county's extensive parishes contained scattered hamlets, villages and market towns where the poor were maintained either in poorhouses or in their own homes. While all three counties had arrangements for farming the poor, a form of contracting out poor relief, it was most prevalent in Cumberland.

Greystoke and Brampton are representative of the seventeen Cumbrian settlements included in the project. Greystoke, four miles west of Penrith, comprised 7,511 acres divided into ten townships and three chapelries and

---

[58] Vaisey (ed.), *Diary of Thomas Turner*, pp. 196, 241, 244.

[59] F. M. Eden, *The State of the Poor, A History of the Labouring Classes in England* (3 vols, London, 1797), ii. 46–100.

[60] Eden, *State of the Poor*, ii. 84.

[61] W. Hutchinson, *History of Cumberland* (2 vols, Carlisle, 1794), ii. 442–4, 451, 468, 657, 664; Eden, *State of the Poor*, ii. 49, 87, 89, 99.

accommodated 2,451 people by 1821.[62] Of these, Greystoke, Little Blencow, Johnby, and Motherby and Gill were united for the relief of paupers. The other nine areas supported their own poor separately.[63] In 1744 the united townships established a poorhouse to maintain their poor and agreed that, when opened, 'all the said poor of the Townships do enter the said Poorhouse otherwise cease asking any further supply'.[64] To help offset costs, common land was enclosed and the yearly rent arising applied to the poorhouse. If parish officials anticipated that this would absolve them of the majority of their responsibilities towards the poor, they were to be disappointed. Indeed, the poorhouse supplemented rather than replaced Greystoke's existing provision of outdoor relief in the form of house rents, house repairs, weekly allowances, fuel, clothing and medical services; and out-parish payments. Greystoke also contracted with individuals to care for fellow parishioners for a fixed fee under stringent conditions. In May 1766 John Hunter was 'put to boarding' with Miles Fleming at the rate of £2 14s 6d a year. Fleming was to mend Hunter's clothes at his own expense but the parish officers agreed to procure new ones 'at their proper charges'. In 1780 the parish agreed with Mary Tydal of Catterlen to nurse Ann Crodas's child for £5 8s for one year.[65] These tailored arrangements may reflect active negotiation between the parties and a shared sense of rights and obligations.

Strategies for managing the poor were more obviously institutional in the market town of Brampton, a parish of 6,466 acres (population: 2,921 in 1821), nine miles east of Carlisle.[66] A workhouse, in operation by 1777, had a capacity of twenty.[67] Ten years later, Thomas Allen was contracting with twelve settlements including Brampton, Hayton and Kirklinton to farm their poor.[68] In 1794, William Hutchinson stated unequivocally that Brampton had no workhouse and that paupers were boarded out at the rate of 2s 3d per week and out-pensions provided at 1s per week.[69] Nonetheless, in 1803 a workhouse in the town is recorded as accommodating twenty-

---

[62] Parson and White, *Directory Cumberland*, p. 473; <https://www.cumbriacountyhistory.org.uk/township/greystoke> [accessed 8 Feb. 2021].

[63] Parson and White, *Directory Cumberland*, p. 473.

[64] CAS, PR5/43, Greystoke, Poor account book, 1740–1812.

[65] CAS, PR5/43, Greystoke, Poor account book, 1740–1812.

[66] Parson and White, *Directory Cumberland*, p. 393; <https://www.cumbriacountyhistory.org.uk/township/brampton> [accessed 8 Feb. 2021].

[67] *A Report from the Committee Appointed to Inspect and Consider the Returns made by the Overseers of the Poor* (Parl. Paper 1777).

[68] CAS, SPUL/4/1, Report of poorhouses, 1787.

[69] Hutchinson, *History of Cumberland*, i. 131.

eight inmates, while a further thirteen adults and fifteen children were in receipt of regular outdoor relief. That year £140 was expended in relieving the poor in the workhouse and £111 11s 11d out of it.[70] By 1828, the poor were once again being farmed, this time for both indoor and outdoor relief. The contractor had use of the former workhouse's furniture but had to provide food and clothing and was also responsible for all casual relief including vagrancy.[71]

The twelve Staffordshire parishes included in the project are notable for their diversity, although none is located round Stoke-upon-Trent, with its burgeoning pottery industry. They include the traditional urban centre of the city of Lichfield with its cathedral, administrative functions, parliamentary representation, quarter sessions and court for the recovery of debts; Wednesbury and Darlaston, with their growing metalwork trades built on plentiful coal supplies; market towns including Uttoxeter, based around agriculture; and rural villages such as Abbots Bromley. Darlaston, located between Wednesbury and Walsall, experienced a 74.4 per cent increase in population between 1801 and 1831 (from 3,812 to 6,647) and Wednesbury 102.8 per cent (from 4,160 to 8,437).[72] As occurred elsewhere, an increasing population placed greater pressure on relief (Table 0.1).

By 1766, Wednesbury's small early eighteenth-century workhouse had been enlarged and enclosed. Twenty years later, it had either been substantially rebuilt or replaced.[73] In 1801–2 relief amounting to just over £951 was expended on an average of fifty-two workhouse inmates (sixteen men and thirty-six women). In the same year, an average of 172 people received outdoor relief at a cost of fractionally over £815.[74]

Table 0.1 Numbers in receipt of outdoor relief in Wednesbury, 1770–96

	Men	**Women**	**Children***	**Total**
March 1770	13	32	6	51
June 1789	15	34		49
November 1796	19	45	24	88

*The accounts do not always distinguish payments made to children.
Source: Adapted from J. F. Ede, *History of Wednesbury*, p. 168.

---

[70] *Abstract ... Expence and Maintenance of the Poor*, p. 79.
[71] CAS, PR60/21/13/6, Public meeting at Brampton Vestry, 3 Apr. 1828.
[72] *VCH Staffordshire*, i. 323–4.
[73] Ede, *History of Wednesbury*, pp. 164–5.
[74] The number of workhouse inmates in March 1775 was 71 and 56 in April 1775: Ede,

In contrast to Darlaston and Wednesbury, Lichfield's population grew by 36.5 per cent (from 4,842 to 6,607) between 1801 and 1831.[75] Parochial administration was divided between the Cathedral Close and the parishes of St Mary's, St Chad's and St Michael's. Only St Mary's, the largest parish, maintained a workhouse throughout the long eighteenth century. Periodic attempts to unite the city's parishes for the purposes of relief were either short-lived or failed to materialize altogether. The result was a shifting collection of relief strategies covering most forms of relief involving shared and independent workhouses, farming the poor, parish poorhouses, pensions, rents, casual relief and recourse to charity.[76] As with the other parishes and townships in the 'Small Bills' project, the survival of overseers' vouchers for St Mary's privileges nothing so much as a combination of administrative efficiency and serendipity.

Overseers' vouchers

The partial life story of Jane Sewell emerged through the bills and receipts generated as part of the administration of the Old Poor Law. At first glance, these overseers' vouchers may appear to be little more than 'indecipherable scrawl'. To dismiss them as such, however, would be to 'miss the chance to enter into an entire social world converging on the page'.[77] It is their very ordinariness and the multiple layers of information embedded within them that makes them important. Indeed, these scraps of paper and their survival, fundamental to the 'Small Bills' project, can be regarded as one of the 'rich, alternative sources for reaching the poor', and the goods and service providers who supplied them.[78]

By detailing daily interactions, overseers' vouchers reveal the degree of complexity and the time-consuming nature of poor-relief administration in the long eighteenth century and the increasing bureaucratization of society. Fleshing out the summaries presented in overseers' accounts, which Tim Wales described as the 'endpoint of processes which are often obscure', the vouchers provide background to hitherto unarticulated stories and illuminate the extent to which local economies were bound up with parish

---

History of Wednesbury, pp. 166–9.

[75] *VCH Staffordshire*, i. 329.

[76] *VCH Staffordshire*, xiv. 87–92.

[77] S. Rockman, 'The paper technologies of capitalism', *Technology and Culture*, lviii (2017), 487–505, at 498.

[78] A. Tomkins, *The Experience of Urban Poverty, 1723–1782: Parish Charity and Credit* (Manchester, 2006), p. 4.

expenditure.[79] Consequently, the vouchers add a new level of quotidian detail to metanarratives of consumption and material culture that frequently omit paupers as consumers. With the exceptions of more durable items such as household goods, tools, clothing and footwear, the vouchers reveal a world of ephemeral consumption designed to satisfy immediate needs: the payment of house rent, medical attention and food.[80] Analysis of the vouchers, therefore, provides the opportunity to show how the provisioning of workhouses and outdoor relief fit into the bigger pictures of purchasing and consumption practices, and how parishes influenced commercial environments and economic development.[81] As illustrated in the chapters on women and business and on clothing, they point to the structural significance of poor relief as a means of sustaining and underpinning local economies.[82]

Alannah Tomkins noted that the 'creation, retention and ultimate survival of records relating to ... labouring and poor populations' faltered in major towns and cities as a consequence of industrial change and rapid population growth.[83] As the eighteenth century turned into the nineteenth, however, those who came into contact with the Old Poor Law, either as parish officers, ratepayers, suppliers or recipients faced an increasingly bureaucratized system. Letters; petitions; parish registers; highway, churchwardens', overseers' and constables' accounts; vestry minutes; election notices; contracts; and bastardy, removal, settlement and apprenticeship papers all multiplied in response to enabling legislation, greater numbers of paupers, more suppliers and demands for greater accountability.[84] Included within such quotidian ephemera are overseers' vouchers. Over time, much of this material was discarded to make way for new accumulations of paperwork. As a result, survival rates between and within counties and parishes vary considerably. Equally important in determining the survival of vouchers is archival and preservation practice.

---

[79] T. Wales, 'The parish and the poor in the English Revolution', in *The Nature of the English Revolution Revisited: Essays in honour of John Morrill*, ed. S. Taylor and G. Tapsell (Woodbridge, 2013), pp. 53–81, at p. 62.

[80] J. Styles. 'Involuntary consumers? Servants and their clothes in eighteenth-century England', *Textile History*, xxxiii (2002), 9–21.

[81] P. M. Solar, 'Poor relief and English economic development before the Industrial Revolution', *The Economic History Review*, xlviii (1995), 1–22; S. King, 'Poor relief and English economic development reappraised', *The Economic History Review*, l (1997), 360–8.

[82] S. P. Walker, 'Expense, social and moral control: accounting and the administration of the Old Poor Law in England and Wales', *Journal of Accounting and Public Policy*, xxiii (2004), 85–127, at 87; Tomkins, *The Experience of Urban Poverty*, p. 3.

[83] Tomkins, *The Experience of Urban Poverty*, p. 4.

[84] Walker, 'Accounting and the administration of the Old Poor Law', 85–127.

Introduction

In 1894, the Local Government Act permitted the newly created county councils to make provision for archives; at the same time parish councils became responsible for non-ecclesiastical records of the parish.[85] It was not until the immediate post-war development of county record offices and the passage of the 1962 Local Government (Records) Act, regularizing the position of county record offices that significant progress was made in depositing and preserving parochial records nationally. This larger story of archival development hides a more regional one. Independent of legislation, pioneering work on establishing local archives was undertaken in the south-east between the 1920s and the late 1940s, laying the foundations for the county archive network. The regional nature of these innovations, however, means that parish archives – including vouchers – survive most completely in the south-east.[86] Arguably, the journey from parish chest to repository in the twentieth century created as many of the archival 'absences' as the records management practices of the eighteenth and nineteenth centuries.

Once individual bills had been settled and overseers' accounts had been written up in the vestry minutes or a separate account book, there was no specific need or requirement to preserve them. As vestry decisions came under greater scrutiny and pressure to reform the Poor Law gradually intensified, however, there was an increasing recognition that vestries had to become more accountable to those who funded parish welfare.[87] In 1744 the Poor Relief Act strengthened requirements to keep registers of expenditure on the poor. Overseers' accounts were to be written up at the end of each year and certified by magistrates.[88] Parishioners were permitted to inspect poor-rate accounts after giving notice and paying sixpence for the privilege. By 1793 further legislation had made it possible to prosecute overseers for neglect of duty, including the mismanagement of parochial funds.[89] It is noticeable that in many parish collections from around 1750, and especially after 1800, more vouchers were preserved. In some parishes, this preservation can be ascribed to the diligence of individual parish officers like Thomas Turner who, in addition to his occasional parochial duties, received two

---

[85] E. Shepherd, *Archives and Archivists in 20th Century England* (Abingdon, 2009), p. 26.

[86] The Parochial Registers and Records Measure (1929) undoubtedly encouraged many parishes to deposit material with the diocesan record office, formally administered by the diocesan registrar. In a few dioceses the county record office was also designated as a diocesan record office. It was not until the measure was revised in 1978 that this became common. Between 1946 and 1951 ecclesiastical archives were surveyed to ensure that future decisions could be taken in a coordinated manner: Shepherd, *Archives and Archivists*, p. 135.

[87] Walker, 'Accounting and the administration of the Old Poor Law', 85–127.

[88] 17 Geo II, c 38.

[89] 33 Geo III, c 55.

pounds per year to act as parish clerk.[90] In other parishes, it was because of established procedures that became resistant to change. From the later 1770s, there were repeated requests by the national government to provide detailed accounts of parochial expenditure. It is evident, however, that a significant gap existed between what was expected and what individual parishes did. In the parish of St Mary's, Lichfield, Frederick Morton Eden reported that the accounts were 'in such a confused state (some years being lost and others not settled) [that] very little information could be collected'.[91] By 1822, however, incoming bills were pasted into two large bound volumes in date order.

Unevenness in the archival record raises questions over how well the vouchers represent spending on the poor. In some instances, records have simply not survived. In others, it is the consequence of the ways in which poor relief was managed. Fewer vouchers survive for Cumberland compared to East Sussex or Staffordshire, posing some problems when assessing aspects of continuity and change. Across a thirty-six-year period, there are only thirty-four vouchers for Irthington and just seventeen covering a ninety-nine-year period for Kirklinton.[92] This pattern is due, in part, to the widespread practice of farming out paupers, since contractors were not expected to provide bills or account for their expenditure. In 1787 thirty parishes or quarters in Eskdale and Cumberland wards farmed their poor. Contractors were paid an annual sum plus a set amount per pauper to maintain and support them.[93] Rent, clothing, beds and bedding, however, remained the responsibility of individual parishes or townships. Consequently, vouchers were generated for items purchased by parishes but not for those purchased by contractors. Some of the parishes also maintained their poor at home. Paupers in receipt of pensions did not produce accounts of their expenditure. Unevenness is also evident in the ways in which information in the vouchers was recorded. This is especially true for payments made to those without settled status. In 1821 John Waltham of Abbots Bromley drew up a list of relief payments given to 'poor travellers': twenty-nine men, twenty-two women and twenty-seven children, none of whom were named. In such instances, discussed in Hitchcock's chapter (Chapter 3), parish authorities were less likely to record individual names. A few pennies to help them on their way was preferable to the more costly and time-consuming expense of vagrant examinations.

---

[90] ESRO, PAR378/31/1/1/, East Hoathly, Overseers' account book, 1761–79.

[91] Eden, *State of the Poor*, ii. 653–4.

[92] King, *Poverty and Welfare*, p. 186; CAS, PR83/16/1–7, Irthington, Overseers' vouchers, 1783–1819; PR156/7/1–17, Kirklinton, Overseers' vouchers, 1735–1834.

[93] CAS, SPUL/4/1, Report of poorhouses, 1787.

Even with seemingly uninterrupted runs of vouchers, there is no certainty that they represent total expenditure on relief or indeed, whether items paid for by the parish, including those destined for the workhouse, were intended for or even reached paupers. During the long eighteenth century, it was commonplace to dispense alcohol as medicinal relief at the same time as it was customary to provide refreshments to the vestry. Thomas Turner recalled in March 1758: 'In the evening I went down to Jones's, where we had a vestry ... We stayed until about 11:30 quarrelling and wrangling. We spent on the parish account 5/–, and also 3½*d* each of our own.'[94] Some expenses, including payments relating to assistant overseers' salaries, legal fees, the outlay of officials who attended local assizes or vestry meetings held in inns, the construction and maintenance of workhouses and their gardens, and administrative expenses 'benefited' the poor indirectly.[95] Payments such as these, however, were increasingly acknowledged in parliamentary statistics as parishes were asked to report administrative costs separately.

Unevenness in the historic record is compounded if corresponding overseers' accounts are absent or if parish workhouses operated according to the provisions of Gilbert's Act. These workhouses were required to draw up their own accounts and present them separately from other vestry expenditure. This financial arrangement was increasingly followed by those administering workhouses in single parishes, making the overseers' accounts progressively opaque. In comparing the vouchers to entries in account books, it is notable that some items are either under-represented or missing entirely. These absences could include labour or services provided by the parish poor, the regular payment of maintenance for illegitimate children and payments towards parish pensions. Paupers undertaking occasional work for the parish rarely presented bills, perhaps because of their inability to write or the associated cost of paper, pen and ink, and possibly because the issue of a bill by a pauper would have been regarded as inappropriate. Overseers, however, sometimes drew them up on their behalf. As occurred in Cumberland, regular payments for pensions or maintenance would generate a voucher only if parish officers chose to be punctilious about disbursements, perhaps wherever the overseers themselves sought reimbursement for pension monies paid out.

---

[94] John Jones was the publican of The Crown public house in East Hoathly where the vestry invariably met. On 3 Mar. 1758 seven men attended the meeting, and the allowance for refreshments was approximately five shillings: ESRO, AMS6532/1–4, Dean K. Worcester, Transcript of Thomas Turner's diaries, 3 Mar. 1758, pp. 672(1)–673(1).

[95] See Interlude 4 (M. Dean, 'The Wilkinsons and the Griffin Inn, Penrith') in this volume.

Overseers' vouchers represent the 'written means of storing and conveying information', although their form and appearance vary significantly.[96] Accustomed to trading on credit, retailers, producers and service providers used them to record what they had supplied. The majority are handwritten. Except for a flurry of vouchers associated with the drawing up of annual accounts at Easter, sampling the data for parishes reveals few consistent patterns regarding days of the week or periods in the year when accounts were settled. A bill or invoice was usually generated by the supplier and passed, by hand, to an overseer. On payment, overseers may have asked recipients to sign the bills or added their own signature to confirm that accounts had been settled, enabling them to write up monthly or annual accounts for the parish. At a time when individual methods of accounting and bookkeeping varied considerably and as bills might remain unpaid for months, retaining vouchers offered proof that goods or services had been supplied or that payment had been made.[97] Retained bills were stored in different ways. In Uttoxeter, Staffordshire, they were folded in thirds, divided into bundles and tied with tape. In a similar manner, Ringmer's vouchers were so numerous during the 1820s that they were sorted into monthly bundles, remaining in the order in which they were received or paid. Others, like those at Kirkby Lonsdale, Westmorland, with their tell-tale holes, were kept on long, metal receipt spikes.

Similar to pauper letters, the orthography of vouchers runs the gamut from uncertain hands with phonetic spellings to others exhibiting clerk-like precision. In addition to business owners, some were drawn up by assistants, apprentices, family members or parish officials. A small number show evidence of reuse, with different orders on each side or contain working calculations. Others, like the one on a fragment of an East India Company report on tea sales, were written on the backs of old handbills, price lists or printed circulars.[98] Some vouchers contain entries for hundreds of items; others are notable for their brevity. Surgeons, apothecaries, doctors, grocers, drapers and haberdashers tended to submit lengthy bills often covering several months. Butchers submitted substantially shorter bills more frequently. Unless notes or letters accompany the vouchers, there is little in the way of personal testimony or comment. Where comments exist, they are mediated through the commercial language common to the period.[99] Printed bill-heads form a minority of the collection. A few,

---

[96] Rockman, 'Paper technologies', 487.

[97] J. Raven, *Publishing Business in Eighteenth-Century England* (Woodbridge, 2014), p. 184.

[98] CAS, Kendal, WPR19/7/1/5/6/19, Kirkby Lonsdale, Overseers' vouchers, *c.*1809.

[99] P. Hudson, 'Correspondence and commitment: British traders' letters in the long-eighteenth century', *Cultural and Social History*, xi (2014), 527–53.

containing illustrations of the wide range of products on offer, are indicative of a business's status and ambitions.[100] Others are pre-printed standard blank forms, including out-parish demands for reimbursement designed to reduce the burden of parish administration around non-resident paupers.[101] As with other printed ephemera like quasi-legal documents, 'unambiguous language and utility of design were paramount ... A typical example left gaps of varying sizes according to what had to be filled in, the structure of the language forming a prompt to the writer.'[102] Surviving bills from stationer Elizabeth Wetton attest to the range of printed ephemera she supplied to Uttoxeter's overseers: certificates, lists of paupers, Board of Health and cholera notices, electoral and voters' lists, 'sets of poor accounts' and handbills.[103] These administrative forms proliferated as the management and administration of the Poor Law became increasingly bureaucratic. John Coles, a stationer from Pulborough in Sussex, with strong family ties there, began to dominate the market for pre-printed forms, particularly those concerning poor relief. By the middle of the eighteenth century, his forms were used nationally, from Westmorland to Sussex, including in East Hoathly.[104] In nineteenth-century Cumberland, Charles Thurnam increasingly supplied parishes with printed materials.[105] Standardized receipts, itemizing commonly purchased goods, were also popular, especially with innkeepers like the Wilkinsons of Penrith: meals and drinks consumed, and hay and corn provided for horses, were marked up alongside the relevant items.[106]

Whatever their form and appearance or the level of literacy displayed, most vouchers tended to conform to standard business conventions. That is, their purpose was to convey information about the goods and services provided in

[100] Raven, *Publishing Business*, p. 53; P. Collinge, 'Chinese tea, Turkish coffee and Scottish tobacco: image and meaning in Uttoxeter's Poor Law vouchers', *Transactions of the Staffordshire Archaeological and Historical Society*, xlix (2017), 80–9. See also Amy Louise Erickson, 'Wealthy businesswomen, marriage and succession in eighteenth-century London', *Business History* (2022), DOI: 10.1080/00076791.2022.2036131.

[101] Raven, *Publishing Business*, p. 7.

[102] M. Twyman, 'Printed ephemera', in *The Cambridge History of the Book, 1695–1830*, ed. M. F. Suarez and M. L. Turner (7 vols, Cambridge, 2009), v. 66–82, at p. 74.

[103] SRO, D3891/6/34/7/19b, Elizabeth Wetton, 30 Oct. 1829; D3891/6/37/12/8, 9 Apr. 1832; D3891/6/39/1/2, 8 Apr. 1833; D3891/6/39/1/13, 20 July 1833; D3891/6/39/8/48, 23 Mar. 1833; D3891/6/39/8/62, 10 May–25 Aug. 1832.

[104] N. Tadmor, 'The settlement of the poor and the rise of the form in England, c.1662–1780', *Past & Present*, ccxxxvi (2017), 43–97.

[105] P. Collinge, '"Exceedingly obnoxious to others in the trade": Carlisle bookseller, printer and publisher Charles Thurnam (1796–1852)', *Northern History*, lviii (2021), 66–85.

[106] See Interlude 4 (M. Dean, 'The Wilkinsons and the Griffin Inn, Penrith') in this volume; CAS, SPC21/8/11/13, Griffin Inn, Penrith, c.1800.

a way that would be intelligible to the recipient. Elizabeth Spencer's chapter on clothing (Chapter 2) brings this need for clarity to the fore. When bills could be submitted a considerable time after the goods were supplied, it was necessary to ensure that their contents were adequately described and priced. The most detailed examples contain the date the bill was submitted; a top line addressed to the parish, overseers or workhouse followed by 'Bt [bought] of' or 'Dr [debtor] to' and the supplier's name. Except for the bills of grocers, drapers and haberdashers (which frequently list several items on the same line), goods and services were typically itemised individually with the unit price, quantity purchased and the total price. At the bottom the overall total and the date the bill was settled is followed either by the business owner's name, that of their assistant, or their mark and is sometimes countersigned by a parish official. Such information is not always evident. Many bills lack specific details about expenditure or the name of the recipient of the relief. In others, only one recipient is named where clearly (given the nature and quantity of goods supplied) the relief was destined for several. The intended use of some goods and services is potentially problematic where uses or quantities are unspecified. Lime, for instance, could be used for improving soil, making limewash, plaster or mortar. Sometimes, unspecified 'goods' were simply delivered 'to the workhouse'. In some instances, notably in Sussex, bills issued by overseers for goods and services they had supplied can be difficult to differentiate from those seeking reimbursement after having already paid for goods and services.

Qualifications aside, by detailing daily interactions, overseers' vouchers reveal the degree of complexity and the time-consuming nature of poor-relief administration in the long eighteenth century and the increasing bureaucratization of society. They also demonstrate that, through their requests, the poor were less marginal in local economies than might be anticipated. Paupers influenced directly and indirectly what everyday goods and services local businesses produced, stocked and offered. One consequence of this was to see returned to those who paid the poor rate some of their outlay through expenditure on the goods and services they supplied to the parish. Even with the tightening of relief criteria in the early 1800s, the vouchers display an astonishingly diverse response to what constituted the relief of poverty. Moreover, by rendering communities of overseers, shopkeepers, tradespeople, producers and professionals visible, the vouchers offer the possibility of a newly granular understanding of the interactions of all the people who came into contact with the Poor Law. The resulting research, evident in this volume, constitutes a new approach to parish welfare and the economics of poverty with the ability to reach new cohorts among the people caught up in the Poor Law, whether as recipients or as providers.

I. Paupers and vagrants

1. Accounting for illegitimacy: parish politics and the poor

Louise Falcini

In the early morning of 15 February 1757 Thomas Turner, the parish overseer, walked the short distance to John Durrant's house and informed John's daughter, Ann, that he would accompany her to see the local magistrate Mr George Courthope later that day. Courthope lived some four miles away in Uckfield, a short walk if you were fit and healthy but an arduous journey if, like Ann, you were heavily pregnant. The previous evening Ann had readily agreed to 'swear the father' of her unborn child 'at any time', and so she set off a short while later in company with Susan Swift, who was paid sixpence for her trouble, with Turner following on behind.[1] The process of an unmarried woman formally naming the father of her expected child set in motion a chain of events that was played out across thousands of local communities during the eighteenth century. This chapter looks at these encounters in one small Sussex village, East Hoathly, in a single decade, the 1750s, when the law, parochial authorities and settled paupers came together over the seemingly simple but nonetheless intractably messy issue of managing unmarried motherhood.

In the eighteenth century parishes across rural England continued to experience a steady rise in illegitimacy. In many parishes, the ratio of illegitimate first births to similar legitimate births increased considerably in the decades around mid-century, creating financial tensions in the systems of support.[2] Parishioners and their vestries became increasingly concerned

---

[1] ESRO, AMS6532/1–4, Dean K. Worcester, Transcript of Thomas Turner's diaries, 15 Feb. 1757, p. 408.

[2] P. Laslett, 'Introduction: Comparing illegitimacy over time and between cultures', in *Bastardy and its Comparative History: Studies in the History of Illegitimacy and Marital Nonconformity in Britain, France, Germany, Sweden, North America, Jamaica and Japan*, ed. P. Laslett, K. Oosterveen and R. M. Smith (London, 1980), pp. 1–68, at pp. 14–15; K. Oosterveen, R. M. Smith and S. Stewart, 'Family reconstitution and the study of bastardy: evidence from certain English parishes', in *Bastardy*, ed. Laslett, Oosterveen and Smith, pp. 86–140. For a brief critique of the methodologies used in these papers see A. Levene, T. Nutt and S. Williams (eds), *Illegitimacy in Britain, 1700–1920* (Basingstoke, 2005), pp. 5–8.

L. Falcini, 'Accounting for illegitimacy: parish politics and the poor' in *Providing for the Poor: The Old Poor Law, 1750–1834*, ed. P. Collinge and L. Falcini (London, 2022), pp. 25–49. License: CC BY-NC-ND 4.0.

with the economics of unmarried motherhood. An impending illegitimate birth, particularly to plebeian women like Ann Durrant, and Jane Sewell, who appeared in the Preface of this book, was especially troubling for the effect it could have on parochial poor rates. The overseers' vouchers can account for part of this story, but the absences outlined in the Introduction identify points where the vouchers or account books are missing or silent or, more frustratingly, where the recorded details are opaque. But the cost alone does not adequately reflect or explain the complex management of unmarried motherhood, pauper marriages and parochial settlement that underpinned social policy across the eighteenth century. To do so, we need to examine the 'politics of procreation' embedded in the day-to-day administration of parochial income in order to explore the workings of power and agency, acted out between neighbours and ratepayers, each with a vested interest.[3] By exploring the microhistories of just a few women, caught in negotiation with one of the smallest of English parishes, this chapter will draw on a wider range of sources to argue that the financial implications of unmarried motherhood for a small rural community, in dialogue with the agency employed by prospective parents, substantially shaped the management of illegitimate births in these parishes, and by extension the lives of hundreds of thousands of unmarried mothers caught in the same net of relations.

Research on illegitimacy began to emerge from the wide-scale population studies of the 1970s and 1980s.[4] This research examined demographic change across England and identified the ebb and flow of illegitimate births, which largely followed the birth rate. Illegitimacy ratios rose as the population was increasing, and slowed when population growth was stagnant or declining. Thus, as the population grew across the later eighteenth century, so did the ratio of illegitimate first births, particularly from mid-century, and it continued to do so well into the nineteenth century. There were, however, notable disparities both within and between regions, where ratios remained at a largely constant rate.[5] Underlying these broad changes, a declining

---

[3] N. Tadmor. 'Where was Mrs Turner? Governance and gender in an eighteenth-century village', in *Remaking English Society: Social Relations and Social Change in Early Modern England*, ed. S. Hindle, A. Shepard and J. Walter (Woodbridge, 2013), pp. 89–112, at p. 98.

[4] Oosterveen, Smith and Stewart, 'Family reconstitution'.

[5] E. A. Wrigley, 'Marriage, fertility and population growth in eighteenth-century England', in *Marriage and Society: Studies in the Social History of Marriage*, ed. R. B. Outhwaite (London, 1981), pp. 155–63; E. A. Wrigley, R. S. Davies, J. E. Oeppen and R. S. Schofield, *English Population History from Family Reconstitution, 1500–1837* (Cambridge, 1997), pp. 421–2; R. Adair, *Courtship, Illegitimacy, and Marriage in Early Modern England* (Manchester, 1996).

age at marriage and economic fluctuations influenced both national and regional ratios of illegitimacy.[6] At the same time, bridal pregnancy increased. It has been calculated that in the period 1750–99 an average of 33 per cent of women gave birth within seven months of marriage. Again, this varied significantly from region to region, with some 20 per cent of women pregnant at marriage in some areas and 40 per cent or more in others.[7] Higher rates of prenuptial pregnancy and illegitimacy suggested that sex was a widely accepted part of courtship for the poor. Both Randolph Trumbach and Tim Hitchcock identified these variations with a rise in heterosexual penetrative sex as a precursor to marriage.[8] While sexual reputation was part of a wider concern for probity, there was a general acceptance of bridal pregnancy among the poor. Likewise, unmarried motherhood did not prove a barrier to a subsequent marriage with a new partner.[9] These early demographic analyses also identified clusters of illegitimate births among specific families. From this, Peter Laslett posited that the propensity to bear illegitimate children was passed from one generation to the next, in what he termed a 'bastardy prone sub-society'.[10] Women who gave birth to more than one illegitimate child were, somewhat pejoratively, termed 'repeaters' in this literature. More recent research by Steven King and Barry Reay have successfully unpicked some of the complexities concerning familial ties and illegitimacy to give further context to regional variation.[11] While older accounts of illegitimacy and unmarried motherhood have, for the most part, emphasized shame, coerced marriage and the moral judgement of others, the agency of unmarried mothers and the fathers of their children,

---

[6] For women mean age at marriage fell from 26.4 years in the first half of the 18th century to 23.9 years 100 years later: Laslett, Oosterveen, Smith (eds), *Bastardy*, p. 21.

[7] Laslett, 'Introduction', p. 23.

[8] T. Hitchcock, 'Sex and gender: redefining sex in eighteenth-century England', *History Workshop Journal*, xli (1996), 72–90; T. Hitchcock, *English Sexualities, 1700–1800* (Basingstoke, 1997); R. Trumbach, *Sex and the Gender Revolution: Heterosexuality and the Third Gender in Enlightenment London* (Chicago, 1998).

[9] Kate Gibson notes this contested notion of shame in the current literature: K. Gibson, 'Experiences of illegitimacy in England, 1660–1834' (unpublished University of Sheffield PhD thesis, 2018), p. 25.

[10] P. Laslett, 'The bastardy prone sub society', in *Bastardy*, ed. Laslett, Oosterveen and Smith, pp. 232–8.

[11] S. King, 'The bastardy prone sub-society again: bastards and their fathers and mothers in Lancashire, Wiltshire, and Somerset, 1800–1840', in *Illegitimacy in Britain, 1700–1920*, ed. Levene, Nutt and Williams, pp. 66–85; B. Reay, 'Sexuality in nineteenth-century England: the social context of illegitimacy in rural Kent', *Rural History*, i (1990), 219–47.

along with the lived experience of the poor, has only recently formed a subject of sustained scholarship.[12]

In the eighteenth century, poor women likely to give birth to an illegitimate child were subject to intrusive questioning as part of the legal process of managing unmarried motherhood. It was difficult to compel a woman to reveal intimate details about her relationships or pregnancy but access to financial support could be curtailed if she refused to do so. Formal procedures were initiated by 'swearing the father' before a magistrate, known as a 'bastardy examination'.[13] Here, pregnant women or new mothers were 'examined' as to the circumstance of their pregnancy and asked to name the father of their child. The examination and resulting document permitted the parish to place financial liability for the infant on a specified man. This man could then either agree to indemnify the parish and make provision for the child by means of a 'bastardy bond', a civil agreement contracted with the parish allowing the father to pay costs as they arose, including a weekly sum for the maintenance of the child.[14] Alternatively, he could pay, if he was able, an agreed sum to cover the entirety of the expense likely to be incurred by the parish, including the expense of apprenticing the child. In 1733 a new statute clarified legal remedies for recouping monies from fathers. It enabled parochial officers to have the man taken up by warrant or summoned to appear before magistrates at petty sessional hearings, where an order of filiation was granted, provided the magistrates were agreed over the likelihood of the child's paternity.[15] These formal proceedings were underpinned by a

---

[12] Adair, *Courtship, Illegitimacy, and Marriage*; D. Levine and K. Wrightson, 'The social context of illegitimacy in early modern England', in *Bastardy*, ed. Laslett, Oosterveen and Smith, pp. 158–77; A. Macfarlane, 'Illegitimacy and illegitimates in English history', in *Bastardy*, ed. Laslett, Oosterveen and Smith, pp. 71–85; Reay, 'Sexuality in nineteenth-century England'; D. Cohen, *Family Secrets: Living with Shame from the Victorians to the Present Day* (London, 2013); E. Griffin, 'Sex, illegitimacy and social change in industrializing Britain', *Social History*, xxxviii (2013), 139–61; S. Williams, '"I was forced to leave my place to hide my shame": the living arrangements of unmarried mothers in London in the early nineteenth century', in *Accommodating Poverty: The Housing and Living Arrangements of the English Poor, c.1600–1850*, ed. J. McEwan and P. Sharpe (Basingstoke, 2011), pp. 191–220; Levene, Nutt and Williams (eds), *Illegitimacy in Britain*.

[13] This process should have taken place before two magistrates but in practice there was very often a single magistrate.

[14] Failure to keep up payments could mean that the entirety of the bond; perhaps twenty, thirty or even forty pounds or more would become forfeit to the parish. These amounts were well beyond the annual earnings of a labouring man.

[15] 6 Geo II, c 31, An Act for the Relief of Parishes and Other Places from Such Charges as May Arise from Bastard Children Born within the Same, 1733.

welfare system predicated on a pauper's place of legal settlement.[16] This often proved contentious, as it defined which community would pay for the care of the mother and child if they were unable to provide for themselves. An illegitimate child would take the settlement of its place of birth. After 1744 this was widely interpreted as the mother's place of settlement, although the 1744 statute specifically identified that this applied only to a child born to a vagrant mother.[17] The wide-ranging assistance supported by this national system was administered locally and financed by a parish poor rate, thereby making it particularly responsive to local conditions. As the economics of providing for the poor became increasingly important, many communities sought to ameliorate parochial costs to benefit their own ratepayers. The subsequent close management of the settlement system, where paupers were quickly returned to their place of legal settlement, fostered a society in which the petty exclusionary politics of the parish became an important element in the economics of poverty across the eighteenth century, thus creating a vast paper trail of both vouchers and entries in overseers' or vestry accounts, as parochial officers sought reimbursement for the administrative and legal costs of settlement and removal.[18] In parallel, many thousands of parishes used the flexibility of the welfare system and the confines of the settlement laws to manage illegitimacy or potential illegitimacy in their own communities. But poor men and women directly concerned with a pregnancy were also able to influence those outcomes, sometimes through collusive arrangements, at other times by their sheer intransigence and on occasion by negotiation – not all of which have left readily available traces. By exploring a series of bastardy cases that arose in East Hoathly within just a few months of each other in 1756 and 1757, the details of which were recorded in Thomas Turner's diary, this chapter illustrates the strategies used in this one small rural community at a point when such births were relatively infrequent. It highlights the approaches and financial pressures at work as the ratio of illegitimate births began to increase much more

---

[16] Settlement was more often than not the place of a pauper's birth; a new settlement might be gained by serving an apprenticeship, by employment of more than a year, by serving as a parish officer or by renting a house for more than £10 per annum. By far the simplest way for a woman to acquire a new settlement was to marry, as she would automatically take the settlement of her husband. See T. Hitchcock, S. Howard and R. Shoemaker, 'Settlement', *London Lives, 1690 to 1800* <https://www.londonlives.org/static/Settlement.jsp> [accessed 20 Mar. 2021].

[17] 17 Geo II, c 5, s 25, Vagrancy Act, 1744.

[18] S. Hindle, *On the Parish?: The Micro-Politics of Poor Relief in Rural England c. 1550–1750* (Oxford, 2004), pp. 300–60; K. D. M. Snell, *Parish and Belonging: Community, Identity and Welfare in England and Wales, 1700-1950* (Cambridge, 2006), pp. 81–161.

quickly than previous years, and by extension in many of the 15,000 parishes in England and Wales.[19]

East Hoathly was a small east Sussex parish of around 350 inhabitants. In the first half of the eighteenth century there was approximately one baptism of an illegitimate first-born child every four years. By the last quarter of the century, approximately one illegitimate first-born child was baptized every year.[20] At the annual meeting of the vestry, just after Easter 1756, the parish acquired a new overseer of the poor, Thomas Turner, a man in his late twenties and a relative newcomer to the parish, who, as a shopkeeper, was familiar with small-scale accounting. This made him ideally placed to pay close attention to parochial expenditure. He was extremely assiduous in this regard, leaving bills and receipts for thousands of items supplied to the poor of East Hoathly. As with other parishes, the East Hoathly vestry was keen to keep the poor rate low, but the pregnancy of an unmarried or widowed woman signalled a significant and ongoing expense to the community. There were few legal options. If the putative father was able to marry, it might be enough to keep the woman off the parish. If he had a settlement elsewhere, all the better, as the newly married couple could be removed to the husband's parish. Where marriage was not a possibility, recovering money from the father became a parochial priority. At the beginning of Turner's first term as overseer, collecting arrears of maintenance became his first real opportunity to demonstrate his effective management of the poor rate.

The first case to involve Thomas Turner concerned the illegitimate child of Ann Cain, born four years earlier in 1752. When Peter Adams fathered

---

[19] In decades around the mid-eighteenth century the ratio of illegitimate to legitimate births in many parishes began to rise at a much higher rate, creating new financial tensions as parishes sought to manage these additional burdens, though this varied enormously by region: Adair, *Courtship, Illegitimacy, and Marriage*, pp. 110–28.

[20] R. Probert (ed.), *Cohabitation and Non-Marital Births in England and Wales, 1600–2012* (Basingstoke, 2014), pp. 1–9; T. Evans, *'Unfortunate Objects': Lone Mothers in Eighteenth-Century London* (Basingstoke, 2005); T. Nutt, 'The paradox and problems of illegitimate paternity in Old Poor Law Essex', in *Illegitimacy in Britain*, ed. Levene, Nutt and Williams, pp. 102–21; S. Williams, '"They lived together as Man and Wife": plebeian cohabitation, illegitimacy, and broken relationships in London, 1700–1840', in *Cohabitation*, ed. Probert, pp. 65–79; E. Griffin, 'Sex, illegitimacy and social change in industrializing Britain', *Social History*, xxxviii (2013), 139–61; J. Bailey, '"All he wanted was to kill her that he might marry the girl": broken marriages and cohabitation in the long eighteenth century', in *Cohabitation*, ed. Probert, pp. 51–64; A. Muir, 'Courtship, sex and poverty: illegitimacy in eighteenth-century Wales', *Social History*, xlii (2018), 56–80; K. Barclay, 'Love, care and the illegitimate child in eighteenth-century Scotland', *Transactions of the Royal Historical Society*, xxix (2019), 105–26.

the child, marriage had been out of the question since he already had a wife and nine children. A month after the birth of his illegitimate daughter, Adams entered into a bond with the parish to maintain the child at eighteen pence per week. The arrangement worked well for the first four years. The parish paid Ann Cain her weekly allowance, which was in turn, reimbursed by Adams, but by 1756 the regular maintenance payments made by Adams had become erratic. As Adams's payments became irregular, the parish came under considerable pressure to continue the maintenance payments for the child (despite Ann's recent marriage to Thomas Ling). When Turner took over as overseer in April 1756, he consulted other parishioners over the best course of action. At first, Turner obtained a warrant requiring Adams to appear before Mr Justice Poole in Lewes to explain his non-payment, but was reluctant to serve it, feeling that a legal letter would be more persuasive. He continued to pressure Adams into paying but was repeatedly fobbed off with excuses and promises. It soon became clear to Turner, following legal advice, that the bond superseded the bastardy order and the only way to recover the money was by suing at common law. As the weeks and months went by, Turner granted various extensions and favours over the payment of Adams's arrears. It was not until July 1758 that Adams finally paid the outstanding debt and a sum to cover the maintenance of the child until she was seven, a total of £8 15s 6d.[21] The affair dragged on for two years and, although Turner saved the parish the considerable expense of legal fees and recouped the loss, the parish had carried the expense of maintaining the child during that time. In decades when an illegitimate birth in East Hoathly happened only every three to four years, 1757 was about to become an *annus horribilis* for parochial expenditure on unmarried mothers and their children, leaving parish finances much depleted and the vestry and ratepayers increasingly fractious.

In the late autumn of 1756, the then twenty-one-year-old Ann Durrant was living in Laughton, a small village in east Sussex, where she received a shilling or two a week from the parish.[22] By February of the following year Ann was visibly pregnant by George Hyland. In 1733 the law had been changed to protect a woman from intrusive questioning about her pregnancy in the time closest to the birth of her child.[23] Overseers and magistrates were prohibited from quizzing her directly about the father of her expected child from a month before the expected birth until a month after the child was born, although of course she could volunteer the information. They were,

---

[21] ESRO, AMS6532/1–4, Worcester, Transcript, 3 July 1758, p. 608(2).
[22] ESRO, PAR409/31/1/2, Laughton, Account book of disbursements, 1723–60.
[23] 6 Geo II, c 31, s 4.

however, able to question her about her settlement status – her right to live in the parish and to claim financial support there. On Friday, 18 February 1757, Ann Durrant was thus taken the few miles to Uckfield where the magistrate, George Courthope, questioned her as to her legal settlement. It was determined as the neighbouring parish of East Hoathly, the parish of her birth and where, for over a year, she had been employed as a farm servant by Thomas Brazier. Following this adjudication, she was no longer entitled to further assistance from the parish of Laughton and the overseers immediately sought a removal order, requiring the signatures of two magistrates. This document permitted the parish of Laughton to 'remove' Ann to her now legally established place of settlement, East Hoathly. Despite Ann being 'big with child', she was delivered to the overseer at East Hoathly, Mr Thomas Turner, that same day.

This process was an entirely legitimate method of offloading the considerable expense of the impending birth, together with the ongoing care and maintenance of an illegitimate child, in this instance to an adjacent parish. Although that parish was able to recover some of this money from the father, this was by no means guaranteed.[24] Laughton's overseers and other parochial officers were almost certainly aware that George Hyland was the child's father and that he was wholly unable to support a family. Indeed, they were already supporting one or possibly two children from his marriage, which had ended on the death of his wife some two years previously. Turner safely received Ann Durrant in East Hoathly, and the following morning he went to see her father, John, who lived locally. Carefully avoiding direct pressure on Ann, Turner confirmed with Ann's father that she was willing to name the father of her expected child. Therefore, for a second day in a row, Ann was voluntarily despatched to Uckfield to swear a further document in front of the local magistrate. This time the signature of only one magistrate was required. As soon as Ann had named George Hyland from Laughton, Turner acquired a warrant to apprehend him. Two ill-advised attempts failed, tipping off Laughton's overseers that their parishioner was to be taken up as the father of Ann's child. A third attempt was then made. A small party of men from East Hoathly set out for Laughton. This time there was more preparation. First, the East Hoathly party ascertained that Hyland was indeed at home. They then visited James Rabson, the Laughton headborough and asked him to serve the warrant. Rabson refused to do this alone, even though Thomas Turner and Robert Hook from East Hoathly

---

[24] Thomas Nutt suggests that samples varied from less than 32 per cent of monies recovered in some Essex parishes during the early 19th century to 85 per cent in a similar sample from parishes in the West Riding of Yorkshire: Nutt, 'Paradox and problems'.

volunteered to accompany him and despite Hyland having the use of only one arm. Turner offered Rabson's son-in-law a shilling to assist but Rabson refused to swear him in. A second individual was proposed and refused; the rather exasperated Turner again pressed Rabson to go alone. This reluctance to cooperate did not go unnoticed. Turner noted in his diary that he had entreated Rabson 'to serve our warrant and not to use us ill'.[25] After extended negotiations, Rabson finally agreed to go and find someone to assist, and landed on Laughton's overseer, William Goad, who lived half a mile in the opposite direction from Hyland's house.

These prevarications suggest that the parochial officers of Laughton were entirely aware of East Hoathly's aim of taking up Hyland as the father of an illegitimate child and of the financial implications if the couple were coerced into marriage. A marriage in this context, dictated by the laws of settlement, would shift the financial burden and the marital home to Laughton. This would not involve a single illegitimate birth but a family with the possibility of several more children, all of whom might require parochial assistance. This exclusionary policing of parochial boundaries using the laws of settlement clearly contributed to the complexity of an already difficult relationship between these parishes.[26] As welfare costs rose through the eighteenth century, the management of welfare processes by local communities came under enormous pressure to keep poor rates as low as possible, or at least static. So, while Turner remained deeply suspicious of Rabson's motives, the men from East Hoathly pressed on.

What followed was a comedy of errors and misdirection. The small party went directly to George Hyland's house, where he was roused from his bed together with Durrant, who, despite the magistrates' order, had returned to Laughton and Hyland's house within days, possibly hours, of her enforced removal. This was clearly an ongoing relationship. The growing band trudged back to East Hoathly together with Durrant and Hyland, where they arrived around midnight. They called on John Watford, a regular attender of the vestry, and proceeded to Jones's, the local public house, where they remained drinking until at least 2 a.m., charging 3s to the parish account. In the early hours of the morning the group breakfasted at Turner's house and in typical Turner fashion dined 'on the remains of yesterday's dinner'.[27] Turner resolved to charge the parish account six shillings for the meal.

The following morning, the Laughton overseers arrived in East Hoathly to

---

[25] ESRO, AMS6532/1–4, Worcester, Transcript, 22 Feb. 1757, p. 414.

[26] Hindle, *On the Parish?*, p. 353.

[27] This phrase is used frequently in Thomas Turner's diary. See D. Vaisey (ed.), *The Diary of Thomas Turner, 1754–1765* (East Hoathly, 1994).

make the parish an offer of eighteen pence per week as maintenance for the child and forty shillings for the lying-in. This was declined in the hope that Hyland would marry Durrant, thus entirely removing the problem from East Hoathly since the new family would be required to live in Laughton. Later that day, Turner and a small party travelled to Uckfield to consult the local magistrate, hoping he could broker a resolution. After some discussion, they agreed to return the following day, together with their now prisoner, Hyland. In the early evening, they made their way back to East Hoathly and again assembled at Turner's house; after a short while, they went on to Jones's public house. Turner retired to bed exhausted, but he was not left in peace.

During the evening Turner was called on several times to go to Jones's, where he eventually arrived at around 12.30 a.m. There he discovered that the party would not go to Uckfield the following morning because Hyland had agreed to marry Durrant. Jeremiah French, on behalf of East Hoathly, had agreed that the parish would pay Hyland five pounds, provide a ring to the value of ten shillings and a wedding breakfast, and pay for the marriage licence. Turner, believing that almost everyone was drunk, returned home to bed. He was called on at 7.30 a.m. that same morning and told that if he obtained the licence from Lewes there would be a marriage. Turner immediately set out for Lewes only to return empty-handed because he had not been accompanied by the groom, Hyland. That afternoon, after borrowing a horse and the money for the licence, Turner wearily set out for Lewes, this time with Hyland. They had ridden only a short way along the road before Hyland decided that he would rather be bound in a bastardy bond. The East Hoathly men agreed to send for the overseers of Laughton and to go to Uckfield to swear the bond. When they got to the turnpike Hyland again changed his mind, agreeing that he would only marry after all, for forty shillings more. They turned back for Lewes. where they met with Joseph Fuller junior, a vestryman from East Hoathly, who gave Hyland a note of hand on behalf of the parish for thirty shillings and promised him five stone of beef to be paid on the day he married Durrant. The marriage licence and ring were duly acquired and the completely exasperated Turner concluded his busy day in the Sussex countryside by smoking a pipe of tobacco at, by now his regular haunt, the White Horse in Lewes, where his fellow parishioners were unlikely to bother him.[28]

By Friday morning, George Hyland had again changed his mind and decided that he would not marry after all. The now familiar parochial party set off for Uckfield to swear a bastardy bond. The infuriated Turner promptly presented

---

[28] Similar vouchers for a licence and ring survive for Sarah Winter, £1 3s 8d (ESRO, PAR378/31/3/26/80, East Hoathly, Overseers' vouchers, 11 Oct. 1820) and for an unnamed recipient in 1770–1 (ESRO, PAR378/31/3/15/21, East Hoathly, Overseers' vouchers).

himself at the Maiden Head and spent eighteen pence on liquid refreshment charged, properly in his opinion, to the parish account. The following Monday, Hyland decided he would marry if the parish was still in agreement over terms. The party, including the bride and groom, set off at pace to Laughton while Jeremiah French was despatched to collect the Laughton parish clerk. When they arrived at Laughton, however, the curate, the Revd Mr Shenton, was absent, so Thomas Fuller was hurriedly sent to fetch the Revd Porter from East Hoathly to perform the ceremony. Finally, on 28 February 1757 at 11.35 a.m. the marriage took place in Laughton parish church by licence. It was witnessed by Stephen Clinch and Joseph Fuller and the service was performed by the Revd Mr Thomas Porter, all of whom were from East Hoathly. The very next morning French, Watford and Turner accompanied Hyland to Uckfield for him to swear his parish. After this, the removal order for Hyland and his new wife was granted. Later that day Turner and French escorted George and Ann Hyland to Laughton and handed them to William Goad, the overseer.

Ann Durrant and George Hyland were not passive actors in this narrative. Their story identifies the use of financial incentives as an important and largely overlooked factor in that well-trodden narrative of coercive marriage and illegitimacy. The offer of money gave the couple a point of negotiation and a lever with which they were able to assert their agency. Hyland clearly used his on-again off-again agreement to marriage to the maximum, extracting six pounds ten shillings, five stones of beef, a wedding ring, a wedding breakfast and the administrative expenses of his marriage from the parish of East Hoathly. Ann's role was less immediately obvious, but undoubtedly her knowledge of parochial administration, gained while living with her sister and illegitimate child when she first became pregnant, was invaluable. It is impossible to say if the Hyland's marriage was a happy one, although it was plainly enduring, since over the next twenty years Ann and George went on to have nine children baptized in Laughton.[29] The parish of East Hoathly believed that it had struck both a reasonable and a seemingly pragmatic bargain, although one suspects the parish of Laughton was less happy.[30] Turner was rapidly gaining experience in the intricacies of illegitimacy. More cases were to follow fast on the heels of these first two.

---

[29] There is no compelling evidence for the baptism of the child she was pregnant with at the time of her marriage. The most likely explanation is that the child died during birth or was perhaps miscarried. It seems unlikely that the couple waited two years to baptize their first child, given that subsequent children were baptized within weeks of their birth.

[30] The same successful tactic of paying a pauper to marry outside of the parish was used again by the parish officers of East Hoathly when, at the end of 1766, the widow Constance Jarman became pregnant by Daniel Carey from the adjacent parish of Chiddingly. The parish of East Hoathly paid for the church fees, a ring costing 5s 6d, the wedding dinner at

In the week or two Turner was busy dealing with the Durrant–Hyland pregnancy and marriage, another case, initially concerning settlement, was beginning to take shape, that of the widow Elizabeth Day and her young daughter, Ann. Elizabeth had a legal settlement in Waldron, an adjacent parish, but lived in East Hoathly on a certificate, which guaranteed Waldron would accept responsibility for her should she require poor relief.[31] Elizabeth was born and brought up in East Hoathly, and in late December 1749 she married Thomas Day. When Elizabeth married, she took on the legal settlement of her new husband in Waldron, and within days of her marriage they were removed there by the parish of East Hoathly. A year later their child, Ann, was baptized in Waldron parish church, and the following summer Thomas Day died. After the death of her husband, Elizabeth and her young child returned to her parents in East Hoathly, where they lived very quietly, just getting by. But in January 1757 the parish of East Hoathly resolved to return Elizabeth to Waldron. It is uncertain why East Hoathly wanted Elizabeth to leave but the two parishes agreed over her return, although it seemed that Elizabeth herself was reluctant to go. On 31 January the parish of East Hoathly ensured there was a settlement examination, which identified Elizabeth and her daughter's place of legal settlement as Waldron. This prepared the way for her formal removal from East Hoathly.[32] Some three weeks later, Thomas Turner arrived to escort Elizabeth to Waldron, but she told Turner that she would not 'go for anyone'.[33] Elizabeth was not a young mother. She was almost forty and certainly not easily persuaded. Her refusal to leave East Hoathly prevailed, and again the parish of Waldron provided a certificate to guarantee its support should she require assistance. It is difficult to say whether Elizabeth's pregnancy was planned or coincidental, and timings are imprecise, but it is clear that she became pregnant around January or possibly February 1757, at the point that she was being pressurized into leaving the parish and her close family.[34] The father of this child was Robert Durrant, an unmarried man in his early forties with a settlement in East Hoathly and the elder brother of Ann Durrant. It was not until the following summer

---

four shillings, and a 'present' of two guineas to encourage the marriage. Their son, Daniel, was baptized on 10 May 1767: ESRO, PAR378/31/3/1/1, East Hoathly, Overseers' account book, Jan. 1766.

[31] ESRO, PAR 499/31/1, Waldron, Vestry minutes and overseers' memoranda, 1749–67, with accounts, 1763–66, Feb. 1787–Apr. 1803.

[32] ESRO, PAR378/32/1/15, Waldron, Settlement certificate, 31 Jan. 1757.

[33] ESRO, AMS6532/1–4, Worcester, Transcript, 22 Feb. 1757, p. 413.

[34] Elizabeth Day's parents, John and Mary Dann, lived in East Hoathly.

that Elizabeth's pregnancy became known to East Hoathly parish officers. Turner was by then churchwarden rather than overseer of the poor, but he remained very much involved with the management of parochial poor relief. Turner consulted both Justice Courthope in Uckfield and Ed Verral, the justices' clerk in Lewes on the matter of her removal to her parish of settlement. All were of the opinion that Elizabeth could not be removed since she had not asked for poor relief.[35] The only small consolation was that her illegitimate child would not gain a settlement in East Hoathly but must take that of its mother in Waldron.[36] East Hoathly settled for the status quo, knowing that as Elizabeth could be removed as soon as she became a burden on the parish. This pragmatic position remained until mid-October, just before Elizabeth was to give birth, when Waldron detained Robert Durrant as the father of Elizabeth's child. Since the child was to have a settlement in Waldron, the parish would become responsible for its upkeep and this, as the law directed, should be recovered from the father. After some discussion, the parochial officers of Waldron agreed to accept fifteen pence per week for maintenance of the child and forty shillings for the lying-in. This cost initially fell on the parish of East Hoathly, since Robert Durrant was ill and almost certainly unable to pay for this from his own pocket. It would be incumbent on the parish to recover their costs from Durrant when or if he was in a position to pay. Jeremiah French, the overseer of East Hoathly, however, would not agree to the fifteen pence, and expressed himself unwilling to go above twelve pence per week. As a result, East Hoathly had no choice but to have the matter settled at the quarter sessions in Lewes some months later, a case they lost.[37] Elizabeth's illegitimate child, Sarah, was born in early November 1757.

When the child was baptized on 27 November 1757, Elizabeth chose to call her Sarah Durrant Day. This caused Thomas Turner to 'remark' on this unusual occurrence in his diary.[38] Both parents' surnames were entered into the baptismal register as part of the child's name. This strategy publicly identified the father of Elizabeth's child and emphasized Elizabeth's own connection with East Hoathly. Her intransigence and assertion that she

---

[35] The law did not formally change until 1795 but it was widely assumed that a pauper could not be removed to their parish of legal settlement until they had asked for relief.

[36] R. Burn, *The Justice of the Peace, and Parish Officer*, ii (London, 1755), p. 198.

[37] ESRO, AMS6532/1–4, Worcester, Transcript, Feb. 1758, pp. 563, 633(1)–634(1).

[38] ESRO, AMS6532/1–4, Worcester, Transcript, 27 Nov. 1757, p. 600. This tactic was also used by Mary Durrant in Laughton when her illegitimate daughter, Lucy Akehurst Durrant, was baptized on 24 Aug. 1765: ESRO, Sussex Family History Group transcript. It was used again when Susannah Eldridge gave birth to an illegitimate son in Aug. 1778, who was named John Cornwell Eldridge.

would not be returned to Waldron, despite it being her place of legal settlement, confirmed her strong sense of belonging to the parish of her childhood and indeed her desire to remain with her aged parents.[39] She never remarried but continued to receive payments of eighteen pence per week from the parish of East Hoathly for 'keeping Robert Durrants girl'.[40] She also appeared as a regular recipient of a charitable bequest distributed to the poor of East Hoathly each Christmas, receiving a penny and a draught of beer.[41] Nonetheless, Elizabeth managed to get by, piecing together a living from occasional agricultural or domestic work, like the three-quarters of a day spent hop-picking for Thomas Turner in 1764 or the few shillings she was paid to nurse her mother in her last illness.[42]

Managing the costs of unmarried motherhood and minimizing its impact on the poor rate was part and parcel of the vestry's and the parish officers' roles. This included recouping maintenance payments whenever they were able. In 1757, when these costs were exceptionally high, the opportunity to relieve the parish of the regular payment for an illegitimate child was seized upon with great zeal. In April 1755 Sarah Vinal's illegitimate son, William, was baptized at the parish church. It was generally known that the father of this child was William Tull, a former labourer who had previously worked for both Will Funnel and Richard Guy, both of whom were local brickmakers.[43] Tull had neither contributed to the upkeep of the child nor remained in the locality. But in March 1757 Dame Martin, the wife of a local famer, informed Thomas Turner that Tull had called at her house that morning. Turner immediately gathered together some of his fellow vestrymen and they set off in pursuit of Tull. He was eventually caught and returned to Turner's house in East Hoathly. The following morning Sarah Vinal joined the company for breakfast and Tull agreed to marry her. The necessary arrangements were made, including the acquisition of a marriage licence in Lewes and the purchase of a wedding ring. The marriage took place the day after, on Thursday, 31 March 1757. In the afternoon Tull was taken to Lewes to swear

---

[39] Snell argues this form of 'parochial pride' and 'self-assertiveness' augmented settlement laws, yet in this instance Elizabeth Day used it to evoke a former settlement. K. D. M. Snell, *Parish and Belonging: Community, Identity and Welfare in England and Wales, 1700–1950* (Cambridge, 2006), p. 110.

[40] ESRO, PAR378/31/1/1, East Hoathly, Overseers' account book, 29 June 1765.

[41] ESRO, AMS6532/1–4, Worcester, Transcript, 21 Dec. 1757 and 21 Dec 1762, pp. 615(1), 1126.

[42] ESRO, AMS6532/1–4, Worcester, Transcript, 15 Sept. 1764, p. 1383. Elizabeth Day's father, John Dann, was buried on 15 Feb. 1763 in East Hoathly; her mother, Dame/widow [Mary] Dann, was buried on 18 Apr. 1768: ESRO, Sussex Family History Group transcript. Elizabeth Day lived until she was eighty-seven and was buried in East Hoathly on 14 Oct. 1804.

[43] It is difficult to determine if this was Richard or his brother David Guy.

a settlement examination, where he identified his parish to be Thatcham in Berkshire. A second justice of the peace's signature was sought for the removal order to make it legally binding. In all, this had cost East Hoathly £2 14s 7¾d on the parish account. The next day, Friday, 1 April, the newly married couple, together with their child, were despatched to Thatcham. They were accompanied by four men from East Hoathly to ensure that they completed their journey, all of which added a further five guineas to the parish account. The following Tuesday evening two of those men returned with the bad news that Tull had escaped, thus leaving his newly acquired wife, Sarah Tull, and his two-year-old son, William, to continue on to Thatcham, where they knew no one and had no connection other than an absent husband.[44] The parish of East Hoathly, however, seemingly found itself free of the expense of maintaining Sarah Vinal. Nonetheless, in a year that had seen them spend £11 15s 7d on the Durrant–Hyland case, at least £7 19s 7¾d was spent on another illegitimate infant and its mother. Out of a total of less than £133, a significant sum had been expended on just two women and their children. For Sarah and pauper women like her, sexual opportunity did not always align itself with economic benefit. Sarah now found herself deserted and more than 100 miles away from the community she had grown up in. There is some evidence to suggest, however, that her son, William, was returned to East Hoathly to live with her parents and that Richard Vinal, her father, continued to receive eighteen pence per week from the parish to support him.[45] Financial amelioration of the situation was largely reserved for a parish and its ratepayers, those willing to enforce the settlement laws. But the strict letter of the law dictated that, despite the child's parents marrying, because he was born prior to the marriage, William remained illegitimate and the parish was required to recover maintenance from the father. A neat solution for the parish was overlaid with layers of complexity, familial ties and a strong sense of belonging that influenced outcomes for the parish poor.

A final case in this clutch of illegitimate births and parochial machinations came on Sunday, 23 October 1757. While Richard Parkes and Sarah's sister, Mary Vinal, were at church for the second reading of their banns, a young woman, Anne Stevenson, leapt to her feet, and dramatically denounced the forthcoming marriage. Anne told the rector, Mr Porter, that she had given birth to a child by Parkes some three years previously and that he had 'many times promised her marriage'.[46] In eighteenth-century common law,

[44] ESRO, PAR378/31/1/1, East Hoathly, Parochial account book, 1763.
[45] 'To Vinal 3 Weeks for Sarah's Boy', ESRO, PAR368/31/1/1, East Hoathly, Account book, 1 Apr. 1761.
[46] ESRO, AMS6532/1–4, Worcester, Transcript, 23 Oct. 1757, p. 567.

Table 1.1 East Hoathly's biannual poor rate, 1757–69

Year	1757	1758	1759	1760	1761	1762	1763	1764	1765	1766	1767	1768	1769
Poor rate (shillings in the £)	3s 6d	2s 8d	3s 6d	2s 2d	4s 3d	1s 6d	–	4s	2s	3s 3d	3s 6d	5s	2s
	–	–	1s 6d	3s	3s	–	–	15d	–	–	–	2s 8d	–

Source: Compiled from ESRO, PAR378/31/3/1/1, East Hoathly, Account book, 1761–79, and AMS6532/1–4, Worcester, Transcript.

a proposal was a legally enforceable contract, and despite the unpropitious circumstances, Anne Stevenson was still hopeful of a marriage. The following day Mary Vinal revealed to Turner and Burgess, the parish officers, that, like many young women about to be married, she was pregnant. The notion of shaming a poor woman because of her unmarried motherhood, particularly in a rural parish, had all but vanished by the second half of the eighteenth century. Sexual activity as a precursor to marriage and bridal pregnancy were widely accepted, and when this occasionally failed parishes made pragmatic decisions according to circumstances.[47] In this instance, Mary was immediately taken to Uckfield to swear the child to Parkes.[48] Turner secured a warrant to apprehend Parkes and early next morning Parkes was taken up. He quickly agreed to the marriage and, together with Thomas Fuller and Thomas Turner, continued on to Lewes to secure a licence. The couple were married in East Hoathly at 11 a.m. that morning. No sooner had they been married than Parkes was taken to Uckfield to be examined as to his parish of settlement, which was discovered to be the nearby Hellingly. By eight o'clock that evening, the newly married couple found themselves delivered to the churchwarden's house in Hellingly, some six or seven miles away. These two days' work cost the parish £2 19s 6d, an expenditure both unexpected and impressive in its timely execution, and in Turner's opinion they 'made a good days work of it'.[49] This entirely pragmatic parochial response from East Hoathly, assisting Parkes and Vinal to marry, left both the parish of Hellingly and Anne Stevenson's parish to deal with the aftermath of Parkes's inconstancy.

---

[47] T. Hitchcock, '"Unlawfully begotten on her body": illegitimacy and the parish poor of St Luke's Chelsea', in *Chronicling Poverty: The Voices and Strategies of the English Poor, 1640–1840*, ed. T. Hitchcock, P. King and P. Sharpe (Basingstoke, 1997), pp. 70–86; N. Rogers, 'Carnal knowledge: illegitimacy in eighteenth-century Westminster', *Journal of Social History*, xxiii (1989), 355–75.

[48] Mary already had an illegitimate child, Anne Thomas Vinal, baptized in East Hoathly on 24 Mar. 1750/1. The child was 'put out' to her mother and Thomas Parkes by East Hoathly at 9d per week in 1762: ESRO, AMS6532/1–4, Worcester, Transcript, 18 Apr. 1762, p. 1045.

[49] ESRO, AMS6532/1–4, Worcester, Transcript, 25 Oct. 1757, p. 572.

Mary, who was already the mother of an illegitimate child, was now resident in Hellingly together with her new husband, while Anne Stevenson was left to appeal to her own parish of settlement for financial redress.

The cases reviewed here offer a brief glimpse of the methods deployed by a small parish in the management of illegitimate births, settlement and marriage. Most required some form of initial parish expenditure to mitigate long-term costs. Like other small communities, East Hoathly used a variety of strategies to manage their finances including passing these costs on to another parish. Even so, the immediate economic impacts of these cases were considerable, especially for a small village of fewer than 400. Between drink, food, travel and legal costs, the single instance of the Hyland–Durrant case cost the parish of East Hoathly at least £11 15s 7d. In the same administrative year, 1756–7, the parish also spent £7 19s 7¾d on the coerced marriage between William Tull and Sarah Vinal. This amounted to a total of £19 15s 2¾d on just two cases concerning illegitimacy or potential illegitimate births. In one of these cases, it was money well spent by the parochial officers seeking to ameliorate a charge on the rates in subsequent years. The coerced marriage between Tull and Vinal however, was much less successful, since the Vinal family retained the eighteen pence per week as maintenance for Sarah's child paid via the vestry, while William Tull remained beyond their grasp. But £19 15s 2¾d out of a total poor-relief budget of less than £133 was just under 15 per cent and a very substantial sum.[50] Although it is worth noting that much of this money remained circulating in the locality, largely spent as cash in support of local businesses.[51] The additional £2 19d 6d spent on hurrying the marriage of Richard Parkes and Sarah Vinal fell into the next parochial accounting period and the parish was able to defer the expenditure. The case of the widow Elizabeth Day was somewhat different: she had a settlement elsewhere and, if necessary, East Hoathly might call on that parish to provide financial support should she require it. Yet it remains slightly puzzling that East Hoathly did not remove her to Waldron immediately after her initial settlement examination in January 1757.[52]

---

[50] This is the figure for 1761, which is the closest that can be found for expenditure on poor relief to 1757: ESRO, PAR378/31/1/1, East Hoathly, Account book, 1763.

[51] Thomas Turner regularly supplied goods to those in surrounding parishes, including items to the Laughton vestry for the use of the poor.

[52] It is entirely possible that East Hoathly allowed Elizabeth Day to remain in the parish to care for her elderly parents, thereby relieving the parish of the expense. Steven King notes the failure to remove some unmarried mothers: S. King, 'Poor relief settlement and belonging in England, 1780s to 1840s: comparative perspectives', in *Migration, Settlement and Belonging in Europe, 1500–1930s*, ed. S. King and A. Winter (London, 2013), pp. 81–101,

Unlike the Hyland–Durrant case, there was no attempt by East Hoathly to encourage a marriage between Elizabeth Day and Robert Durrant; rather, the economics of the situation allowed them to play the long game. If Elizabeth remained a widow and was to make a claim for poor relief, East Hoathly would be able to return her and her children to Waldron. If Robert Durrant was able to work, he would be liable to make some contribution to the upkeep of his child. Encouraging a marriage, thereby allowing Elizabeth a settlement, would bring the whole of the expense of an impoverished couple with children on East Hoathly.

In most years there was sufficient flexibility in the system of payments made under the Poor Law to maintain the occasional illegitimate child or to cover for poor harvests. By the 1750s these regular outgoings in East Hoathly were relatively small, given that only six parishioners received a regular pension, two of whom were receiving it for an illegitimate child. In addition, one or two parishioners were paid for spinning, carding or twisting yarn. As well as pensions, there were regular deliveries of fuel, flour and meat, together with rental payments, and further ad hoc payments were made for burying the dead, occasional nursing and medicines, clothing and the mending of shoes. However, managing the parochial finances of illegitimacy could be an exceedingly erratic business. At a point when the ratio of illegitimate births was beginning to rise across the country, East Hoathly's finances were put under considerable stress by a sudden rise in cases of illegitimacy and unmarried motherhood. These tensions became more explicit when, a handful of years later, Turner noted the 'quarrelling and bickering' among his fellow vestrymen when they tried to set the annual poor rate so that everyone 'might pay his just quota'.[53] The following year, discussions became more contentious still, when Turner suggested the 'avaricious views' of the overseer prevented a rate from being agreed. He went on to suggest that one particular, unnamed, office-holder wished 'to serve his own private ends and to be assessed lower according to the law than anyone else'.[54] When years were particularly difficult with several illegitimate births, like those of 1756–8 in East Hoathly, parishes had to make complex calculations about immediate benefits and longer-term solutions for more lasting benefits – that of lower rates. When such births were occasional, small parishes had the flexibility to commit significant resources to mitigate costs in subsequent years. But, when illegitimacy ratios rose significantly, tensions over poor rates increased. The small amount of slack in the system

at pp. 87–8.
[53] ESRO, AMS6532/1–4, Worcester, Transcript, 26 Mar. 1763, p. 1161.
[54] ESRO, AMS6532/1–4, Worcester, Transcript, 10 Apr. 1764, p. 1298.

was reduced, leaving East Hoathly and small parishes like it struggling to manage multiple illegitimate children. The tensions already inherent in the system began to spill over from vestrymen to the wider community, and this played out across thousands of English parishes. The system for managing the financial vagaries of poor relief, however, enabled minor shortfalls to be made up within a year. Thus in small parishes the poor rates were usually set and collected twice yearly.[55] Much larger parishes, with far greater expenses, set and collected rates four or more times per year. But smaller agricultural parishes were especially hard hit since the rate base was narrow and the smaller vestry was very much prone to manipulation by one or two stronger voices. The men who made up the East Hoathly vestry, however, were very much embedded in the microeconomics of the parish. Men like Thomas Turner, Robert Hook, Joseph Fuller, Joseph Durrant Sr and John Watford Jr, who were all regular attendees at the vestry meetings during the 1750s and 1760s.[56] Most were small businessmen or service providers – variously a shopkeeper, a shoemaker, a butcher, a blacksmith and a small-scale farmer, all of whom submitted bills to the parish. Any increase in spending by or on the poor was invariably spent locally on goods or services supplied by these men. Most of the vestry had an eye to what they themselves might supply, such as Thomas Turner renting a bedpan and candlestick when these were needed by Thomas Woolgar in 1775.[57] An increase in the poor rate might be resented by other vestrymen, like Jeremiah French, a wealthy local farmer, who constantly haggled about petty disbursements made by the overseers.[58] As with other rural parishes, there was a very fine line to be followed in setting the poor rate, which needed to be sufficient to cover expenses but not so high as to push marginal families into poverty.[59]

Part of the business of balancing parochial finances was knowledge, and between 1756 and 1758 Thomas Turner appears to have developed a substantial store of it. In a small village, personal relationships, business interactions or gossip might easily influence perceptions about a neighbour's honesty, their ability to pay or their moral probity. It was the overseer's duty to begin sifting through this information before further proceedings

---

[55] For an explanation of the rating system and poor rates see S. Williams, *Poverty, Gender and Life-Cycle under the English Poor Law, 1760–1834* (Woodbridge, 2011), pp. 69–100.

[56] N. Tadmor, 'Where was Mrs Turner? Governance and gender in an eighteenth-century village', in *Remaking English Society: Social Relations and Social Change in Early Modern England*, ed. S. Hindle, A. Shepard and J. Walter (Woodbridge, 2013), pp. 89–112.

[57] See Interlude 1 (J. Irvin, 'Thomas Woolgar, the mystery man') after this chapter.

[58] For a short description of French see Vaisey (ed.), *Diary of Thomas Turner*, p. 331.

[59] Williams, *Poverty, Gender and Life-Cycle*, p. 79.

were initiated. At the end of July 1756 Turner was called to interview Richard Hope's servant, who was thought to be 'with child'. Turner was very sceptical about a possible illegitimate pregnancy, writing that he was 'doubtful there is reason to suspect she is with child'.[60] But nonetheless he made enquiries about the woman's settlement and the parish's liability to support her. As elsewhere, welfare processes in East Hoathly were largely predicated on this local knowledge and personal trust, together with a great deal of intrusive questioning. When Turner talked to Mary Evenden in 1758, she admitted her pregnancy but would not 'swear the father'. Tuner wrote in his diary that night, 'I think according to all circumstances nobody need think of any other person for the father but Mr Hutson'.[61] By the 1760s, the by now more experienced Turner had become somewhat cynical, referring to a hurried marriage by licence as a 'country sort' of a match where the woman 'is pregnant if her own word is to be taken for it'.[62] And as the only shopkeeper in East Hoathly, Thomas Turner was only too well aware of the importance of maintaining good business relationships across the locality. These relationships included Peter Adams, the father of Ann Cain's child, who was part of Turner's wider social circle. In the 1750s Adams, like Turner, attended vestry meetings at Jones's public house. Turner lent him money and drank with him, and on occasion they dined together. The friendship continued over several years.[63] When Adams defaulted on his maintenance payments Turner's reluctance to involve the full power of the law and his willingness to allow Adams time to pay his arrears, eventually paid off. The parish was able to recoup the money owed to it without recourse to an expensive legal case. It was these social bonds, often between men, that greased the wheels of parochial finances.[64] Indeed, at the same time as Turner was attempting to recover these parochial arrears, he was also pursuing Adams for a business debt, which might explain some of his hesitancy in having Adams prosecuted and thus imprisoned for his parish liabilities. Yet, this economic reciprocity, which largely benefited male ratepayers like Peter Adams, was often granted to the detriment of women like Ann Cain and their illegitimate children. When Adams first defaulted on his payments, the

---

[60] ESRO, AMS6532/1–4, Worcester, Transcript, 31 July 1756, pp. 274–5.

[61] ESRO, AMS6532/1–4, Worcester, Transcript, 3 May 1758, pp. 714(1)–715(1). James Hutson, widower, married Mary Evenden on 9 Sept. 1759 at East Hoathly.

[62] ESRO, AMS6532/1–4, Worcester, Transcript, 8 Dec. 1763, p. 1243.

[63] Vaisey (ed.), *Diary of Thomas Turner*, p. 326.

[64] Naomi Tadmor discusses this form of 'social alignment' and Turner's involvement with the 'politics of the parish': N. Tadmor, *Family and Friends in Eighteenth-Century England: Household, Kinship and Patronage* (Cambridge, 2001), p. 273.

parish continued to pay the agreed eighteen pence per week but eventually Turner stopped the payments. In his diary, he noted that Thomas Ling and his new wife, Ann (formerly Cain), were 'continually harassing me for the money'.[65] Men lower down the social scale, or without the necessary economic leverage, were not given the opportunities to prevaricate in quite the same way and relied on personal interventions and reminders of monies 'owing' to them. Nonetheless, these persistent requests were effective.

The matter of who would care for the infant and in turn receive the maintenance money was entirely dependent on local conditions. East Hoathly did not possess a workhouse, so family members nominally cared for an illegitimate child, although occasionally a neighbouring family would take the child. A new household was formed only if the couple subsequently married; otherwise, illegitimate children were subsumed into existing households.[66] After the birth of her daughter Sarah, the widow Elizabeth Day received the agreed maintenance payments of eighteen pence per week directly from the parish, although she was living with her parents, John and Elizabeth Dann. Richard Vinal, father to both Sarah and Mary Vinal, however, received maintenance payments for 'keeping Sarah's boy' and similarly 'keeping Ann Thomas Vinal Mary's daughter' in April 1762. By this point both Vinal women had married and left the family home to live elsewhere as their new settlements dictated. Keeping an illegitimate child in the parish while they were infants or small children had the advantage of keeping any maintenance money local: small necessities were inevitably purchased close by to the benefit of local traders and shopkeepers.

Women were not just recipients of maintenance payments but also customers spending money in the local economy. As illegitimacy ratios rose, parishes increasingly acknowledged women's economic responsibility in maintaining their illegitimate offspring. After a mother had ceased nursing an infant, she was expected to return to the workforce. Bastardy bonds began to stipulate financial contributions to be made by mothers. Women like Susannah Eldridge, who gave birth to an illegitimate child in East Hoathly in 1778, were expected to pay sixpence per week for the child, although she was much less likely to be formally pursued for non-

---

[65] ESRO, AMS6532/1–4, Worcester, Transcript, 24 July 1757, p. 268.

[66] Ashurst Majendie's report to the Poor Law Commissioners suggested that payment of cottage rents by vestries in Sussex encouraged the artificial rise in rents generally. There is no indication that this included housing for unmarried mothers, although it did include housing for widowed women and their children: *Report from His Majesty's Commissioners for Inquiring into the Administration and Practical Operation of the Poor Laws* (Parl. Papers 1834), appendix A, no. 8, Report from Ashurst Majendie, p. 165A.

payment.[67] By the early nineteenth century, pre-printed forms left space for a woman's contribution for maintenance of her illegitimate child to be noted. This did not mark any substantive change in policy, but it did reflect growing concerns over the financial burdens created by the birth and maintenance of illegitimate children.

As illegitimacy ratios rose across England from the mid eighteenth century onwards, parishes more readily deployed strategies to manage the financial implications of such births. East Hoathly provides a remarkably detailed set of examples, which took place at a point when illegitimacy and unmarried motherhood were beginning to have a powerful effect on both community relationships and the parochial poor rate. This single parish is not indicative of a common approach to parochial management, but there is evidence to suggest that some of these practices were more widespread, particularly offering a financial incentive to affect a marriage. Elaine Saunders has identified petty constables across Hertfordshire who were involved in offering similarly large sums to induce a marriage, particularly when a pregnant woman might be in a position to make a match in an alternative parish.[68] In Gnosall, Staffordshire, two cases reflect this same strategy. On 4 November 1740 the vestry minutes recorded that it was 'agreed at the said Vestry to allow Hannah Parton £3. 8s 0d provided she solemnizes marriage with Richd Worrall'. In a similar manner, in 1780 John Edge managed to agree the sum of five guineas for marrying the pregnant Ann Fox; this, together with various accrued expenses, cost the parish £8 12s 0d.[69] Samantha Williams noted the case of Elizabeth Hart and John Darling in the parish of Campton and Shefford in Bedfordshire, where the overseers recorded the sum of £14 paid to secure their marriage.[70] Williams, however, did not differentiate a specific sum paid to the couple, quite possibly because it was never recorded separately, but a majority of it almost certainly went to the new family. These cases are particularly difficult to identify in parochial records, as paupers did not issue vouchers for these essentially verbal agreements, although remnants of their agreements sometimes appear in vouchers as parochial officers recouped monies owed from the parish. Occasionally, small traces are left through a bill for a ring or a

[67] John Cornwell Eldridge, illegitimate son of Susannah Eldridge and John Cornwell, baptized on 9 Aug. 1778 at East Hoathly: ESRO, Sussex Family History Group transcript.

[68] E. Saunders, '"Men of good character, strong, decent and active": Hertfordshire petty constables, 1730–1799' (unpublished Open University PhD thesis, 2018), pp. 254–6.

[69] Identified in W. E. Tate, *The Parish Chest: A Study of the Records of Parochial Administration in England*, 3rd edn (Chichester, 1983), pp. 218–19.

[70] Williams, *Poverty, Gender and Life-Cycle*, p. 108. Further cases are noted by Keith Snell in *Parish and Belonging*, pp. 142–3.

licence. Much of the detail in the East Hoathly cases, however, is noted in the diary of Thomas Turner. By the 1830s the Poor Law Commissioners reported these marriages as commonplace, particularly as a collusive action between a pregnant woman and her parish of settlement, noting that an opening gambit for a single pregnant woman thrown on the parish was: 'He's willing to marry me *if he could afford it*, and he does not belong to you.'[71] The commissioners noted that settlement by marriage had become a 'fertile source of fraud', and it remained a significant component of the parish accounts.[72]

While there was a great deal of common experience shared between paupers in East Hoathly and parishes across rural England, it is important to acknowledge some important differences. There were just over 300 parishes or places in Sussex, and by 1803 about half of them maintained some or all of their poor in a workhouse or had arrangements for contracting out their care. Unlike East Hoathly, these parishes were able to deploy differing strategies in their management of illegitimacy. In some places, pregnant women were admitted to the workhouse as a matter of policy or perhaps of expediency, to give birth and complete a period of lying-in with their infants. The mothers might remain in the workhouse while nursing, sometimes for brief periods, or at other times; the child might be maintained in the workhouse while the mother returned to work. In these cases, overseers would keep any financial contribution made by the father to offset the expenses incurred by the workhouse. After Gilbert's Act in 1782, parishes were permitted to unite for the purpose of building and administering a workhouse, whereon several were established and operated across west Sussex.[73] Between two and twenty adjacent parishes participated in these Sussex unions.[74] The necessity of policing the borders between these parishes to manage legal settlements was greatly diminished since multiple parishes were contributing to the same poor relief 'pot'. Despite the existence of workhouses, many mothers choose to live outside of these institutions and were permitted to do so by local vestries. Making these complex calculations of legal costs and maintenance payments, or being aware of other potential costs to the parish, allowed for a certain flexibility in parochial decision-making. Turner's pragmatic approach to illegitimacy and that of many like him, enabled women such as Ann Cain, Elizabeth Day and countless others to access financial support

---

[71] *Report ... into the Administration and Practical Operation of the Poor Laws*, p. 90.

[72] *Report ... into the Administration and Practical Operation of the Poor Laws*, p. 90.

[73] S. A. Shave, *Pauper Policies: Poor Law Practice in England, 1780–1850* (Manchester, 2017).

[74] The 'hundred houses' of Suffolk and Norfolk provide a very different landscape, where as many as 200 parishes were incorporated to form a single large workhouse. These incorporations began in the mid 18th century, implementing single policies across large swathes of these counties.

when they needed it most. Some fifty years after Turner, following a significant growth in illegitimate births, there was an expectation among the poor that an unmarried mother would receive the local 'rate' to support her illegitimate child. By the early nineteenth century, the average payment across rural England for the care and maintenance of an illegitimate child was a little under two shillings per week, albeit the parish might occasionally provide a little more.[75] In Sussex, parishes tended to pay maintenance to mothers of illegitimate children, whether or not they had received the money from the father, even though rates of default were high. In Mayfield, less than ten miles from East Hoathly, the parish supported forty-six illegitimate children in the community and six more in the workhouse in the early 1830s. The annual expense of supporting these children was £208, only £85 of which was recovered from fathers.[76] The amount awarded as maintenance payments for each illegitimate child created particular community tensions of its own. By the time of the 1834 Poor Law Commissioners' report, the associated national survey, *Rural Queries*, identified this as a common grievance of rural respondents. Here, the frequent complaint was that unmarried mothers received a greater sum in maintenance payments than a married couple did for a legitimate child as part of a parochial wage subsidy.[77] There was a particular dependence on these family subsidies in Sussex. These small sums of money supplied as maintenance payments circulated from parish to pauper, to providers of goods and services, and thence back again, embedding this exchange in the microeconomics of the parish. Indeed, the circulation of cash in the Old Poor Law system provided pecuniary opportunity for the small-scale trader. In 1832 the overseers in Lewes were described as being

> chosen from so low a class of petty tradesmen, that it is notorious that they use the balance of parish money in their hands to carry on their own businesses; being little removed above the paupers, they are not able to resist them, and there is the constant temptation to lavish relief supplied on the articles in which they deal.[78]

---

[75] *Report … into the Administration and Practical Operation of the Poor Laws*, p. 93. Analysis by Margaret Lyle suggests that the reported average figure for England was 20*s* 7*d* per week, while unmarried mothers in Sussex received a relatively generous 24*s* 9*d* per week in 1832: M. E. Lyle, 'Regionality in the late Old Poor Law: the treatment of chargeable bastards from rural queries', *The Agricultural History Review*, liii (2005), 141–57.

[76] Lyle, 'Regionality', pp. 177–8.

[77] These subsidies had become increasingly common during the later 1790s after a series of failed harvests, and continued into the early 19th century during times of extreme economic hardship: K. D. M. Snell, *Annals of the Labouring Poor: Social Change and Agrarian England, 1660–1900* (Cambridge, 1985), pp. 15–66.

[78] *Report … into the Administration and Practical Operation of the Poor Laws*, p. 58.

These economic ties played an increasing role in the circulation of cash between and across localities, sometimes generating vouchers and at other times an entry in the account books. In addition, the legal costs associated with illegitimacy were a significant cause for concern, and the fees levied on recovering unpaid money from fathers did not always achieve their end.[79] In general, legal fees associated with welfare payment were increasing at a significant rate. By 1785, the fees, including all removal expenses and those incurred by overseers, for Sussex were £2,741 11s 3d. By 1803 this had more than doubled to £5,746 17s 11½d.[80] These significant sums, replicated across the country, added to the already contentious burden of supporting unmarried women and their children at higher rates than their married counterparts.

The tiny Sussex parish of East Hoathly displayed an enormous variety of circumstance, epitomizing the pragmatic management of illegitimate births and unmarried motherhood, and the flexibility of the parochial Poor Law system across the long eighteenth century. Much of this management was contingent on maintaining a longer-term financial strategy, with local ratepayers shouldering the financial burden should all else fail, and being willing to invest large sums to avoid a longer-term drain on the parish account. On the whole, management of the Poor Law system was undertaken by men cognizant of the wider implications for the local economy and financial benefits that might accrue to themselves or their near neighbours. This said, the vestry sought to mitigate costs whenever possible, particularly through managing the settlement system to their advantage. A coerced marriage undoubtedly offered a neat solution, but a small financial inducement for such a marriage often produced a more equitable result, with potential pauper parents negotiating and agreeing settlements with the added bonus of significant sums of money remaining in circulation across the locality. But 'solutions' of the sort described here remained largely dependent on local knowledge, personal relationships and prudent management of parochial finances. The reality of eighteenth-century illegitimacy, the experience of unmarried motherhood and the management of this particular mini-welfare state emerged from the micro-negotiations of Thomas Turner, Ann Durrant, George Hyland, Sarah Vinal and their fellow parishioners and lovers. This particular parochial *annus horribilis* did not extend beyond the boundaries of east Sussex, but it exposes the pressures and systems at play across the 15,000 parishes of England and Wales.

---

[79] See, for example, replies from the parish of Framfield: *Report … into the Administration and Practical Operation of the Poor Laws*, appendix B, p. 504.

[80] *Abstract of Answers and Returns relative to the Expence and Maintenance of the Poor* (Parl. Papers, 1803-4 [C.175], xiii), p. 533.

Interlude 1

Thomas Woolgar, the mystery man

Jean Irvin

We don't know a great deal about Thomas Woolgar.[1] We don't know exactly when or where he was born or when and where he died, but we do know that he was living somewhere in the village of East Hoathly in Sussex in 1775, when the surgeon Mr Nathaniel Paine amputated his leg.

East Hoathly's account book records that the parish shared the expenses of the amputation and Thomas's subsequent care with the parish of St John sub-Castro in Lewes.[2] This was an unusual arrangement since the costs of medical care usually fell on the patient's parish of legal settlement. Perhaps the amputation was the result of an accident that occurred during Thomas's employment in East Hoathly. Whatever the reason, no clue was left in the parish records as to the reason for these shared expenses.

Thomas's ongoing care was undertaken in East Hoathly, including subsequent dressing of the wound and medicines. He was also provided with wine and 'liquor', no doubt to help with pain relief. The aptly named surgeon, Mr Paine, who also lived in the village, checked on Thomas's progress and dressed the wound on at least one occasion. Mr Paine's itemized bill, including the professional fee of three guineas for the amputation itself, medicines and treatments indicates that this took place sometime before April 1775.[3] On 7 January 1775 Thomas received a generous quantity of 'liquer' from Thomas Turner's general store and two 'rollers' (or bandages), a sponge and 'rags'.[4] From then

---

[1] For the fuller story of Thomas Woolgar see J. Irvin, 'The Mystery Man – Thomas Woolgar', The Poor Law <https://thepoorlaw.org/the-mystery-man-thomas-woolgar> [accessed 20 Mar. 2021]. The blog post is made available under a Creative Commons Attribution-NonCommercial 4.0 International License (CC BY-NC 4.0).

[2] ESRO, PAR378/31/1/1, East Hoathly, Overseers' account book, 1775.

[3] ESRO, PAR378/31/3/14/17B, East Hoathly, Overseers' vouchers, Apr. 1775.

[4] ESRO, PAR378/31/3/14/13, East Hoathly, Overseers' vouchers, 7 Jan 1775.

on he received a regular supply of fuel, food, drink and household items that comprehensively addressed his personal care needs.

Thomas's hygiene appears to have been a continuing priority. Turner provided copious supplies of soap together with a rented bedpan (two shillings) and candlestick (1s 2d), all at parish expense.[5] The quantity of candles was increased, no doubt to ensure there was enough light to properly wash and dress Thomas's wound. On 19 April, James Marchant was paid four shillings for having shaved Thomas on eight occasions.[6] The last overseers' receipt paid on behalf of Thomas, dated 21 April 1775, was for the attendance of and services provided by the surgeon, Mr Nathaniel Paine.[7]

For Thomas Woolgar to have survived life-threatening surgery without any of the advantages of modern medicine and hygiene was probably not just a result of the skill of the surgeon but also an indication of his robust constitution and of the good pre- and post-operative care he was given. The parish supported Thomas financially throughout the first three months of 1775, providing cash, goods and services, costing a total of £28 2s. At today's prices this approximates to £2,419.54, which suggests that East Hoathly was a parish with a settled community that could afford to take its responsibilities for relief of the poor seriously, and in Thomas' case it did not stint.[8]

Sadly, Thomas Woolgar then disappeared from the records as mysteriously as he had arrived.

---

[5] ESRO, PAR378/31/3/14/12, East Hoathly, Overseers' vouchers, 13 Apr. 1775.
[6] ESRO, PAR378/31/3/15/2, East Hoathly, Overseers' vouchers, 19 Apr. 1775.
[7] ESRO, PAR378/31/3/14/17A, East Hoathly, Overseers' vouchers, 21 Apr. 1775.
[8] Currency converter, The National Archives <https://www.nationalarchives.gov.uk/currency-converter> [accessed 20 Mar. 2021].

2. Clothing the poor

Elizabeth Spencer

In 1828 the widow Elizabeth Newell wrote to her home parish of Yoxall in Staffordshire to make a request of the overseer of the poor:

> Sir I have taken the liberty to send for my small account for I am now ill and in need of it if you please to send me a dark gown and a small print [?] yards I am sorry to say I can make no return for your good will to me at present But will take the first opertunity I hope your goodness will [excuse] my freedom.[1]

A later note shows that Newell received '13 weeks pay' at £1 19s, but with no hint of whether her accompanying plea for a gown and fabric was answered.[2] However, while she asked the overseer to 'excuse her freedom', Newell was clearly confident that in writing she might meet with success.[3] Indeed, hers was not an unusual or unreasonable request; the provision of clothing and textiles was a consistent feature of the Old Poor Law as it was issued as 'relief in kind' alongside a range of other goods and services.[4] Alongside a pension, a pauper might receive clothing on a regular, semi-regular, occasional or one-off basis in response to acute material need. In turn, this provision of clothing had broader consequences for the scale of the local economy, as well as for the circulation of money within and beyond the parish. Drawing on 404 overseers' vouchers across eight settlements in Cumberland and nine parishes in Staffordshire, this chapter explores the range of practices involved in this provision of clothing between 1769 and

---

[1] SRO, D730/3/13, Yoxall, Overseers' vouchers, 1828.

[2] SRO, D730/3/13, 1828.

[3] S. King and A. Stringer, '"I have once more taken the leberty to say as you well know": the development of rhetoric in the letters of English, Welsh and Scottish sick and poor, 1780s–1830s', in *Poverty and Sickness in Modern Europe: Narratives of the Sick Poor, 1780–1938*, ed. A. Gestrich, E. Hurren and S. King (London, 2012), pp. 69–92, at p. 88.

[4] S. Williams, 'Poor relief, labourers' households and living standards in rural England, c.1770–1834: a Bedfordshire case study', *The Economic History Review*, lviii (2005), 485–519, at 485.

E. Spencer, 'Clothing the poor' in *Providing for the Poor: The Old Poor Law, 1750–1834*, ed. P. Collinge and L. Falcini (London, 2022), pp. 53–79. License: CC BY-NC-ND 4.0.

1834.[5] It looks first at the purchase of textiles and haberdashery items across these seventeen locations, then at the items of clothing distributed to men, women and children by these Poor Law authorities, and finally traces some of the differing practices surrounding this.

Pauper clothing has been subject to increasing attention since the turn of this century, both in studies of the day-to-day operation of the Old Poor Law and as a topic in its own right. This scholarship has thus far followed two strands. The first is concerned with the material reality of clothing provision. Drawing primarily on accounts, bills and receipts, it seeks to understand what was purchased and in what quantities and qualities; how, when and to whom this was distributed; and how 'generous' this provision was.[6] Early studies suggested that overseers were primarily focused on supplying basic needs by the cheapest means possible.[7] It was Steven King, however, who largely set the terms for subsequent debate in 2002 when he suggested that most paupers 'could expect to see regular replacement of their clothes' and contended that Poor Law authorities were willing to buy expensive and fashionable fabrics.[8] Focusing on the early nineteenth century, Peter Jones broadly agreed with King that paupers were 'well clothed' but argued that this was a 'compassionate pragmatism' with an emphasis on functional, hard-wearing textiles and a high degree of standardization, driven partly by the importance of apprenticeship. One of the most important aspects of clothing relief, Jones suggested, was that it remained significant even in the crisis years leading up to the Poor Law Amendment Act of 1834.[9] Vivienne Richmond, in contrast, has disagreed with both King and Jones, drawing on Poor Law records in Sussex and Kent to argue that parish clothing relief 'virtually ceased' in the 1820s. Moreover, while Richmond found a brief rise in clothing provision in the first two decades of the nineteenth century, she argued that the clothing supplied was inferior and 'possibly stigmatic'.[10]

---

[5] The 240 vouchers for Cumberland are divided as follows: Wigton, 65; Brampton, 39; Threlkeld, 29; Hayton, 28; Dalston, 26; Greystoke, 21; Papcastle, 18; Skelton, 14. There were 164 vouchers for Staffordshire: Wednesbury, 90; Lichfield, 27; Abbots Bromley, 11; Darlaston, 9; Uttoxeter, 9; Gnosall, 5; Hamstall Ridware, 5; Yoxall, 5; Endon-with-Stanley, 3.

[6] H. French, 'How dependent were the "dependent poor"? Poor relief and the life-course in Terling, Essex, 1762–1834', *Continuity and Change*, xxx (2015), 193–222, at 195.

[7] A. Buck, *Dress in Eighteenth-Century England* (London, 1979), p. 155; B. Lemire, '"A good stock of cloaths": the changing market for cotton clothing in Britain, 1750–1800', *Textile History*, xxii (1991), 311–28, at 317.

[8] S. King, 'Reclothing the English poor, 1750–1840', *Textile History*, xxxiii (2002), 37–47.

[9] P. Jones, 'Clothing the poor in early-nineteenth-century England', *Textile History*, xxxvii (2006), 17–37.

[10] V. Richmond, '"Indiscriminate liberality subverts the morals and depraves the habits of

The literature therefore reflects differing levels of agreement on the overall generosity, scale and significance of clothing provision under the Old Poor Law, though there is general consensus that clothing provided by parishes was on the whole hard-wearing and possibly even uniform compared to that of the wider population. John Styles, for instance, has argued that, while the poor were able to exercise some choice, clothing provided by parishes was 'consistently cheap, coarse, and undecorated', with the dress of paupers 'barely matching, let alone surpassing, non-pauper adults at the lower point of the family poverty cycle'.[11] An issue related closely to clothing provision is badging the clothing of paupers with red or blue cloth, a requirement introduced in 1697 and repealed in 1810.[12] However, there is little evidence for the practice in the vouchers, save for frequent purchases of blue textiles.

A second strand of scholarship has turned from questions of quantity and quality to focus on letters written by, for or about paupers, though attention has rested largely on requests for relief by paupers themselves, whether written in their own hand or by an intermediary.[13] These letters were generated by the out-parish system whereby someone living beyond their parish of settlement wrote 'home' to the parish authorities.[14] As Elizabeth Newell's letter demonstrates, clothing and textiles could form part of a written request for relief; indeed, in a sample of 3,271 letters, King found that, after sickness and housing, 'issues around cloth or clothing' were 'the most important motifs of pauper narratives'.[15] These letters reveal a rich resource for attitudes towards and understandings of clothing, as well as a rhetoric surrounding insufficient clothing, nakedness and raggedness

---

the poor": a contribution to the debate on the Poor Law, parish clothing relief and clothing societies in early nineteenth-century England', *Textile History*, xl (2009), 51–69; V. Richmond, *Clothing the Poor in Nineteenth-Century England* (Cambridge, 2013), pp. 187, 210.

[11] J. Styles, *The Dress of the People: Everyday Fashion in Eighteenth-Century England* (New Haven, 2007), pp. 261–75.

[12] The parish poor of Stone, Staffordshire, may have been required to wear badges between 1697 and 1784: S. Hindle, 'Dependency, shame and belonging: badging the deserving poor, c.1550–1750', *Cultural and Social History*, i (2004), 6–35, at 10, 23–34.

[13] S. King and P. Jones, 'Testifying for the poor: epistolary advocates and the negotiation of parochial relief in England, 1800–1834', *Journal of Social History*, xliv (2016), 784–807, at 788; S. King and P. Jones (eds), *Navigating the Old English Poor Law: The Kirkby Lonsdale Letters, 1809–1836* (Oxford, 2020).

[14] T. Sokoll, 'Institutional context: the practice of non-resident relief', in *Essex Pauper Letters: 1731–1837*, ed. T. Sokoll (Oxford, 2016), pp. 10–17, at p. 11.

[15] S. King, '"I fear you will think me too presumtuous in my demands but necessity has no law": clothing in English pauper letters, 1800–1834', *International Review of Social History*, liv (2009), 207–36, at 216.

frequently deployed to support pleas for assistance.[16] As Jones has argued, paupers were aware of 'wider cultural discourses on issues such as clothing, decency and propriety', which fed into their requests for relief.[17] Pauper letters concerning clothing – or a lack thereof – were sometimes combined with a specific request for clothing or money with which to buy it, and were often accompanied by the recurring threat that, without relief, writers would be forced to 'come home' or to send dependents 'home' to their parish of settlement.[18] This was a particularly effective threat, as it was often cheaper to relieve an out-parish pauper than it was for their equivalent living within the parish.[19] In drawing primarily on accounts, bills and receipts, this chapter inevitably engages in more depth with scholarship focused on the material reality of clothing provision, though there are letters written by paupers, their advocates or intermediaries dotted throughout the sample of vouchers. These letters are invaluable in that they can reveal 'coincidental' details about the material lives of the poor, but clothing could form an important part of a strategic request for relief in its own right.[20] Pauper letters as a source 'from below' have been much discussed, and their overall credibility as accounts of poverty established.[21] However, they are also complex, strategic and performative pieces of writing that hint at processes of negotiation often obscured by entries in accounts, bills and receipts.[22]

---

[16] King, '"I fear you will think me too presumtuous"', 224–7; S. King, 'Negotiating the law of poor relief in England, 1800–1840', *History*, xcvi (2011), 410–35, at 426; S. King, *Writing the Lives of the English Poor, 1750s–1830s* (Montreal, 2019), pp. 265–6; T. Sokoll, 'Negotiating a living: Essex pauper letters from London, 1800–1834', *International Review of Social History*, xlv (2000), 19–45, at 36; King and Stringer, '"I have once more taken the leberty"', pp. 73–4; P. D. Jones, '"I cannot keep my place without being deascent": pauper letters, parish clothing and pragmatism in the south of England, 1750–1830', *Rural History*, xx (2009), 31–49, at 33; T. Hitchcock, *Down and Out in Eighteenth-Century London* (London, 2004), pp. 107–8.

[17] Jones, '"I cannot keep my place"', 31–2.

[18] K. D. M. Snell, 'Belonging and community: understandings of "home" and "friends" among the English poor, 1750–1850', *The Economic History Review*, lxv (2012), 1–25, at 9; Sokoll, 'Negotiating a living', 28.

[19] S. King, 'Pauper letters as a source', *Family & Community History*, x (2007), 167–70, at 167.

[20] A. Tomkins, '"I mak bould to wright": first-person narratives in the history of poverty in England, c.1750–1900', *History Compass*, ix (2011), 365–373, at 369.

[21] T. Sokoll, 'Pauper letters as a historical source', in *Essex Pauper Letters*, ed. Sokoll, pp. 3–8, at p. 3; T. Sokoll, 'Writing for relief: rhetoric in English pauper letters, 1800–1834', in *Being Poor in Modern Europe: Historical Perspectives, 1800–1940*, ed. A. Gestrich, S. King and L. Raphael (Oxford, 2006), pp. 91–112, at p. 108; Snell, 'Belonging and community', 2; King, *Writing the Lives of the English Poor*, p. 56.

[22] A. Levene, 'General introduction', in *Narratives of the Poor in Eighteenth-Century Britain*, ed. A. Levene (5 vols, London, 2006), i. pp. vii–xix, at p. xix; King, 'Negotiating

In any discussion of clothing provision under the Old Poor Law two things must be kept in mind. First, it was rare for any pauper to be clothed entirely by the parish.[23] Much has been written on the 'economy of makeshifts', in which the poor could 'make do' through various formal and informal strategies.[24] The pauper wardrobe might therefore be supplemented by charity, prizes, gifts, clothing societies or clothing produced in the home, and even through less legitimate avenues such as theft.[25] Indeed, Styles has highlighted that 'involuntary consumption' of clothing chosen by someone else was a widely shared experience for the eighteenth-century plebeian population beyond those on parish relief.[26] It is also usually impossible to determine what clothing a pauper owned at the point at which they sought relief, though sometimes inventories appear in the vouchers. As Alannah Tomkins has highlighted, those on parish relief 'might encompass a wide range of material wealth'.[27] For instance, while a young servant might have opportunity to build up a wardrobe of fashionable clothing, a family with

---

the law of poor relief', 417; P. D. Jones and N. Carter, 'Writing for redress: redrawing the epistolary relationship under the New Poor Law', *Continuity and Change*, xxxiv (2019), 375–99, at 379; T. Sokoll, 'Old age in poverty: the record of Essex pauper letters, 1780–1834', in *Chronicling Poverty: The Voices and Strategies of the English Poor, 1640–1840*, ed. T. Hitchcock, P. King and P. Sharpe (Basingstoke, 1997), pp. 127–54, at pp. 131, 146.

[23] S. Hindle, *On the Parish? The Micro-Politics of Poor Relief in Rural England, c.1550–1750* (Oxford, 2004), p. 270.

[24] A. Tomkins and S. King, 'Introduction', in *The Poor in England, 1700–1850: An Economy of Makeshifts*, ed. S. King and A. Tomkins (Manchester, 2003), pp. 1–38, at p. 1; Hindle, *On the Parish?*, pp. 4, 9; S. Williams, *Poverty, Gender and Life-Cycle under the English Poor Law, 1760–1834* (Woodbridge, 2011), p. 7; J. Boulton, '"It is extreme necessity that makes me do this": some "survival strategies" of pauper households in London's West End during the early eighteenth century', *International Review of Social History*, lxv (2000), 47–69, at 56.

[25] S. King, *Poverty and Welfare in England, 1700–1850: A Regional Perspective* (Manchester, 2000), p. 258; Styles, *Dress of the People*, p. 258; Hindle, *On the Parish?*, p. 4; Richmond, *Clothing the Poor*, p. 298; Richmond, '"Indiscriminate liberality"', pp. 51–69; D. MacKinnon, '"Charity is worth it when it looks that good": rural women and bequests of clothing in early modern England', in *Women, Identities and Communities in Early Modern England*, ed. S. Tarbin and S. Broomhall (Aldershot, 2008), pp. 79–93; J. Broad, 'Parish economies of welfare, 1650–1834', *The Historical Journal*, xlii (1999), 985–1006, at 1002.

[26] Styles, *Dress of the People*, p. 247.

[27] A. Tomkins, 'Pawnbroking and the survival strategies of the urban poor in 1770s York', in *The Poor in England*, ed. King and Tomkins, pp. 166–98, at p. 184. Pauper inventories also highlight that they had differing levels of domestic goods: J. Harley (ed.), *Norfolk Pauper Inventories, c.1690–1834* (Oxford, 2020); J. Harley, 'Material lives of the poor and their strategic use of the workhouse during the final decades of the English Old Poor Law', *Continuity and Change*, xxx (2015), 71–103.

young children would see this stock depleted.[28] Second, and significantly, it must be remembered that there were regional differences in practice that inevitably impact on any consideration of clothing provision, while the strategies of different authorities within a region or a county might still vary significantly.[29] Provision could vary even within a single location as, for example, it experienced a period of significant economy.[30] This exacerbates difficulties with determining the overall significance and scale of clothing provision as different parishes, counties and regions may yield very different conclusions. Indeed, this is reflected in an ongoing lack of consensus in existing literature on clothing provision.

In focusing on Cumberland and Staffordshire, this chapter adds further case studies for building up regional and intra-parish perspectives on the provision of clothing and textiles. However, its aim is not to reconstruct precisely the scale of spending or to establish in their entirety specific details about the clothing provided by each settlement, parish or county. Indeed, the chapter will demonstrate some of the difficulties involved in doing so, not least that there are simply more vouchers for some places than others. Even for places where vouchers provide a fairly strong picture of what was purchased, when and how much it cost, there remain difficulties in determining how, when and to whom it was distributed. This is exacerbated by inconsistent accounting practices, different descriptive words and significant gaps in the record; as Stephen Walker has demonstrated, badly kept accounts were a particular target for Poor Law reform in the 1830s.[31] More importantly, as King has argued, an entry in an account book or name

---

[28] J. Styles, 'Involuntary consumers? Servants and their clothes in eighteenth-century England', *Textile History*, xxxiii (2002), 9–21; J. Styles, 'Custom or consumption? Plebeian fashion in eighteenth-century England', in *Luxury in the Eighteenth Century: Debates, Desires and Delectable Goods*, ed. M. Berg and E. Eger (Basingstoke, 2003), pp. 107–15.

[29] J. Kent and S. King, 'Changing patterns of poor relief in some English rural parishes circa 1650–1750', *Rural History*, xiv (2003), 119–56, at 119; French, 'How dependent were the "dependent poor"?', 215; H. French, 'An irrevocable shift: detailing the dynamics of rural poverty in southern England, 1762–1834: a case study', *The Economic History Review*, lxviii (2015), 769–805, at 773; R. Dyson, 'The extent and nature of pauperism in five Oxfordshire parishes, 1786–1832', *Continuity and Change*, xxviii (2013), 421–49, at 443; P. Sharpe and J. McEwan, 'Introduction: accommodating poverty: the housing and living arrangements of the English poor, c.1600–1850', in *Accommodating Poverty: The Housing and Living Arrangements of the English Poor, c.1600–1850*, ed. J. McEwan and P. Sharpe (Basingstoke, 2011), pp. 1–21, at pp. 2–3; Tomkins and King, 'Introduction', p. 9.

[30] King, 'Introduction', p. xxxiv.

[31] S. P. Walker, 'Expense, social and moral control: accounting and the administration of the Old Poor Law in England and Wales', *Journal of Accounting and Public Policy*, xxiii (2004), 98–9, at 104.

listed in a bill for clothing simply records the end of what could be a lengthy process of negotiation, while those who made unsuccessful requests are entirely obscured by these records.[32] The very nature of the vouchers provide yet further challenges. This chapter draws on overseers' vouchers ranging from accounts, bills, receipts and notes to letters written by, about or on behalf of out-parish paupers. The key criterion for inclusion in the sample is that vouchers relate to clothing and textiles in some way, whether through purchase, provision, inventorying or requests for relief.[33] The chapter does not draw in detail on vouchers relating to footwear, focusing instead on the 'soft' clothing and accessories issued by parishes, though both shoes and clogs appear across overseers' vouchers more broadly.[34] Nevertheless, as Peter Jones has argued, the issue of 'shoeing the poor' is a topic unto itself.[35]

This patchwork of sources makes it difficult to extract data concerning the overall scale and cost of clothing provision with any certainty; any 'final figures' must be regarded as an estimate at best. However, this chapter demonstrates that the strength of the vouchers lies in highlighting adaptability and diversity (as well as inconsistency) in the ways in which clothing and textiles were purchased, made and distributed from the 1770s up to the final years of the Old Poor Law, something often overlooked by attempts to determine the overall generosity of clothing provision.

Purchasing textiles

Evidence from the overseers' vouchers across Cumberland and Staffordshire suggests that, aside from accessories such as shoes and hats, clothing was not often purchased ready-made. Rather, echoing the consumption practices of much of the wider population, cloth was purchased first and then 'made up' into items of clothing. This pattern is consistent with that identified by Styles, whereby overseers outside London and larger provincial towns continued to source clothing in this way despite the increasing availability

---

[32] S. King, '"Stop this overwhelming torment of destiny": negotiating financial aid at times of sickness under the English Old Poor Law, 1800–1840', *Bulletin of the History of Medicine*, lxxix (2005), 228–60, at 248; King, *Writing the Lives of the English Poor*, p. 10.

[33] The sample contains 404 vouchers tagged under the major field 'Clothing, shoes and textiles' and under the subfields 'Men's clothing', 'Women's clothing', 'Children's clothing', 'Textiles' and 'Haberdashery' on the project data capture programme. The sample does not reflect the entirety of the collection of vouchers for each county.

[34] For example, see P. Collinge, 'Women, business and the Old Poor Law', for discussion of Ann Keen, supplier of ready-made shoes.

[35] Jones, 'Clothing the poor', 22–3.

of ready-made garments.[36] The vouchers can therefore provide significant information on what textiles were purchased by parishes but remain relatively underused in studies of eighteenth-century consumption, which tend to focus on individual 'choice'.[37] This section extracts details about the types of textiles that were purchased, as well as information about price and quantity, while the vouchers also hint at some of the practices involved in the purchase and distribution of textiles. This exercise, however, comes with three important caveats; first, the vouchers that survive may not necessarily reflect a parish's overall textile consumption in any given year or period. Second, not all textiles purchased by the Poor Law authorities were intended for clothing but were used for other household items such as bedding. Sometimes it is straightforward to determine when this was the case as, for instance, parishes purchased 'sheeting'. However, these distinctions are easily lost in generic descriptions such as 'cloth'. Finally, there is usually little way of knowing how the textiles purchased were distributed: the vouchers do not always make clear distinctions between indoor and outdoor relief, for instance, and it is also possible that some of these textiles did not end up in the homes or on the backs of parish paupers at all.

Despite these limitations, it is possible to explore textile consumption at both parish and county level. An examination of Cumberland in Table 2.1 shows the kinds of fabrics purchased and the average price per yard across the eight locations. This is based on 616 purchase entries gleaned from the sample of 404 vouchers, including accounts, bills and receipts where a named fabric is listed, and sometimes accompanied by the length purchased and a price. Often the price per yard of a fabric was specified, but where it is not this has been calculated based on the length purchased and the final price (if available). The categories listed in Table 2.1 obscure a greater diversity of descriptive terms and identifiers, and therefore deserve explanation. The table demonstrates that linens appear most often across the sample at an average of 12½*d* per yard. Fabrics were sometimes straightforwardly described as 'linen' or 'linen cloth', but this category also includes linen textiles such as tow cloth, fustian, canvas and harden, harden being especially popular across parishes. Very few purchases of more expensive linens such as lawn, Holland or cambric are in evidence, while the cloths that were purchased most often tend towards the coarse and hard-wearing. These textiles might have been used to make aprons, caps or bedding, as well as shifts and shirts. It is also probable that some of the textiles in Table 2.1 simply described as 'cloth' were linen or linen

---

[36] Styles, *Dress of the People*, pp. 164–5.
[37] Styles, *Dress of the People*, p. 247.

Table 2.1 Fabrics and prices across 240 overseers' vouchers, Cumberland, 1770–1837

Fabric	Years	Average price per yard (*d*)	Most expensive per yard (*d*)	Cheapest per yard (*d*)	No. of entries
Linens	1770–1837	12½	18	4	185
Duffel	1770–1831	20¼	28	15	73
Calico	1809–1837	7	12	3	65
Stuff	1770–1801	10½	15	8	46
Flannel	1773–1837	13	18	10	41
Plaid	1771–1796	10	22	7½	39
Check	1773–1836	12	22	8	21
Cottons	1809–1837	18	42	9	16
Serge	1771–1817	16	18	14½	12
Cloth	1770–1825	–	–	–	66
Other	1772–1837	–	–	–	52
Total					616

mixes; however, some of the 'cloths' costing 20*d* to 30*d* per yard would have referred to woollen or woollen mixes.

Duffel, a coarse woollen cloth used to make outerwear such as coats and cloaks, is the second most popular fabric in the sample after linen. Though the average price across the parishes was 20¼*d* per yard, it was repeatedly purchased at 22*d* per yard, suggesting that there may have been an agreed price between different suppliers or a price stipulated by parish overseers. The purchase of calicoes and cottons is discussed in more detail below, but Table 2.1 shows that parishes also purchased a range of woollen and woollen-mix fabrics; the manufacturer Elizabeth Proud, for example, supplied Hayton near Brampton with grey woollen cloth.[38] 'Stuff' refers to a woven material and was used as a generic descriptor for a mixed fabric probably used to make women's gowns. Specific to the parish of Brampton was 'Wildbore' stuff, probably an unglazed worsted mix.[39] Woollen textiles such as flannel and serge were used to make garments like petticoats and breeches. Plaid or 'pladen', at an average of 10*d* per yard, might have referred

---

[38] E. Berry, Elizabeth Proud, Woollen Mill Owner and Manufacturer, Hard Bank Mill, Hayton <thepoorlaw.org/elizabeth-proud-...bank-mill-hayton> [accessed 25 Oct. 2021].

[39] 'Wildbore', in C. W. Cunnington, P. E. Cunnington and C. Beard, *A Dictionary of English Costume, 900–1900* (London, 1960), p. 280; P. Collinge, 'Wild boar stuff', <https://thepoorlaw.org/wild-boar-stuff> [accessed 21 July 2020].

both to a plaid woollen cloth or to a fabric with a checked pattern; the most expensive, at 22d per yard, was probably woollen, and the cheapest, at 7½d, a cotton, linen or linen mix. This lighter fabric, along with 'check', which was a feature of much textile production in Cumberland, might be used for various purposes; 'chack' for lining garments was purchased by Brampton in 1781, which also purchased an 'Apron check' in 1817.[40] The category of 'other' includes fabrics that appear only infrequently or are not possible to identify. Focusing on Wigton provides an understanding of how the averages across Cumberland relate to the expenditure of an individual township. As Table 2.2 demonstrates, purchases in Wigton closely follow the pattern for Cumberland as a whole, with the exception that there are no purchases of calico. Looking at the year 1772 alone, there are purchases of 'blue stuff', 'broad Lin cloth', 'white tow cloth', 'Pladden', 'Blue duffel', 'cloth', 'harden', 'Strong blue duffel', 'cloth sheary', 'dark strip[e]', 'gray stuff', 'strip[e]', 'green stuff' and 'black [calamanco]'.[41] This gives some idea of the diversity of descriptive terms deployed, as well as the range of textiles purchased by one location. Figure 2.1 shows the detail of a bill drawn up by Joshua Harrison of Wigton. Aside from serge, the average price per yard for fabrics purchased by Wigton falls slightly below the averages for Cumberland as a whole, probably as a result of inflation in later years.

Looking across textile consumption in the nine Staffordshire parishes highlights both similarities and differences. As Table 2.3 demonstrates, a key contrast is that, where Cumberland shows a marked reliance on duffel, Staffordshire demonstrates a greater diversity of woollen and woollen-mix fabrics. These were probably used for a range of garments such as coats and cloaks, as well as waistcoats, gowns, petticoats and breeches. Under this category are several woollen and woollen-mix textiles including 'woollen and jersey' as well as woollen and terry, linsey woolsey, jersey, kersey, worsted and frize.[42] These textiles cost an average of 18d per yard which was cheaper than duffel, though this obscures a wide range of prices. Again, the category of linens includes a range of textiles including canvas, drabbit, harden, Irish linen and 'Barnsley linen'. However, in contrast to Cumberland, there are also four entries for finer 'Holland' purchased by Abbots Bromley in the 1820s and for cambric purchased by Lichfield in 1831.[43] There is again the possibility that some of the fabrics described as

---

[40] T. W. Carrick, *The History of* Wigton (Carlisle, 1949), p. 30; CAS, PR60/21/13/2/36, Brampton, Overseers' vouchers, 1781; PR60/21/13/5/47, 1817.

[41] Calamanco was a woollen stuff.

[42] Frize, a coarse woollen cloth, appears only once in 1769.

[43] SRO, LD20/6/7/242, 1831.

Table 2.2 Fabrics and prices across 65 overseers' vouchers, Wigton, Cumberland, 1770–8

Fabric	Average price per yard (*d*)	Most expensive per yard (*d*)	Cheapest per yard (*d*)	No. of entries
Linens	10½	14	7	39
Duffel	17½	22	14	21
Stuff	10	14	8	16
Plaid	8½	9	7½	14
Check	11½	16	8	11
Flannel	12½	18	6½	10
Stripe/dark stripe	13	14	12	7
Serge	16	18	14½	4
Cloth	–	–	–	25
Other	–	–	–	4
Total				151

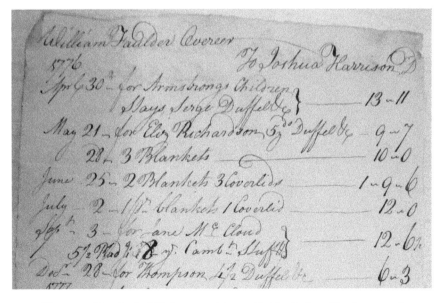

Figure 2.1 Detail of a bill for material supplied by Joshua Harrison, 1776

Table 2.3 Fabrics and prices across 164 overseers' vouchers, Staffordshire, 1769–1831

Fabric	Years	Average price per yard in pence	Most expensive per yard in pence	Cheapest per yard in pence	Number of entries
Woollen/woollen mix	1769–1827	18	42	12	85
Linens	1779–1827	11¾	26	7	78
Calico	1804–1831	6½	16	4	71
Flannel	1778–1831	16½	26	10½	62
Hemp cloth	1769–1793	12	18	9½	38
Cottons	1782–1827	15¼	32	6	19
Gingham	1822–1831	9½	12	4	18
Stuff	1793–1831	13	15	12	4
Serge	1785	23	21	24	3
Cloth	1779–1830	–	–	–	56
Other	1779–1827	–	–	–	21
Total					455

'cloth' were also linen or linen mixes, but of significance in Staffordshire is the large quantity of 'Hemp cloth' purchased by the parish of Wednesbury between 1778 and 1793. Though this cloth was woven from hemp rather than flax, it was probably put to much the same use as linen. Further down Table 2.3 are calico, cottons and gingham, as well as flannel at an average of 16½d per yard. The most expensive flannels were 'milled' or 'double milled' at 22d to 24d per yard, and there is also 'Welch' and 'fine Welch' flannel in the sample. Stuff and serge appear only infrequently. The average price per yard for textiles across Staffordshire is slightly lower than for Cumberland, but this may simply be the result of a smaller sample.

Table 2.4 shows the fabrics purchased by the parish of Wednesbury between 1778 and 1801.[44] Indeed, with 262 entries for textile purchases, Wednesbury dominates the entire sample for Staffordshire and therefore, unsurprisingly, follows closely the overall pattern for the county. Linens and hemp cloth, when combined, appear most often across the vouchers, at an average of 11d to 12d per yard. There are also payments for weaving

---

[44] Wednesbury has good records between 1778 and 1794, though there are no textile bills for 1780 and only one textile purchase recorded in 1787. There is a gap between 1794 and the seven entries for 1801.

Clothing the poor

Table 2.4 Fabrics and prices across 90 overseers' vouchers, Wednesbury, Staffordshire, 1778–1801

Fabric	Average price per yard (*d*)	Most expensive per yard (*d*)	Cheapest per yard (*d*)	No. of entries
Woollen/woollen mix	14¾	32	12	59
Linens	11	17	9	46
Hemp cloth	12	18	9½	31
Flannel	21	26	12	27
Striped cotton	14	16	14	7
Serge	23	21	24	3
Cloth	–	–	–	48
Other	–	–	–	3
Total				224

cloth in the Wednesbury vouchers, which is not something that appears in the Cumberland sample; for example, William Russell was paid for '58 yds of shirt cloth wove at 3d per yard' in 1779.[45] Woollen and woollen-mix fabrics appear second at a relatively low average of 14¾*d* per yard, with a 'woollen and jersey' mix purchased most frequently. Flannel appears next at a high average of 21*d* per yard when compared with the overall average for Staffordshire, largely because the parish frequently purchased expensive 'milled flannel'. One difference when compared with other vouchers in both Cumberland and Staffordshire is that Wednesbury purchased 'striped cotton' seven times between 1782 and 1794, which was relatively early for the consumption of cotton. The parish usually only purchased around two yards of this at a time, which suggests that it may have been used for aprons, handkerchiefs, lining garments or for children's clothing.

Neither Wigton in Cumberland nor Wednesbury in Staffordshire demonstrate the increasing purchase of cotton and cotton-mix textiles reflected in Tables 2.1 and 2.3. In both counties the cotton textile calico appears after 1800 and increases in frequency in the 1820s. Dalston and Papcastle in Cumberland clearly illustrate this shift; in Dalston bills for the period 1778 to 1787 show no purchases of calico, but five entries alone for 1831 to 1836 show 'Grey calico' twice in 1831 at 4½*d* per yard and 'Calico' at 7¾*d* per yard in 1836. In Papcastle, of forty entries for textile purchases between 1821 and 1837, there are sixteen for calico at an average of 5½*d* per yard but only two for linens. Abbots Bromley in Staffordshire follows a

[45] SRO, D4383/6/1/9/1/5/3, Wednesbury, Overseers' vouchers, 1779.

similar pattern; there are only eleven vouchers for the period 1822 to 1827, but they contain rich detail about textiles, showing fifty-two purchases of calico including olive, white, dyed, black glazed, unbleached and 'print' calico at an average of 6*d* per yard. There are only eleven entries for linens, and even the cheapest linen at 7*d* was more expensive than the average price per yard for calico. The purchase of calico by parishes was identified by King as an indication of relative generosity, most likely based on an assumption that the term referred to fashionable printed calicoes.[46] However, it is probable that by this point 'calico' referred rather to a plain cotton cloth, something supported by the prices recorded and descriptive terms such as 'unbleached'. This does not rule out the possibility that some of these calicoes came in prints used for women's gowns; for example, Abbots Bromley purchased 'Print Callico' at 3*d* and 6*d* per yard in 1827.[47] However, their primary purpose was probably as a cheaper replacement for linen and linen-mix textiles. Indeed, this may have formed a deliberate attempt to reduce clothing expenditure, as Richmond found for Sussex and Kent in the 1820s.[48] This would not necessarily have resulted in significant savings in the long term, however, as calico was less hard-wearing than linen. As Styles has outlined, it was only after 1825 that cottons began to offer a meaningful price advantage over linen for making shifts and shirts.[49]

In addition to calico, the vouchers demonstrate a wider shift towards cotton or cotton-mix textiles after 1800, which fall under the category of 'cottons' in Tables 2.1 and 2.3. These included corduroy, cotton, dyed cotton, muslin, nankeen, printed cotton, gingham, striped cotton velveteen and jaconet. Corduroy and the silk-like velveteen might have begun to replace woollen textiles for outerwear like waistcoats and breeches, and were the most expensive of the cotton fabrics, accounting for high averages in Tables 2.1 and 2.3. Greystoke in Cumberland, for example, purchased corduroy four times between 1820 and 1836 at an average of 24*d* per yard. Abbots Bromley purchased gingham sixteen times between 1822 and 1827 at an average of 10*d* per yard, while it also purchased corduroy at 32*d* per yard, velveteen at 21*d*, stripe cotton at 13*d*, muslin at 12*d* and dyed cotton at 6*d*. There were also various iterations of 'prints' purchased by authorities across both Cumberland and Staffordshire which may have been cotton or cotton-

---

[46] King, 'Reclothing the English poor', pp. 43–5.

[47] SRO, D1209/4/3/1/152, Abbots Bromley, Overseers' vouchers, 1827.

[48] Richmond, '"Indiscriminate liberality"', pp. 51–69; Richmond, *Clothing the Poor*, p. 187.

[49] Styles, *Dress of the People*, p. 95; J. Styles, 'What were cottons for in the early Industrial Revolution?', in *The Spinning World: A Global History of Cotton Textiles, 1200–1850*, ed. G. Riello and P. Parthasarathi (Oxford, 2013), pp. 307–27.

mix textiles used for women's gowns; for example, 'blue & white print' was purchased by Hayton in Cumberland in 1831.[50] Cotton textiles had by no means entirely eclipsed other fabrics by 1834, as linens appear across all years of the sample. However, their increasing presence does reflect an important shift in textile consumption after 1820.

It is possible to extract some detail about the lengths of fabrics purchased by parishes, but extremely difficult to determine averages. The vouchers in Cumberland suggest that overseers purchased an average of four yards of linen at a time, but in Brampton this ranged from one yard of harden purchased on several occasions between 1781 and 1796 to thirty-one yards of 'Housewife linen' purchased in 1794 and 1795. Duffel seems to have been supplied at around four yards at a time with slightly more consistency, perhaps in response to specific need, for instance, to provide a coat for an apprentice.[51] Nevertheless, in Hayton purchases of duffel still ranged from one to thirty-five yards. The Staffordshire parishes are broadly similar.[52] The average purchase of linen was slightly higher than in Cumberland at eight and a quarter yards, but in Wednesbury this ranged from 141 yards of 'strong linen cloth' purchased in 1779 to half a yard of harden in 1789.[53] This shows differing practices even within parishes, as some may have kept a store of fabrics purchased in bulk but also purchased textiles in response to need and for specific individuals. This might reflect distinctions between indoor and outdoor relief as parishes stockpiled textiles for use in workhouses, but the vouchers often make these distinctions difficult to confirm, particularly when these purchases appear in a bill issued by a vendor. The parish of Wednesbury did purchase textiles intended for 'the house' a number of times, though no clear pattern emerges in terms of the lengths supplied; in 1789, for example, purchases ranged from five yards of linen, sixteen yards of jersey, thirty-five yards of 'white jersey', four yards of harden, and one and a half yards of linen.[54] The 1789 manual *Instructions for Cutting Out Apparel for the Poor* emphasized that purchasing textiles wholesale contributed to considerable savings.[55] However, contrary to this advice, parishes continued to purchase a mix of longer and shorter lengths up to the end of the Old Poor Law.

[50] CAS, PR102/112/16, Hayton, Overseers' vouchers, 1831.
[51] J. Lane, *Apprenticeship in England* (London, 1996), pp. 28–9.
[52] Some Staffordshire parishes used 'nails', around one-sixteenth of a yard, as a measurement.
[53] SRO, D4383/6/1/9/1/5/8, 1779; D4383/6/1/9/2/114, 1789.
[54] SRO, D4383/6/1/9/2/65; D4383/6/1/9/2/126, 1789.
[55] Anon., *Instructions for Cutting Out Apparel for the Poor; principally intended for the Assistance of the Patronesses of Sunday Schools, and other Charitable Institutions, but Useful in all Families* (London, 1789), p. 1.

The nature of the vouchers, as well as inconsistent descriptive practices, makes it difficult to reach overall judgements about textile consumption by different authorities. There are some purchases of more expensive fabrics such as lawn in evidence but never in significant numbers and, as Jones, Styles and others have found, the textiles purchased across Cumberland and Staffordshire were relatively inexpensive, coarse and perhaps even uniform in some instances. There are certainly none of the expensive damasks and camlets purchased by the plebeian Latham family between 1724 and 1767, for instance.[56] No parish purchased additional decorative trimmings such as ribbons or lace, which were relatively cheaply available. Striped fabrics, plaids, checks, ginghams and prints may have provided some colour variation and pattern, but textiles were most consistently described as blue, white, grey, brown, black and sometimes as green. The most striking consistency of colour is in the purchase of duffel across Cumberland as, of seventy-three entries, forty-five are described as blue. As duffel was probably used to make outerwear such as coats and cloaks, this suggests a degree of uniformity.[57]

In addition to purchasing lengths of fabrics, authorities across Cumberland and Staffordshire were consistently supplied with haberdashery items. In Cumberland, vouchers record purchases of coat, breast and shirt buttons, horn and metal buttons, tape, whalebone (baleen), hooks and eyes, laces, apron strings, twists and yarn. There is a similar picture across Staffordshire with purchases of buttons, laces, inkles, pins, thread, binding, tape, yarn, sewing cotton, silk and even needles. In both counties it can be difficult to disentangle the prices of these items as they are often listed alongside each other as in the typical entry 'to Tape thread Whail Bone and Laces'. However, they usually never cost more than a shilling at a time as thread could be little as $1d$ to $2d$ an ounce, while a dozen buttons could be had for $4d$ to $9d$. There is evidence to suggest that some parishes purchased haberdashery items in bulk; Lichfield, for example, purchased '6 dozen buttons at $9d$' in 1822.[58] However, the overall picture is one of consistent, if small, expenditure alongside lengths of textiles. This expenditure has frequently been overlooked in studies of pauper clothing, perhaps because it is difficult to map onto 'final figures' for clothing provision, but it is important to understandings of the processes by which parishes acquired and distributed clothing and textiles as relief.

---

[56] Styles, *Dress of the People*, p. 263.

[57] P. Collinge, 'Blue duffle', The Poor Law (2019) <https://thepoorlaw.org/blue-duffle> [accessed 21 July 2020].

[58] SRO, LD20/6/6/51, 1822.

Distributing clothing

Clothing and textiles might be distributed through a range of practices, some revealed and some obscured by the vouchers. Providing clothing or cloth rather than cash may have been a way to ensure that relief was not 'frittered away', but parishes seem to have been fairly flexible in meeting demand.[59] It is also difficult to determine from the vouchers alone how pauper requests for relief shaped provision. Elizabeth Newell's letter shows that she made a clear request for clothing, and letters such as this hint at interactions and negotiations that must have taken place within the parish.[60] King has demonstrated that both requests by and attitudes towards in- and out-parish paupers differed little, and so one might imagine similar requests being placed – and fulfilled – in person.[61] Sometimes requests were fairly general, but Newell's reflects that paupers might also make more specific demands. The vouchers can also work to obscure differences between recipients of clothing relief, particularly in attempts to extract general trends and patterns of expenditure.[62] There were many different people in receipt of relief, of which in- and out-parish paupers are just two examples.[63] Gender and life cycle impacted significantly on poverty and there must have been clear differences between regular recipients who could build up a more extensive 'pauper wardrobe' and those who received one-off relief.[64] For the parish of Campton in Bedfordshire, for example, Samantha Williams found that 80 per cent of clothing went to regularly paid pensioners.[65]

If we turn to look at what items of clothing were distributed, the vouchers demonstrate that hats, handkerchiefs, stockings and sometimes garments like aprons could be purchased ready-made. In Cumberland, a 'Hat' ranged from 1*s* to 1*s* 6*d*, while handkerchiefs appear across the sample at an average price of 13½*d*.[66] With these items it is often difficult to determine whether the intended recipient was a man, woman or child unless they were named. Wednesbury purchased an 'aporn for John Wolson' at a high price of 3*s* 3*d* in 1801, but an apron was also an important part of a working woman's

---

[59] Hindle, *On the Parish?*, pp. 264–5.

[60] Sokoll, 'Institutional context', p. 11.

[61] King, 'Introduction', p. l; King, 'Negotiating the law of poor relief', 416.

[62] French, 'How dependent were the "dependent poor"?', 195.

[63] Kent and King, 'Changing patterns of poor relief', 119.

[64] A. Levene, 'Poor families, removals and "nurture" in late Old Poor Law London', *Continuity and Change*, xxv (2010), 233–62, at 235; S. R. Ottaway, 'Providing for the elderly in eighteenth-century England', *Continuity and Change*, xiii (1998), 391–418, at 404.

[65] Williams, *Poverty, Gender and Life-Cycle*, p. 44.

[66] Based on twenty-eight entries for handkerchiefs which usually cost around 10*d* to 14*d*.

wardrobe.[67] Stockings were usually purchased ready-made, though there are some payments for stocking yarn. In Cumberland, prices ranged from 10d for a 'pare of hose' in 1770 to two pairs of stockings at 20d each in 1824.[68] In Staffordshire the average cost of a pair of stockings was 1s 4d, but they increased in price from the 1790s onwards. Beyond these items, it is very difficult to determine prices for individual garments, or to estimate how many individual items of clothing were distributed. However, what the vouchers do reveal are frequent payments for making clothing; Dalston, for instance, paid 2s to 'Timothy Crosier for making Cartnors Cloaths' in 1785.[69] These payments appear across the vouchers and could range from 8s to 10s for making a suit or several items to 4d to 10d for making a single garment. Sometimes payments were made to tailors, as in a bill 'To a Taylor's week and wages for making cloaths' for 'Olive Munkers child' at 1s 4d in 1774.[70] Some of the women who issued bills for making to the parish were also likely mantua-makers or milliners by trade. As Pam Inder has demonstrated, there were dressmakers catering to all levels of society in this period.[71] However, parish paupers might also be paid to make up garments that only required plain sewing such as shirts and shifts. In these instances, not only did this provision benefit the recipients of clothing but also those who undertook this work, as the parish paid them for a service rather than simply providing financial relief. Again, from these costs alone it remains difficult to place an overall price on an item of clothing, particularly when payments were simply made for 'making clothes'; in Skelton, for instance, £1 4d was paid for 'Mary Stubs Cloaths making etc' in 1796 or 1797.[72] Nevertheless, these payments demonstrate broader practices of provision across parishes and hint at hidden economies of making that may have taken place inside the pauper household, poorhouse or workhouse; it is possible that some textiles and haberdashery items were issued directly to paupers, as bills appear only when someone other than the recipient was paid to make clothing (Figure 2.2).

It is clear from the overseers' vouchers that, after providing shoes, a parish's biggest undertaking when it came to clothing was the purchase and distribution of linen garments, and in particular of women's shifts and

[67] SRO, D4383/6/1/9/3/146, 1802.

[68] CAS, PR36/V/1/23, Wigton St Mary, Overseers' vouchers, 1770.

[69] CAS, SPC44/2/37/5, Dalston, Overseers' vouchers, 1778–9.

[70] SRO, D730/3/6, 1820.

[71] P. Inder, *Busks, Basques and Brush-Braid: British Dressmaking in the 18th and 19th Centuries* (London, 2020), pp. 78–9.

[72] CAS, PR10/V/20, 1797.

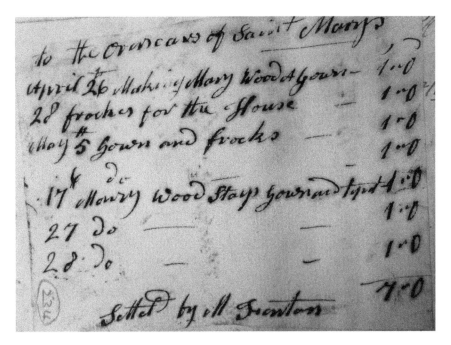

Figure 2.2 Margaret Fenton's bill for making gowns, frocks and stays

men's shirts, which were worn close to the body, washed often and required regular replacement. These body linens were essential to understandings of cleanliness and decency.[73] As Alice Dolan has highlighted, pawning linen had severe implications, as the absence of clean linen was a marker of poverty that might provoke disgust.[74] Crucial to this was owning a change so that one shift or shirt could be worn while the other was laundered. Indeed, a number of overseers' vouchers record the purchase of blue and starch.[75] On average, two and a half yards of cloth were needed to make a shift, three and a half to make a shirt and just under two yards for a child's shift or shirt. Overseers across Cumberland and Staffordshire frequently purchased linen, linen mixes, cloths and cottons, and some of the lengths purchased closely match these quantities; for instance, Dalston often purchased two and a half

[73] S. North, *Sweet and Clean? Bodies and Clothes in Early Modern England* (Oxford, 2020), p. 196.
[74] A. Dolan, 'Touching linen: textiles, emotion and bodily intimacy in England, c.1708–1818', *Cultural and Social History*, xvi (2019), 145–64, at 148, 159.
[75] For example, CAS, PR36/V/6/33, 1776, and SRO, D4383/6/1/9/1/16/4, 1790.

yards of linen or cloth at a time and in the 1790s Wednesbury purchased two and a half to three and a half yards of harden on several occasions. A 1777 Wigton bill reflects the distribution of linen to thirteen recipients including Suse Morrow, Ruth Betterton and Molly Akin who each received '2 yards and a halfe of white tow cloth' at 10*d* a yard between May and September.[76] Suse Morrow, who appears to have been in the poorhouse, had also received two yards of tow cloth at 11*d* in December 1776.[77] This suggests that some parishes distributed lengths of fabric specifically intended for shifts and shirts directly to paupers. Conversely, the 141 yards of 'strong linen cloth' purchased by Wednesbury in 1779 would have made forty shirts, fifty-six shifts or, with over half a yard spare, seventy shifts and shirts for children.[78] It is possible to glean some details about prices for linens from the vouchers, though there are marked difficulties with calculating individual costs for these items. However, it is likely that an adult's shift or shirt cost around 2*s* to 3*s* 6*d*, depending on when it was purchased, how it was purchased and who made it up.[79] Prices for making a single shift or shirt were usually 4*d* to 6*d*, and payments might be made at different times, as a parish purchased fabric that was then made up at a later date.

Beyond linens, a basic set of outerwear for a man consisted of a suit made up of coat, waistcoat and breeches, as well as a shirt, stockings, hat and a pair of shoes, all of which are in evidence in the vouchers. The majority of entries for men's outerwear across Cumberland and Staffordshire reflect payments for making up these items rather than for purchasing them ready-made, though, again, there are difficulties with estimating an individual price for these items; in Cumberland, for instance, costs for making men's outwear ranged from 2*s* to 8*s*. *Instructions for Cutting Out Apparel for the Poor* suggested that coats, waistcoats and breeches could be issued separately as 'it is seldom found that a poor labouring man can afford a whole suit of cloaths at once', and it is clear from the vouchers that parishes frequently provided these items individually.[80] Often they were directed for a named individual, particularly in the case of suits, which were expensive to purchase and make up. In the Staffordshire vouchers there are also payments for

[76] CAS, PR36/V/7/44, 1777.

[77] CAS, PR36/V/6/81, 1776.

[78] SRO, D4383/6/1/9/1/5/8, 1779.

[79] Taking the average price of linen in Cumberland as 12½*d* per yard plus 5*d* for making, a shift comes to 3*s* ¼*d* and a shirt 4*s* ¾*d*. Taking the average price of linen in Staffordshire as 11¾*d* per yard plus 5*d* for making, a shift comes to 2*s* 10½*d* and a shirt 3*s* 10*d*. These are high estimates, illustrating the difficulties of establishing the total cost of a garment from the vouchers.

[80] Anon., *Instructions for Cutting Out*, p. 54.

men's smock frocks, a garment worn by agricultural labourers in the south and Midlands; for instance, Lichfield paid 10*s* for 'A blue mans frock' in 1830.[81] Women's clothing tended to be cheaper to purchase and make than men's but consisted of more individual items. Ann Stubs of Skelton received a relatively full set of clothing in 1792 including a gown, two shifts, a handkerchief, a petticoat, a pair of stockings and an apron, while her child received two shifts and a bedgown.[82] A gown was the equivalent of a suit, though the vouchers suggest that they were purchased less frequently. Nevertheless, it may be that women made up their own or paid someone else to do so; costs for making a single gown ranged across the vouchers from 12*d* in 1775 to 8*d* in 1797, to 1*s* 6*d* in 1831. As already highlighted, parishes were certainly purchasing textiles often used for gowns. A full gown would require around seven yards of fabric, but there are also shorter bedgowns across the sample that required only three yards.[83] Some women received petticoats – for example, Mary Acwood received one at 3*s* 10*d* in 1780 – though they do not appear regularly in the vouchers.[84] This is also the case for cloaks, though again this does not mean that they were not being made from duffel or woollen fabric purchased by the parish.[85] A bill was issued to Lichfield in 1830 for four cloaks at a total of £1 16*s*, which were perhaps purchased ready-made, for example, while a bill to Dalston in 1831 listed 'To making a cloake & Lining'.[86] One key component of a woman's wardrobe that appears relatively infrequently in the sample are stays; in Cumberland there are only seven entries between 1770 and 1776, including three pairs purchased in 1771 at 4*s* 6*d*, 4*s* and 3*s* 6*d* 'for the use of the Poor'.[87] The overseer of Greystoke also made a payment of 1*s* 4*d* in 1822 for 'Making a pair of Stays', but in both Cumberland and Staffordshire purchases of whalebone, 'stay tape', binding and laces hint at the making of stays beyond this (Figure 2.3).[88]

Children also appear as named recipients across the vouchers, and indeed might require a significant outlay as their clothing wore out or became too small. This was especially the case with younger children who required frequent changes, a cost all the more prohibitive for unmarried or single

---

[81] SRO, LD20/6/7/162, 1830.
[82] CAS, PR10/V/17, Skelton, Overseers' vouchers, 1792.
[83] Anon., *Instructions for Cutting Out*, pp. 16–17; Styles, *Dress of the People*, pp. 41–2.
[84] SRO, D4383/6/1/91/6/10, 1780.
[85] Anon., *Instructions for Cutting Out*, p. 68.
[86] SRO, LD20/6/7/203, 1830; CAS, SPC44/2/48/136, 1831.
[87] CAS, PR36/V/2/66, 1771.
[88] CAS, PR5/67-D/6, Greystoke St Andrew, Overseers' vouchers, 1822.

Figure 2.3 Coarse linen stays, 1760–80. York Castle Museum

mothers.[89] Looking again at Ann Stubs of Skelton, a 1788 bill for her child lists a wide range of items including three caps and one bib, striped linen, blue flannel and a yard of Irish linen for two shawls at a total of 5s 11d.[90] Moreover, naked or poorly clothed children were representative of extreme deprivation, placing an obligation on a parish to provide urgent relief.[91] Younger children received frocks and skirts, but older ones received much the same clothing as adults. For instance, Wigton purchased two pairs of stays for 'the use of Stalker's wife's children' in 1771.[92] The vouchers suggest that it was, unsurprisingly, slightly cheaper to clothe a child as, for example,

---

[89] For the rising cost of illegitimate children see S. Williams, *Unmarried Motherhood in the Metropolis, 1700–1850: Pregnancy, the Poor Law and Provision* (Cham, 2018); S. Williams, 'The maintenance of bastard children in London, 1790–1834', *The Economic History Review*, lxix (2016), 945–71, at 968.

[90] CAS, PR10/V/14/4, 1788.

[91] J. Bailey, '"Think wot a mother must feel": parenting in English pauper letters, c.1760–1834', *Family & Community History*, xiii (2010), 5–19, at 16.

[92] CAS, PR36/V/23, 1771.

a child's bedgown cost 9*d* compared to the 2*s* 11*d* spent on a 'Bedgown for Ann Stoker' in 1792.[93] In Wigton in 1772, four boys hats were purchased at 10*d* each while 'a 'Mans Hat' cost 1*s* 2*d*, and payments for making boys' suits were usually lower than for men's. It is well established that a parish might purchase a full set of clothing for children about to go into employment or apprenticeships, and this could again require significant one-off expenditure.[94] In an undated voucher from Lichfield, for instance, is a payment for five days' work at 2*s* 'for making Michael Done a new sute of clothing for his apprenticeship', while the overseer of Threlkeld paid 5*s* 'To Cloaths' for Thomas Hudson's daughter 'going in to Service' in 1790.[95] Indeed, pauper writers often asked parishes to provide clothing to enable their children to secure employment; in 1829, for instance, the Essex pauper Samuel White asked for '20 or 30 shillings' to send his daughter 'out a little respectable' to work in a shop.[96]

In addition to making clothing, payments for mending and repairing clothing appear across the vouchers. They by no means form a large part of expenditure but often remain overlooked in discussions dominated by newly purchased or issued clothing. In Wigton in 1770, for instance, alongside 'Quarter of a years Board and Lodgings for Mary Tremble' was a payment of 2*s* for 'Mending and repairing old cloths'.[97] In Cumberland, payments ranged from 4*d* spent on mending clothes in 1796 to payments of 2*s* 6*d* and 5*s* for 'mending the pa[u]pers close' in 1788 and 1789.[98] Mending is not as much in evidence in Staffordshire, though in 1828 payments for 'Mending etc' and 'Mending shoes and clothes W Harris' at 3*s* each appear in the Yoxall vouchers.[99] Abbots Bromley also purchased '3 yds Callico' and 'Cotton Worsted' for 'mending at the workhouse' in 1822, suggesting that some of the textiles and haberdashery supplies purchased by parishes went towards the repair of clothing.[100] Indeed, this again hints at broader practices of mending and repair, and suggests that the parish could provide clothing relief by a range of means. While mending and repair might not reflect

[93] SRO, D4383/6/1/9/3/210, 1792.
[94] Jones, 'Clothing the poor', p. 28; Jones, '"I cannot keep my place"', 39.
See also K. Honeyman, 'The Poor Law, the parish apprentice, and the textile industries in the north of England, 1780–1830', *Northern History*, xliv (2007), 115–40.
[95] SRO, LD20/6/7/21, undated; CAS, SPC21/8–11/8A, Threlkeld, Overseers' vouchers, 1794.
[96] Sokoll (ed.), *Essex Pauper Letters*, no. 264.
[97] CAS, PR36/V/1/11, 1770.
[98] CAS, PR60/21/13/2/94, Brampton, Overseers' vouchers, 1788; PR60/21/13/2/72, 1789.
[99] SRO, D730/3/14, 1828.
[100] SRO, D1209/4/3/1/9, 1822.

expenditure on new clothing, they do demonstrate that the parish could play a wider role in the maintenance and upkeep of the pauper wardrobe. Indeed, as with making, poorer members of the community may have been paid for mending to relieve pressure on poor relief.

While it is therefore possible to glean some details about the distribution of clothing from the vouchers, other practices are only hinted at. For example, it is difficult to determine whether some of the payments issued to paupers in 'distress' were intended for clothing, though a 1780 receipt in the vouchers from Margaret Huet to the parish of Brampton for 'Five shillings for to help buy cloathes' demonstrates that money could be provided for this purpose.[101] The practices of pawning and redeeming clothing, which appear again and again across pauper letters, are not reflected in the sample of the vouchers at all, though they probably took place.[102] Several letters from Philip and Frances James to Uttoxeter mention pawning goods; for instance, Frances wrote in 1833 that 'I have been [obliged] to Pledge & Sell Almost every thing we had'.[103] Though it did not form direct expenditure on clothing, payments that enabled paupers to fetch clothing out of pawn again reflect broader involvement and investment by the parish in the pauper wardrobe. The overseers' vouchers therefore reveal diverse and flexible practices in the distribution of clothing, as well as parish assistance with the maintenance of the pauper wardrobe, though it remains clear that parishes were far more likely to provide paupers with textiles or to have something made up than they were to purchase clothing ready-made or second-hand, despite a thriving second-hand market.[104] Extracting a 'final' price or quantity for specific items of clothing necessarily excludes some of these strategies.

How clothing provision was received by paupers is difficult to determine, though scholarship on pauper letters has gone some way towards uncovering popular understandings. However, clothing in these letters is always filtered

---

[101] CAS, PR60/21/13/2, 1780.

[102] For discussion of the pawning practices of York paupers see Tomkins, 'Pawnbroking and the survival strategies of the urban poor', pp. 166–93.

[103] 'Letters from Philip and Frances James and others at Leicester to the parish of Uttoxeter in Staffordshire, 1832–7', in *Narratives of the Poor in Eighteenth-Century Britain*, ed. A. Levene (5 vols, London, 2006), i. pp. 273–81.

[104] For the second-hand clothing trade see B. Lemire, 'Consumerism in preindustrial and early industrial England: the trade in secondhand clothes', *Journal of British Studies*, xxvii (1988), 1–24, at 4; B. Lemire, 'The theft of clothes and popular consumerism in early modern England', *Journal of Social History*, xxiv (1990), 255–76; M. Lambert, '"Cast-off wearing apparell": the consumption and distribution of second-hand clothing in northern England during the long eighteenth century', *Textile History*, xxxi (2004), 1–26.

through the need to construct a successful request for relief. Therefore, while a few writers did express surprise or disappointment that a parish had not provided cloth or clothing, they were unlikely to be critical of clothing they had received; rather, requests centred on insufficient, ragged or absent clothing. The repeated purchase of blue duffel in Cumberland suggests that pauper clothing could certainly be uniform in some respects and may have marked out recipients of relief within or even beyond their home parish. However, much like the practice of badging, the meanings of clothing provided by the parish were probably ambiguous rather than straightforwardly reflective of shame or dependency.[105] It is also important to remember that parish relief was just one way in which labouring men, women and children might receive clothing through channels without 'choice'.[106] Finally, it is clear that paupers were more than capable of supplementing parish clothing; when he entered the Skelton poorhouse in 1781, for instance, John Matthews had in his possession one silk handkerchief, which was unlikely to have been acquired through relief.[107]

Conclusion

A shroud or winding sheet marked the last time a pauper might be clothed by the parish; Ann Garnet of Papcastle received four yards of flannel in November 1825, for instance, while 2s was paid shortly afterwards in January 1826 for her shroud.[108] For some this represented the end of a regular supply of clothing, for others it was the end of an occasional or one-off source of relief, while many more may have relied on different strategies that made up the makeshift economy when they were alive. Some may have even been involuntary consumers of parish clothing through inheritance, recycling, theft or pawning; clothing and textiles issued by the parish did not necessarily stay with their initial recipient, though the vouchers usually fix them at the point of purchase or distribution.

By looking across overseers' vouchers in Cumberland and Staffordshire, this chapter has further highlighted regional and inter-parish differences in the ways overseers purchased, supplied, distributed and recorded the clothing and textiles issued to paupers between 1769 and 1834. This demonstrates the importance of further research at both a regional and a

---

[105] Hindle, 'Dependency, shame and belonging', p. 29; S. King, 'The clothing of the poor: a matter of pride or shame?', in *Being Poor in Modern Europe*, ed. Gestrich, King and Raphael, pp. 365–88, at p. 369.

[106] Styles, *Dress of the People*, p. 247.

[107] CAS, PR10/V/15, 1781.

[108] CAS, SPC110/1/3/2/3/199, Papcastle, Overseers' vouchers, 1826–8.

parish-by-parish level to unpick this patchwork of practices. The findings outlined here broadly confirm the utility and potential uniformity of clothing provided in Cumberland and Staffordshire, but demonstrate that, rather than focusing on the 'final' point of distribution, clothing provision needs to be understood as a network of practices. In attempting to determine how many items of clothing were distributed by parishes and how much they cost, there is a risk of obscuring a wider range of strategies evident across the vouchers that included the consistent purchase of haberdashery items as well as the repair of pauper clothing. Not only do difficulties with the source material make sweeping conclusions about quantity and quality tricky, but the adaptability and diversity of these practices is in itself significant. As King has highlighted, end-of-process spending is an 'inadequate guide' to the range of experiences of provision.[109] Clothing provision came in different guises and was added to different wardrobes at different points in the life cycle.

Whether paupers were beneficiaries or losers by way of this diversity is more difficult to say. It highlights, in theory at least, the potential for overseers to exercise flexibility in responding to requests for clothing. Indeed, this flexibility was important for authorities in responding to the varying circumstances of different paupers; the parish of East Hoathly, for instance, was invoiced by Bethlehem Hospital for clothes provided for Elizabeth Overing.[110] Nevertheless, it is likely that in practice it generated mixed experiences. The example of Sarah Sowerby of Threlkeld, an out-parish pauper living in Kendal, is certainly evidence that the system could create marked difficulties for paupers in need of clothing. Between 1801 and Sowerby's death in 1812, three different letter writers addressed the authorities to request relief for her in the form of linen and other items of clothing, including the master of the Kendal workhouse, Daniel Dunglinson. In 1807 Dunglinson twice requested permission from Threlkeld to supply Sowerby with 'necessary Clothing' but was met with silence, and so found it necessary to mobilize the overseer of Kendal who wrote in December 1807 to reiterate Sowerby's 'great Want of Clothing'.[111] Dunglinson's attempts to secure payment for these items show that in some cases clothing relief required repeated negotiation and interaction with the parish authorities, particularly when distributed via the out-parish system. When the range of practices found across the vouchers is taken into account, the 'generosity' of clothing provision also proves a slippery system of measurement; how

---

[109] King, *Writing the Lives of the English Poor*, p. 344.

[110] See Interlude 2 (E. Hughes, 'Elizabeth Overing, sent to Bedlam') after this chapter.

[111] CAS, SPC21/8–11/47, 43, 37, 1807.

should the generosity of a parish that provided linen cloth and thread to a family who deployed the scraps as rags be compared to that of a parish that paid to have a family's shifts and shirts made up? Indeed, paying to have clothes made may even have formed part of a wider parochial strategy, as making up might be given to another individual or family on the margins to help tide them over in a difficult time or to keep them from the workhouse. Moreover, how is generosity to be understood when these different practices were found within the same parish?

Some of the overseers' vouchers for Cumberland show purchases made after the Poor Law Amendment Act of 1834, though it is not clear what these textiles were for; in 1837, for instance, Papcastle purchased 'Blue & Yellow Print' at 6½*d* per yard.[112] As already outlined, scholars have differed in their interpretation of the scale and significance of clothing provision in the final years of the Old Poor Law. The vouchers alone do not provide enough information to determine whether clothing provision was significantly impacted in Cumberland and Staffordshire in particular years of 'crisis', though, unlike Richmond's Sussex and Kent parishes, it certainly continued into the 1820s.[113] What is clear is that in the dying days of the Old Poor Law a number of parishes supplemented the purchase of linen and heavy woollen fabrics with lighter cotton textiles, and particularly calico, which perhaps reflected a broader attempt to make savings. Nevertheless, as King has highlighted, an established sense of entitlement among many paupers often made it difficult for parishes to sustain meaningful savings in the years leading up to 1834.[114] It has already been demonstrated that the shift to the New Poor Law was not automatic or uncontested, and it is not difficult to imagine that this was also the case with the provision of clothing and textiles.[115] Customary rights, expectations and understandings surrounding pauper clothing were unlikely to be transformed overnight.[116]

---

[112] CAS, SPC110/1/3/2/3/125, 1837.

[113] Richmond, '"Indiscriminate liberality"', pp. 51–69; Jones, 'Clothing the poor', p. 34.

[114] King, 'Negotiating the law of poor relief', 413.

[115] Jones and Carter, 'Writing for redress', 384–6.

[116] T. Hitchcock, P. King and P. Sharpe, 'Introduction: Chronicling poverty – the voices and strategies of the English poor, 1640–1840', in *Chronicling Poverty*, ed. Hitchcock, King and Sharpe, pp. 1–18, at p. 10.

Interlude 2

Elizabeth Overing, sent to Bedlam[1]

Elizabeth Hughes

Elizabeth Overing was probably Elizabeth, the daughter of John and Mary Overing, who was baptized in Wilmington, Sussex on 21 September 1746.[2] Her father died in 1773, leaving a will acknowledging all four of his children and leaving £3 a year for Elizabeth but only after her mother's death.[3]

Things seem to have gone wrong fairly soon afterwards, as Elizabeth was admitted to Bethlem Hospital in London on 17 May 1774 by Wilmington parish. Bethlem Hospital, colloquially known as Bedlam, cared for the 'insane' poor, taking in patients from across the country. It was usual for new patients to spend about a year in the hospital's general ward, after which, if they were not cured, they were assessed as to whether they were 'fit' to receive the hospital's charity in the incurable ward. Elizabeth Overing was discharged as 'not fit' on 19 May 1775.

She returned to Wilmington, and by 3 September 1775 she was the subject of a removal order from Wilmington to East Hoathly. The order records that Mary Overing, Elizabeth's mother, was examined as to her daughter's settlement. Since Elizabeth would by now have been twenty-nine, this suggests that she may not have been considered able to answer for herself. There is no explanation as to how she had gained a settlement in East Hoathly but gain it she did. From this time, Elizabeth appears regularly in the East Hoathly overseers' accounts, where payments

---

[1] For the fuller story of Elizabeth Overing see E. Hughes, 'Elizabeth Overing, sent to Bedlam (1746–1815)', The Poor Law <https://thepoorlaw.org/elizabeth-overing-sent-to-bedlam-1746-1815> [accessed 23 Nov. 2021]. This blog post is made available under a Creative Commons Attribution-NonCommercial 4.0 International License (CC BY-NC 4.0).

[2] ESRO, PAR510/1/1, Wilmington, Register of baptisms, marriages and burials, 1538–1812.

[3] ESRO, PBT1/1/62/692, Registered will of John Overing, 1772.

record her maintenance at 3s 6d a week, later increasing to 5s.[4] By January 1782, the process had begun to admit Elizabeth Overing to Bethlem Hospital once more.

Parish maintenance payments for her ended on 12 January 1782, which was the original date for her planned admission to Bethlem. Instead, she was conveyed to Hoxton, where she was maintained by a Mr Robert Harrison from 12 to 26 January at 10s 6d a week. Hoxton was the location of a number of 'madhouses' for private mental health patients in the later eighteenth century. It may be that Elizabeth was accommodated in one or other of these institutions until Bethlem was able to accept her.

She was finally transferred to Bethlem as an incurable patient on 26 January 1782. Elizabeth Overing's expenses were passed on to East Hoathly. Vouchers show that the parish paid deposits of £4 1s 0d towards her board and £3 3s 0d towards her bed, bedding and funeral if she were to die at the hospital.[5] Invoices for Elizabeth's expenses were received in East Hoathly at the end of December each year. For example, in the year ending 28 December 1784, the parish was invoiced £6 10s 0d for board and £2 15s 0d for clothing, which included shoes and stockings, a gown, petticoat and undercoat, shifts, caps, aprons, handkerchiefs and buckles, provided at Bethlem's standard charge.[6] The provision of clothing for the parochial poor was an important element of relief and included responsibility for those parishioners cared for beyond the parish.[7]

In August 1815 Bethlem's patients were transferred to new premises in Southwark. Elizabeth did not live to see it, for she died on 2 June that year. Her burial place has not so far been identified.

---

[4] ESRO, PAR378/ 31/3/1/1, East Hoathly, Overseers' account book, 1761–79.

[5] ESRO, PAR378/ 31/3/19, 20, 21, 22, 23, 25, East Hoathly, Overseers' vouchers.

[6] ESRO, PAR378/31/3/21/24, East Hoathly, Overseers' vouchers, 1784.

[7] See Chapter 2 in this volume for further discussion on the nature and extent of clothing supplied to the poor.

3. Vagrancy, poor relief and the parish
Tim Hitchcock

Late in the evening on a quiet Sunday in late September 1756, Thomas Turner, the diarist and overseer of the poor at East Hoathly in Sussex was alarmed 'by a drunken travelling woman, swearing and rolling about the street'. Turner probably gave her a few pence and hurried her to the parish boundary. Having dealt with the interruption, Turner spent the rest of the evening reading three of Archbishop Tillotson's sermons.[1]

The identity of the drunken traveller is unknown. She is not mentioned again in the diary, nor does she appear in the parish records. This is not unusual. In general, the travelling poor, vagrants and disorderly paupers do not figure largely in the parish records of late eighteenth- and early nineteenth-century Britain. Of approximately 41,500 payments transcribed as part of the 'Small Bills and Petty Finance' project, a vanishingly small percentage – 0.0035 per cent, around 150 – record payments made to 'travellers' or paupers with a 'pass', or to sailors returning from duty at sea: people who appear momentarily, only to move beyond the eye, pen and dubious care of the overseer. This reflects the extent to which, by the latter half of the eighteenth century, the system of parish relief was substantially focused on the 'settled' poor.[2] Having a legal settlement was normally the first condition that a pauper needed to satisfy in order to access regular and ongoing parish relief.

This chapter explores one of the hidden boundaries that marked the realities of life for the English poor – the boundary between a settled pauper,

---

[1] D. Vaisey (ed.), *The Diary of Thomas Turner, 1754–1765* (East Hoathly, 1994), p. 64.

[2] How to interpret the English system of pauper settlement has been the subject of a large body of literature. See, for example, J. S. Taylor, 'The impact of pauper settlement, 1691–1834', *Past & Present*, lxxiii (1976), 42–74; J. S. Taylor, *Poverty, Migration, and Settlement in the Industrial Revolution: Sojourners' Narratives* (Palo Alto, Calif., 1989). See also A. Winter and T. Lambrecht, 'Migration, poor relief and local autonomy: settlement policies in England and the southern Low Countries in the eighteenth century', *Past & Present*, ccxviii (2013), 91–126. There has been an ongoing debate between Norma Landau and Keith Snell on how to interpret the implementation of 'settlement'. See, for example, N. Landau, 'The eighteenth-century context of the laws of settlement', *Continuity and Change*, vi (1991), 417–39; N. Tadmor, 'The settlement of the poor and the rise of the form in England, c.1662–1780', *Past & Present*, ccxxxvi (2017), 43–97.

T. Hitchcock, 'Vagrancy, poor relief and the parish' in *Providing for the Poor: The Old Poor Law, 1750–1834*, ed. P. Collinge and L. Falcini (London, 2022), pp. 83–102. License: CC BY-NC-ND 4.0.

who could normally rely on their parish *in extremis*; and the vagrants and travellers who very frequently could not. By exploring the characteristics that emerge from alternative sources – the lists of vagrants removed from London in the 1780s produced by the 'vagrant contractor', Henry Adams; the parliamentary returns of vagrants prosecuted in the early 1820s; and the overseers' vouchers transcribed by the 'Small Bills' project – this chapter seeks to provide a wider context for the parish pump politics of poverty that dominates our understanding of the workings of the Old Poor Law. It is an attempt to view the world of late eighteenth- and early nineteenth-century poverty from the perspective of those excluded from the supposedly comprehensive Old Poor Law.[3] In addition, it seeks to illuminate the boundaries of relief and punishment, acknowledging along the way that the sources on which it is based were created and designed to measure neither poverty nor its relief.

The late eighteenth- and early nineteenth-century countryside hosted substantial numbers of poor travellers.[4] With the population growing overall, both internal and overseas migration was increasing during these decades. Competing for migrants with London, the industrial regions of the north and Midlands were drawing to themselves generations of working people. To take the single example of the industrial parish of Darlaston, in Staffordshire, on the Birmingham canal, 'famous for the manufacture of gun-locks, bits, stirrups, buckles, nails, screws, cast iron articles, &c.', the population almost doubled in just thirty years.[5] The 1801 census recorded

---

[3] P. M. Solar, 'Poor relief and English economic development: a renewed plea for comparative history', *The Economic History Review*, c (1997), 369–74.

[4] 'Vagrancy' has been the subject of an extensive literature that tends to move unproblematically between the crime of 'vagrancy', the literary depiction of 'vagrants' and the experience of the migratory poor. For the early modern period see C. J. Ribton-Turner, *A History of Vagrants and Vagrancy, and Beggars and Begging* (London, 1887; repr. Montclair, N.J., 1972); A. L. Beier and P. Ocobock (ed.), *Cast Out: Vagrancy and Homelessness in Global and Historical Perspective* (Athens, Ohio, 2008); C. Dionne, *Rogues and Early Modern English Culture* (Ann Arbor, Mich., 2006); A. L. Beier, *Masterless Men: The Vagrancy Problem in England, 1560–1640* (London, 1985); and most recently D. Hitchcock, *Vagrancy in English Culture and Society, 1650–1750* (London, 2018). The 18th and early 19th centuries have generated a largely separate literature, including P. W. Coldham, *Emigrants in Chains: A Social History of Forced Emigration to the Americas of Felons, Destitute Children, Political and Religious Non-conformists, Vagabonds, Beggars and Other Undesirables, 1607–1776* (Baltimore, 1992); T. Hitchcock, 'The London vagrancy crisis of the 1780s', *Rural History*, xxiv, special issue 1 (2013), 59–72, N. Rogers, 'Policing the poor in eighteenth-century London: the vagrancy laws and their administration', *Historie Sociale/Social History*, xxiv (1991), 127–47; A. Eccles, *Vagrancy in Law and Practice under the Old Poor Law* (Farnham, 2012).

[5] W. White, *History, Gazetteer, and Directory of Staffordshire, and the City and County of*

3,812 inhabitants; by 1811 this had increased by over 1,000. The parish continued to grow. In 1831 the census recorded a population for Darlaston of 6,647 souls, most of whom were first-generation inhabitants, who were unlikely to possess a 'settlement' in the parish. Yet the 1803 Poor Law returns suggest that Darlaston was relieving just two non-parishioners out of 258 paupers.[6] Like most internal migrants of the period, they probably found their way to the parish through a complex pattern of either 'stepwise' or 'circular' migration.[7] For the thirteen parishes in Staffordshire whose vouchers the 'Small Bills' project has transcribed, the population increased by just under 80 per cent in the four decades after 1800, while the equivalent figure for the seventeen parishes included in the data for Cumberland is 42 per cent. Even the small rural parish of East Hoathly in Sussex grew in these decades – from 395 in 1801 to over 600 in 1841. Indeed, the only parish whose vouchers are included in the project that failed to see substantial growth was the tiny, isolated township of Cumwhitton in Cumberland, just east of Carlisle.[8]

Beyond the migratory poor, the English countryside also played host to whole communities of travellers. 'Gypsies' had resisted oppression and prosecution for at least 300 years, being described by even a nominally sympathetic contemporary commentator as 'numerous bands of semisavages dispersed amidst our highly civilised countrymen'.[9] While there are no credible population statistics, their prominent place in the statistics of vagrancy and the frequent reference to 'Gypsies' in both literature and

---

the City of Lichfield (Sheffield, 1834), p. 330.

[6] *Abstract of Answers and Returns relative to the Expence and Maintenance of the Poor* (Parl. Papers 1803–4 [C. 175], xiii). It should be noted that the number of 'non-parishioners' listed for England, excluding London, is substantially higher than this, at 19.2 per cent – 190,107 non-parishioners against a total number of relieved at 989,201 – but this figure hides substantial variations between parishes, counties and regions.

[7] *Abstract Return Pursuant to the Act for Taking an Account of the Population of Great Britain* (Parl. Papers enumeration abstract, 1841) (1843). For population growth see E. A. Wrigley and R. S. Schofield, *The Population History of England, 1541–1871: A Reconstruction* (London, 1981), appendix 7, 'Rickman's parish register returns of 1801 and 1841', pp. 597–630; and T. Wrigley, 'English county populations in the later eighteenth century', *The Economic History Review*, lx (2007), 35–69. For internal migration see C. Pooley and J. Turnbull, *Migration and Mobility in Britain since the Eighteenth Century* (London, 2005), and for migration as reflected specifically in the records of vagrancy, see A. Crymble, A. Dennett and T. Hitchcock, 'Modelling regional imbalances in English plebeian migration to late eighteenth-century London', *The Economic History Review*, lxxi (2018), 747–71.

[8] *Abstract ... for taking an Account of the Population of Great Britain*.

[9] Quoted in M. Saxby, *Memoirs of a Female Vagrant Written by Herself* (London, 1806), p. v.

legislation reflect their presence on the roads.[10] To these numbers can be added Irish travellers, who were frequently on the tramp in search of seasonal work.[11]

To 'Gypsies' and Irish travellers can be added discharged soldiers and sailors, left to make their way home on foot at the conclusion of each of the innumerable wars of the period. In 1763, 1784, 1802 and 1817 Britain's roads and lanes were awash with young men discharged from the army and navy.[12] Even in years of peace, the quarterly pension payments that needed to be collected in person at the Chelsea Hospital ensured that disabled and retired soldiers could be found on the roads, in a constant circulation of broken bodies.[13]

Through the spring, summer and autumn, the roads of late eighteenth- and early nineteenth-century Britain were heavily populated by what Henry Mayhew would later dub the 'wandering tribes':[14] navvies employed to dig the new canals and lay the new rails, and showmen tramping to a regular rhythm from village to village and from fair to fair. There were building workers, stonemasons and fishermen hoping for a season's work; pedlars and cheapjacks; sellers of crockery, earthenware and small goods with their packs on their backs and walking sticks in their hands. There were the harvest workers making hay in June, hoeing turnips in July and harvesting the corn in August. September brought hops and fruit in need of picking. For many, half their year was taken in a slow perambulation from south to north and back again.[15] In 1834 Jeremiah

---

[10] For a recent overview see D. Cressy, *Gypsies: An English Story* (Oxford, 2018); see also Hitchcock, *Vagrancy in English Culture and Society*; S. Houghton-Walker, *Representations of the Gypsy in the Romantic Period* (Oxford, 2014).

[11] R. Harris, 'Seasonal migration between Ireland and England prior to the famine', *Canadian Papers in Rural History*, vii (1990), 363–86; R. Swift and S. Campbell, 'The Irish in Britain', in *The Cambridge Social History of Modern Ireland*, ed. E. F. Biagini and M. E. Daly (Cambridge, 2017), pp. 515–33.

[12] For the classic statement of the impact of demobilization on the social order see D. Hay, 'War, dearth and theft in the eighteenth century: the record of the English courts', *Past & Present*, xcv (1982), 117–60, at 138–41.

[13] A. Cormack, *'These Meritorious Objects of the Royal Bounty': The Chelsea Out-Pensioners in the Early Eighteenth Century* (2017); C. L. Nielsen, 'The Chelsea Out-Pensioners: Image and Reality in Eighteenth-Century and Early Nineteenth-Century Social Care' (unpublished University of Newcastle upon Tyne PhD thesis, 2014); C. L. Nielsen, 'Disability, fraud and medical experience at the Royal Hospital of Chelsea in the long eighteenth century', in *Britain's Soldiers: Rethinking War and Society, 1715–1815*, ed. K. Linch and M. McCormack (Liverpool, 2014), pp. 183–201.

[14] See Henry Mayhew, *London Labour and the London Poor* (London, 1851), i, chs 1–2.

[15] R. Samuel, 'Comers and goers', in *The Victorian City: Images and Realities*, ed. H. J. Dyos

Jackson, a magistrate at the Isle of Ely, felt entirely confident that he could enumerate the varieties of 'tramps':

> In hay time and harvest many labourers from Norfolk, Suffolk, &c., as well as from Ireland ... many weavers, cotton-spinners &c., in knots of three or four, wearing aprons, driven ... by necessity .... Often sailors two or three together. ... The class of blind and maimed fiddlers and singers ... They often carry matches, a few balls of cotton, ballads, &c.; pretend to be recent widowers or widows ... and drag about with them families of helpless children.[16]

Many workhouses swept their winter inhabitants out through the door as soon as the weather permitted, hoping to save the parish shilling by joining their own paupers to this summer throng. Of the over 84,000 paupers either discharged or absconding from the parish workhouse belonging to St Martin-in-the-Fields between 1725 and 1825, most left – or were pushed out of – the house between March and June.[17]

Raphael Samuel characterized these wandering tribes as the 'comers and goers' of nineteenth-century Britain.[18] Whether migrants or nomads, soldiers, sailors or hop-pickers, they filled the roads, sleeping in barns or the cheapest of lodgings. They were welcomed when there was work to do – 'rendering valuable assistance' – and hurried on their way when it was finished.[19]

The poverty – the real need – of these nomads is beyond question, yet they do not appear to have been treated with compassion by many overseers. Most would have agreed with Jeremiah Jackson that 'Parish officers have enough to

---

and M. Wolff (2 vols, London, 1973), i. 123–60.

[16] *Report from His Majesty's Commissioners for Inquiring in the Administration and Practical Operation of the Poor Laws* (Parl. Papers 1834), appendix E, 'Vagrancy', no. 1, Harrison Codd, 'Report regarding the State and Operation of the Laws relating to Vagrancy', p. 68.

[17] See St Martin in the Fields Pauper Biographies Project, Westminster Archives Centre, St Martin in the Fields, Alphabetical lists of the poor taken in to the House of Maintenance, with the date of admission, date of death or discharge, the age and the number of each pauper, and subsequent Day Books, F4002–F4022, July 1724–March 1819 <https://research.ncl.ac.uk/pauperlives> [accessed 18 Oct. 2021]. The relevant dataset can be accessed via *London Lives, 1690 to 1800* <www.londonlives.org> [accessed 18 Oct. 2021]: 3,113 inmates 'absconded' – 10 per cent in March compared to 6.3 per cent in November; and 43,437 were 'discharged', of whom 11 per cent were removed from the house in March, compared to 6 per cent in December.

[18] Samuel, 'Comers and goers'.

[19] *Report regarding the State and Operation of the Laws relating to Vagrancy* (Parl. Papers 1834), Harrison Codd, p. 68.

do with their own poor'.[20] For Thomas Turner the hop-pickers were a mild irritation. A few days before the 'drunken travelling woman' interrupted his evening, he noted that the hop-pickers, 'very unsensible' with drink, were carousing in the village. Searching barns and outbuildings for vagrants was part and parcel of the overseer's job, but Turner recorded doing so only once, over the course of a weekend on Saturday and Sunday, 4 and 5 February 1758, long after the agricultural workers had departed.[21] A 'Gypsy' like Mary Saxby could spend a vagrant's lifetime travelling the roads of England, work in half a dozen occupations, raise a family on the move and suffer life-changing tragedy, but receive relatively short shrift from her parish of legal settlement: Olney in Buckinghamshire. On the sudden death of her husband, Mary was left a widow with five children. She 'sold what [she] ... had, and discharged all our debts; except a few shillings at alehouses ... I then applied to the parish for assistance: and, for a short time they gave me three shillings weekly, but soon reduced this allowance.' The parish also paid her house rent for a period, before threatening 'that, if I did not remove, they would put a man and his wife, and six children, into it with me'.[22] In the words of one parliamentary report written by George Chetwynd, member of parliament (MP) for Stafford, many vagrants, even when removed to their parish of settlement, either 'immediately leave them to resume their previous pursuits, or are dismissed by the parish officers with trifling relief'.[23]

Drawing on parliamentary returns, historians have noted the wide discrepancy in the percentage of the people dependent on poor relief and the strong regional patterns contained within them. In 1803 only 6.7 per cent of the population of the rapidly industrializing county of Lancashire were in receipt of relief, compared to 22.6 per cent in Sussex.[24] Historians have attempted to build on this material and to use more complex methodologies to relate this measure of poverty 'relieved' to poverty experienced. Tom Arkell and Steven King have developed strategies built around aggregating

---

[20] *Report regarding the State and Operation of the Laws relating to Vagrancy*, p. 68.

[21] Vaisey (ed.), *Diary of Thomas Turner*, pp. 64, 135.

[22] Mary Saxby's memoirs represent the fullest extant personal account of 'Gypsy' life in Britain in the 18th and early 19th centuries: *Memoirs of a Female Vagrant Written by Herself* (London, 1806), pp. 54, 57.

[23] *Report from the Select Committee on the Existing Laws relating to Vagrants* (Parl. Papers 1821), p. 5.

[24] A. Kidd, *State, Society and the Poor in Nineteenth-Century England* (Basingstoke, 1999), p. 18; T. Arkell, 'The incidence of poverty in England in the later seventeenth century', *Social History*, xii (1987), 23–47; S. King, *Poverty and Welfare in England 1700–1850: A Regional Perspective* (Manchester, 2000), pp. 77–140 and table 5.1 on p. 131.

sources, including charities and tax exemptions, to estimate the level of 'unrelieved' poverty, and concluded that this figure could encompass well over half the population.[25] There remains, however, a 'dark figure' of unrelieved poverty that historians cannot fully or accurately measure. By exploring the gap between the evidence of poverty relieved by the parish and poverty punished through the system of vagrant removal, this chapter seeks to identify the silence in between. It is an attempt to acknowledge the partial character of all the sources interrogated, and to identify more firmly what we do not know as well as what we do.

At the heart and root of the system of parish relief and the parallel system of vagrant removal that caught so many of the wandering tribes lay a single concept – settlement. Regularized in the 1690s and developed through endless case law over the course of the eighteenth century, settlement implied that everyone had a claim to a parish of settlement: a parish of origin and a parish of obligation. And, while there was no guarantee of being relieved, a settled pauper did have a parish they could appeal to and appeal against.[26] Built around a life cycle of birth, apprenticeship, service, marriage and household, settlement seems at first sight inclusive and powerful. You could inherit a settlement from your parents, receive one at birth if you were illegitimate or earn one through apprenticeship or service for a year. You could marry into one (women took their husband's settlement), you could buy one (by renting a house worth £10 per year and paying the relevant taxes) and you could gain a settlement (by serving in one of the numerous parish offices).[27] For the middling sort and elite, a settlement came with little effort through property ownership and paying the associated taxes. For the poor, however, it was something to be sought out and evidenced with difficulty. In the words of Adam Smith, 'There is scarce a poor man in England, of forty years of age … who has not, in some part of his life, felt himself most cruelly oppressed by this ill-contrived law of settlements.'[28]

---

[25] See T. Arkell, 'The incidence of poverty'; King, *Poverty and Welfare*, pp. 113–20.

[26] See n. 2. For an account of the development of the administration of settlement in the 1690s, see T. Hitchcock and R. Shoemaker, *London Lives: Poverty, Crime and the Making of a Modern City, 1690–1800* (Cambridge, 2015), pp. 42–52.

[27] The 1793 edition of the most popular justicing manual of the period devoted 282 pages to the single issue of 'pauper settlement'; and a further 80 pages to pauper removal. See R. Burn, *The Justice of the Peace and Parish Officer*, 17th edn (4 vols, London, 1793), iii. 341–683. The examination and treatment of vagrants is dealt with separately in Burn, *The Justice of the Peace and Parish Officer*, iv. 376–406.

[28] A. Smith, *An Inquiry into the Nature and Causes of the Wealth of Nations* (London, 1910), ii. 128.

Parish archives and justices' papers are full of 'examinations' designed to establish a settlement.[29] There were three types of examination: into 'bastardy', pauper settlement and vagrancy. The first required two justices sitting in petty sessions and was supposed to occur either a month before or after a birth.[30] These examinations were designed to identify the father and to allow the parish to seek financial indemnity for the costs involved. The process was necessary to establish the child's settlement and hence which parish would be obliged to foot the bill for its upbringing.[31]

The second type of examination – pauper examinations – could be heard by a single justice, and normally wound through a series of questions as to place of birth, apprenticeship, service, marriage and householding. These examinations could result in issuing a settlement certificate and a removal order and pass, mandating that a pauper up sticks and return to their parish of settlement. The mass of case law that grew decade by decade through the eighteenth century was built around this variety of settlement examination. At their extreme, the legal niceties involved could be absurd.[32]

The final variety of settlement examination was a vagrancy examination, conducted by a single justice. Many of the same issues of birth, apprenticeship and service were addressed in this type of examination, with the addition of the examinee's recent behaviour. The outcome determined both where a vagrant was 'settled' and how they should be punished. Vagrants were regularized in 1744 and classified in one of three categories, as 'idle and disorderly persons', as 'rogues and vagabonds' or as 'incorrigible rogues', with a steep hierarchy of penalties associated with each classification. Unlike a pauper examination, a vagrancy examination would normally lead to between a week and a month of hard labour in a house of correction, a whipping, and enforced removal to one's parish of settlement in the back of a cart, via a system of county contactors (from 1792 women were no longer whipped and from 1819 Irish and Scottish 'vagrants' were excluded from

---

[29] Large numbers of pauper examinations are now available online via commercial services such as Findmypast. For a representative published collection see T. Hitchcock and J. Black, *Chelsea Settlement and Bastardy Examinations, 1733–1766*, xxxiii (London, 1999). This volume is also available on open access at <https://www.british-history.ac.uk/london-record-soc/vol33> [accessed 18 Oct. 2021].

[30] For a comprehensive guide to how eighteenth-century justices understood the administration of bastardy examinations, see Burn, *The Justice of the Peace and Parish Officer*, i. 174–211.

[31] This issue was complicated from 1744, when 17 Geo II, c 5 determined that henceforth the children of those deemed 'vagrant' under the law took the settlement of their mother. See Burn, *The Justice of the Peace and Parish Officer*, iv. 395.

[32] C. Steedman, 'Lord Mansfield's women', *Past & Present*, clxxvi (2002), 105–43.

these punishments).[33] Besides the punishments suffered by vagrants, there are two components of the vagrant examination and removal system that set it substantially apart from pauper removal. First, from 1700 the cost of the examination and removal fell to the county rather than the parish; and, second, a parish identified as being a vagrant's settlement could not appeal against a vagrancy removal.

It was through these alternative systems of examination that one was pigeonholed as deserving of relief or subject to punishment and removal as a vagrant. This process also determined who picked up the tab. Both systems of removal were costly. The legal expenses involved in enforcing pauper settlements could be huge. In 1803 the parish of Brampton in Cumberland reported spending £68 4s 7d on legal expenses – 'Expenditure in any suites of Law; Removal of Paupers; and Expences of Overseers and other Officers' – out of a total of just £403 spent on poor relief as a whole. That year, the parishes of Cumberland spent £3,064 on legal fees, out of a total of £34,896 on poor relief. Staffordshire expended £5,390 out of £110,624 and Sussex, £5,747 out of £206,592.[34] From the approximately 41,500 payments transcribed by the 'Small Bills' project, 3842 relate specifically to legal expenses and record £3973 17s $6\frac{1}{2}d$ worth of costs.

Equally expensive was the system of vagrant arrest and removal. Between 1820 and 1824 Staffordshire spent £4,511 on 'apprehending, maintaining and passing Vagrants', while Cumberland spent £1795 and Sussex £804.[35] This was before the costs of building and supporting the houses of correction are accounted for. Staffordshire was particularly affected, as it formed a weigh station on the journey from London and the agricultural regions of the south-east to the port of Liverpool, whence most Irish travellers were transhipped homeward. In 1821 Staffordshire processed some 6,154 Irish and Scottish vagrants at a total cost of £1,369.[36] Towns such as Lichfield,

[33] See A. Eccles, *Vagrancy in Law and Practice under the Old Poor Law* (Farnham, 2012). For contemporary accounts of the history and workings of this system see *Report from the Select Committee on the Existing Laws relating to Vagrants*, and Burn, *The Justice of the Peace and Parish Officer*, iv. 376–406.

[34] *Abstract of the Answers and Returns ... Relative to the Expence and Maintenance of the Poor in England* (Parl. Papers 1804), pp. 82–3, 474–5, 531–2.

[35] *Returns of Persons committed under Vagrant Laws to Prisons in England and Wales; Sums paid for Apprehension and Maintenance of Vagrants, 1820–1823* (Parl. Papers 1824), pp. 138, 136–7, 127.

[36] *Report from His Majesty's Commissioners for Inquiring in the Administration and Practical Operation of the Poor Laws* (Parl. Papers 1834), appendix E, 'Vagrancy', no. 1, Harrison Codd, 'Report regarding the State and Operation of the Laws relating to Vagrancy', p. 24. Towns such as Lichfield that straddled the major route north were particularly affected. With a population of just over 6,000, the town was obliged to relieve some 1,943 travellers in 1822 alone.

which straddled the major route north, was particularly affected. With a population of just over 6,000 in 1822, the town was obliged to relieve some 1,943 travellers.[37]

As can be seen in the case of Elizabeth Malbon, the workings of these systems were complex and confusing, and frequently administered in an inconsistent manner.[38] There was no obvious reason for Elizabeth Malbon to be removed as a vagrant rather than a pauper. By categorizing her as a vagrant, however, the parish shifted the cost of her removal to the county. In theory it also meant that the receiving parish, Butterton-in-the-Moors, would have had no choice but to acknowledge her settlement. Yet Elizabeth Malbon remained in St Bartholomew, Wednesbury, where she was treated as a settled pauper despite the letter of the law.

The remainder of this chapter interrogates two related but quite different sources. The first is a dataset of some 14,789 vagrants removed from London and Middlesex between 1776 and 1786.[39] These data were derived from the monthly bills submitted by the 'vagrant contractor' for Middlesex, Henry Adams, and provide a unique early overview of the system of vagrant removal. They are particularly important as they incorporate Irish and Scottish travellers, and the unsettled migratory poor taken up as vagrants. The second source surveyed here is the comprehensive parliamentary returns of vagrants punished in England and Wales between 1820 and 1823. These returns provide details, county by county, of everyone punished in a house of correction as a vagrant over these years. Full lists of names and offences are included for a proportion of counties including Sussex, Staffordshire and Cumberland. Because this source relates to the period after 1819, when Irish and Scottish travellers were effectively excluded from punishment as vagrants, it does not reflect their experience, but it illuminates how local justices of the peace (JPs) and constables used the system to police local disorder and the unsettled poor. Together, they provide a detailed overview of both unsettled seasonal travellers, and of paupers punished as vagrants.

For the migratory vagrants, the best sources are the long lists of men, women and children who passed through the hands of Henry Adams during the last decades of the eighteenth century. Eight times a year, at each session of the Middlesex Bench, Adams submitted lists of vagrants conveyed as

---

[37] *The Victoria History of the County of Staffordshire* (London, 1908), i. 325.

[38] See Interlude 3 (D. Shenton, 'Elizabeth Malbon (*c.*1743–1801)') after this chapter.

[39] A. Crymble, L. Falcini and T. Hitchcock, '*Vagrant lives: 14,789 vagrants processed by Middlesex County, 1777–1786*' (2014) <https://zenodo.org/record/13103#.VgFE-pcYHCY> [accessed 18 Oct. 2021].

Table 3.1 Demographic distribution of vagrants removed via Middlesex, 1777–1786

Category	No.	% of total
Solo adult males	4,031	35
Solo adult females	3,015	26.2
Males with dependents	584	5.1
Females with dependants	1,026	8.9
Unknown gender	37	0.3
Dependents	2,829	24.6
Individuals (Total)	11,522	100

Source: Data from Crymble, Falcini and Hitchcock, '*Vagrant lives*' dataset.

proof of his having transported these individuals to the county boundary, after which he would be paid for his services. The original records were created as part of the system for conveying vagrants from Middlesex gaols and holding compounds to the edge of the county, whence they would be sent onwards to their parish of legal settlement. Adams's role also involved picking up vagrants expelled from elsewhere on their way back to Middlesex, as well as those being shepherded through to counties beyond, as part of the national network of removal.[40] The picture that emerges is distinctive.

Men and women are both well represented, as are men and women travelling with children. Vagrants returned to the counties that form the basis for the 'Small Bills' project are also well represented. Industrial areas of the north generated a higher than expected proportion of removals, despite their distance from London. Irish and Scottish migrants are heavily represented, as are discharged soldiers. The seasonality reflecting the role of harvest work is also present, with December, January and February witnessing high levels of vagrant removal as local demands for labour fell. There remains, however, little overlap between the vagrants removed from London and those exposed in the 'Small Bills' data. To take a single example where they do overlap, Elizabeth Fletcher was arrested somewhere in the East End of London – probably Whitechapel – in September 1781, was examined by a magistrate, John Staples esq., and was committed to the Clerkenwell house of correction. She does not appear to have been put to

---

[40] This material has been subject to extended analysis in three interrelated articles: T. Hitchcock, 'The London vagrancy crisis of the 1780s', *Rural History*, xxiv (2013), 59–72; T. Hitchcock, A. Crymble and L. Falcini, 'Loose, idle and disorderly: vagrant removal in late eighteenth-century Middlesex', *Social History*, xxxix (2014), 509–27; A. Crymble, A. Dennett and T. Hitchcock, 'Modelling regional imbalances in English plebeian migration to late eighteenth-century London', *The Economic History Review*, lxxi (2018), 747–71.

hard labour for the required seven days, nor is there any evidence she was whipped. Instead, after two days at Clerkenwell, she was handed over to Henry Adams and taken by cart to a holding station at Ridge, just on the Hertfordshire border with Middlesex. From there Elizabeth Fletcher was passed from contractor to contractor back to her parish of settlement in Darlaston, Staffordshire.[41] The kind of reception she received is unknown, but two years later the parish spent 1*s* 3*d* for a new cord to repair her bed. She appears in the vouchers only on this one occasion and does not appear to have been a regular parish pensioner.[42] Fletcher stands out precisely because of the rarity of this evidential overlap. None of the other three vagrants removed to Darlaston in the data appear in the vouchers for whatever reason. Equally, none of the thirteen vagrants removed to parishes in Staffordshire for which vouchers have been transcribed appear in the parish-level material, nor do the thirty-four vagrants removed from Middlesex to the project's parishes in Cumberland.

Regardless of their reception in their parish of settlement, Lancashire, Yorkshire and the south-western counties of Gloucestershire, Somerset and Devon stand out for the large number of migratory vagrants who gave these counties as their home (Figure 3.1). Once population size is factored in, the West Midlands, Lancashire and Northumbria emerge as areas where a much higher proportion than expected on the basis of their population were removed (Figure 3.2). These data have been analysed in detail for what they say about migration and about the policing of vagrancy in London, but they also simply illustrate the existence of a mobile Britain – made up of men, women and children going from job to job, from harvest work to winter work, from military encampment to home. These sources also reflect a distinctive national pattern of migration, in which the West Midlands, the north-east and Lancashire contributed disproportionately to the migratory stream exposed via vagrant removal. While this helps expose a mobile, constantly moving population, it was a population that was apparently not substantially catered for by the system of parish relief.[43]

The Middlesex lists reflect one image of vagrancy, which is consonant with many literary tropes and older histories of vagrants as travellers, but

---

[41] Crymble, Falcini and Hitchcock, '*Vagrant lives*' dataset.

[42] Small Bills data, D951/5/81/149/50.

[43] The sheer uncertainty surrounding the workings of parish settlement in this period has exercised a generation of historians and been further complicated by the addition of vagrant removal. For settlement removal see S. King, 'Poor relief, settlement and belonging in English, 1780s to 1840s', in S. King and A. Winter, *Migration, Settlement and Belonging in Europe, 1500–1930s: Comparative Perspectives* (New York, 2013), pp. 81–101.

Vagrancy, poor relief and the parish

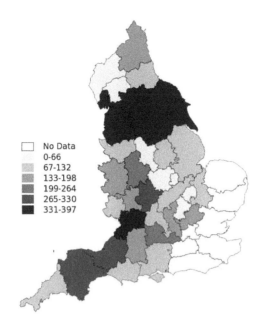

Figure 3.1 Settlement data recorded by Henry Adams, 1777–86

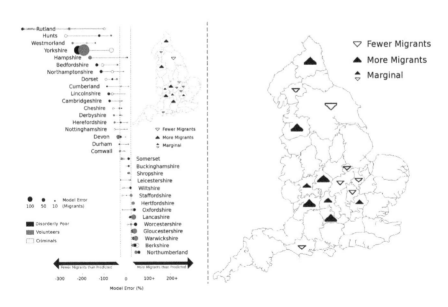

Figure 3.2 The origin of vagrants, 1777–86, moderated by population

it does not reflect the full implications of the system of vagrant policing, particularly as, following the passage of Acts in 1819 and 1822, much of the system of vagrant removal was dismantled, with Irish and Scottish vagrants being incorporated into pauper removal.[44] As a result, the records of vagrancy increasingly reflected the policing of local disorder. Whipping was largely eliminated, first for female vagrants from 1792 and then, largely through negligence, for all vagrants.[45]

Stewarded through Parliament by the Stafford MP, George Chetwynd, the 1822 Vagrancy Act shifted the focus of the system to rest more fully on disorderly behaviour rather than on the mobile poor. In the words of Edward Littleton, the 1822 Act 'had saved the counties of England and Wales the sum of 100,000*l*. annually, which had been heretofore expended in passing vagrants from one part of the country to another … [and] consolidated about fifty acts relative to vagrancy into one act.' To demonstrate the efficacy of that Act, Littleton moved that data about the implementation of the new law should be collected, including 'the number of persons committed under the vagrant laws to the respective prisons in England and Wales, specifying the particular act of vagrancy for which each person was committed, from the 1st Jan. 1820, to the 1st Jan. 1824'.[46] The resulting published report is unique and remarkable. It records some 49,115 vagrants punished in houses of correction between 1820 and 1823.[47] The returns also give us the names and offences of individuals for a subset of these vagrants, and include approximately 14,000 listings of individuals by name and according to sub-offence, including lists of individuals convicted in Cumberland, Staffordshire and Sussex. This is not a comprehensive list of all vagrants in these years; the Cumberland returns, for example, are limited to 1822 and 1823. They, nevertheless, provide a more complete picture than is available in any other source of who was punished for vagrancy and why. And, while the data support the conclusion that the 1822 Act substantially changed local practice, their historical importance lies primarily in the long lists of names and offences recorded.

The circular letter used to generate the returns does not appear to have specified how vagrants should be categorized, and different counties and

---

[44] 59 Geo III, c 12, 1819, An Act to Amend the for the Relief of the Poor; and 3 Geo IV, c 40, 1822: An Act for Consolidating into One Act and Amending the Laws Relating to Idle and Disorderly Persons, Rogues and Vagabonds, Incorrigible Rogues and Other Vagrants in England.

[45] 32 Geo III, c 45, 1792, An Act to Explain and Amend an Act Made in the Seventeenth Year of His Late Majesty King George the Second. See also Eccles, *Vagrancy in Law and Practice*, pp. 52, 162–3.

[46] *Hansard*, HC, Parl. Deb., vol. 10, col. 86, 4 Feb. 1824.

[47] *Returns of Persons committed under Vagrant Laws*.

respondents used different descriptors. Surrey, for example broke down its vagrants into twelve categories, including:

> Idle and disorderly persons …
> Reputed thieves …
> Wandering abroad, lodging in out-houses, and in the open air …
> Wandering abroad and begging …
> Neglecting to maintain family …
> Exposing naked persons …
> Betting and playing at unlawful games …
> Gambling on Sunday …
> Apprehended with implements to commit felony in possession …
> Attempting to commit felony …
> Found in houses and inclosed places, with intent to commit felony …
> Leaving parish, and going to another.[48]

'Wandering' and sleeping rough are certainly there, reflecting the continuing role of vagrancy in policing migration. There is also some evidence of the gypsy and traveller communities. In Essex, for example, 'Sophia Smith, Mary Buckley, Lydia Martin; – wandering abroad and lodging in their tilted cart, camps, or tents, in lanes and other places, they being persons commonly called gipsies'.[49] There is also a very strong emphasis on more localized forms of disorder, including being 'idle and disorderly', 'reputed thieves' and 'neglecting to maintain family'.

The returns also include a new category of disorder for the 1820s – men exposing themselves as a form of sexual assault. They list exemplars of Romantic era sexualities such as Thomas Birch from Essex, who,

> having at sundry times, and particularly on Tuesday the 15th day of April, come to the residence of Elizabeth Cooper, and exposed his person to her, by unbuttoning his breeches and exposing his private parts to the said Elizabeth Cooper, whereby he has committed an act of vagrancy.[50]

In other words, the returns provide a very different picture of the vagrant poor than that revealed by the Middlesex removals. While the 1780s lists reflect a mobile population, the returns from the 1820s reflect the punitive use of vagrancy legislation to control more localized forms of disorder.

Of the counties for which vouchers have been transcribed in the 'Small Bills' project, Sussex provided the most extensive and detailed returns to Parliament.

---

[48] The list is taken from the returns for Surrey: *Returns of Persons Committed under Vagrant Laws*, p. 104.

[49] *Returns of Persons Committed under Vagrant Laws*, p. 20.

[50] *Returns of Persons Committed under Vagrant Laws*, p. 33.

Sussex imprisoned and set to labour some 1,076 men and women in the first years of the 1820s (Figure 3.3). Of these, 'wandering and begging' and forms of 'sleeping rough' amount to just under half the total, though it is unclear whether these were travellers or locals, while over half were convicted of 'offences under the statute', as the Sussex returns describe it, including deserting one's family or being idle and refusing to work. This reflects the policing of a settled population rather than an attempt to regulate internal migration.

A clear measure of the difference between the images of the vagrant population reflected in these two sources can be found in the gender balance. In the parliamentary returns for Sussex, for example, almost three-quarters were male (72 per cent male and 28 per cent female); compared to the Middlesex vagrants of the 1780s, almost half of whom were women (53 per cent male and 47 per cent female).

The national pattern revealed in the 1824 returns suggests that northern England, the south-east and the south-west were particularly active in prosecuting vagrancy, with Lancashire, Lincolnshire, Devon and Middlesex emerging as particularly active counties, both in real terms and per 100,000 of the population (Figure 3.4). While the south-east is not included in the 1780s data, a comparison of the national pattern suggests that the industrializing north, the south-east and the south-west were particularly active in both producing vagrants (who were then returned to their settlements via Middlesex) and prosecuting the disorderly poor *in situ*.

A similar pattern emerges if expenditure is mapped, figures for which are also given in the returns. A comparison of expenditure per vagrant with vagrants per 100,000 of the population suggests in turn that areas that prosecuted large numbers of vagrants spent proportionately less per vagrant and that places with few vagrants spent more (Figures 3.5, 3.6).

The question remains whether the vagrants detailed in the 1824 returns had greater access to the system of parish relief than those removed from London and recorded in the Middlesex returns. Perhaps surprisingly, the answer appears to be no, despite the apparently self-conscious use of the legislation to police idleness and 'refusal to work', and family abandonment. In Sussex, around 15 per cent of all vagrants were charged with either being 'idle and disorderly and refusing to work' or with some form of abandonment – of a wife, a husband or children – to the care of the parish. Even '*threatening*' to 'run away, and leave his family chargeable' resulted in Leonard Lewer being charged and convicted.[51] As a result, an intimate relationship might be expected between the lists of vagrants returned to Parliament and the paupers whose names appear in the parish vouchers. Yet

---

[51] *Returns of Persons Committed under Vagrant Laws*, p. 97.

Vagrancy, poor relief and the parish

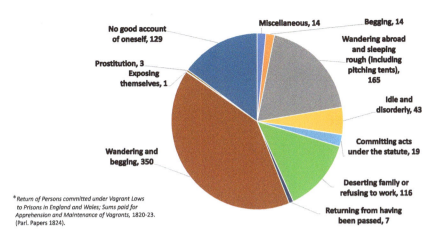

Figure 3.3 Sussex vagrants, 1820–3 (1,076)

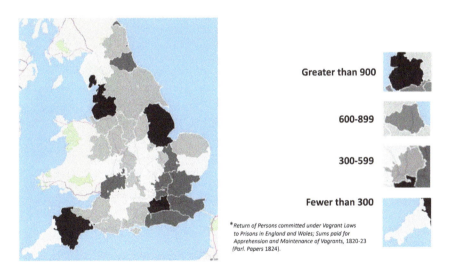

Figure 3.4 Distribution of vagrants by county, 1820–3, per 100,000 of the population

99

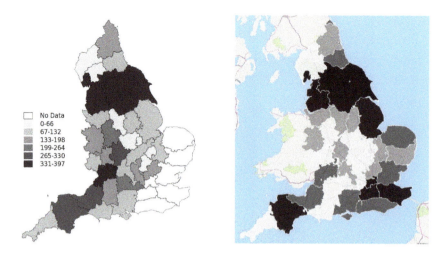

Figure 3.5 Distribution of vagrants, 1777–86 and 1820–3

Figure 3.6 Expenditure per vagrant by county, 1820–3

Vagrancy, poor relief and the parish

for Sussex there is not a single example of a clear and demonstrable presence of the same person in both the vouchers and the parliamentary returns.

The evidence from Staffordshire is equally stark. If anything, the magistrates in Staffordshire were more keen than their Sussex colleagues to use vagrancy to police settlement. The vagrants committed to the county prison at Stafford in 1820 were representative:

> William Tomkinson, John Haywood, James Blakemore; – idle and disorderly, and refusing to work.
> Thomas Bromwich; – leaving his wife chargeable to the parish.
> Thomas Hall; – idle and disorderly and spending his money in alehouses.
> Henry Price; – leaving children chargeable to the parish.
> William Wharton, Thomas Sparrow, – returning to parish after being legally removed.[52]

Each of the 'offences' listed had an impact on a local parish, and in the cases of William Wharton and Thomas Sparrow the prosecution that resulted in their appearance on this list would appear to have been instigated by a parish. Yet there is no single instance in which a name listed in the returns appears unambiguously in the 'Small Bills' data. At the same time, there are a few tantalizing glimpses of how the two systems worked in tandem.

In 1821, for example, Mary Millard was convicted in company with Catherine Trindle, Mary Trindle and Mary Hannon of 'lodging in barns, and not giving a good account of themselves'.[53] In the following year, in early June, Mary was issued a pair of shoes by Thomas Horton, the overseer of the poor at Darlaston, at the cost of 6s 6d. The voucher records her as a resident in the workhouse.[54] William Rock was first punished, along with William Pointon, Thomas Mills and Samuel Smith in 1821, for 'leaving their families chargeable to the parish'. He was convicted again in 1823 for 'leaving family chargeable, &c.'.[55] That year the overseer at Abbots Bromley paid £2 'for half a year's Rent for Mary Rock. Due Lady Day Last'.[56]

The evidence presented here is largely negative but highly suggestive in character. Despite the scale of data collection undertaken by Parliament in 1824, and involved in the 'Small Bills' project and in the digitization of the

---

[52] *Returns of Persons Committed under Vagrant Laws*, p. 88.

[53] *Returns of Persons Committed under Vagrant Laws*, p. 89.

[54] Small Bills data, D1149/6/2/7/6.

[55] *Returns of Persons Committed under Vagrant Laws*, pp. 89, 90. This is probably the same William Rick born at Abbots Bromley.

[56] Small Bills data, D1209/4/3/1.

Middlesex vagrancy records, there is no clear overlap between these three datasets. This should force historians to question how they think about the workings of the Old Poor Law in the late eighteenth and early nineteenth centuries. It suggests that the systems of settlement and removal simply did not work as intended – and could be ignored or gamed by both paupers and overseers. Many fell through the gaps, and the poverty and need of many failed to be recorded or addressed, but in the silence that exists between the sources examined here is evidence of the substantial size of the dark figure of unrecorded poverty. It also suggests, or perhaps simply reminds us, that England was a much more mobile – migratory – country than has frequently been supposed.

The impact and workings of the Old Poor Law were actively debated in the decades up to 1834, and an increasingly popular view was that it worked as a safety net, discouraged the poor from working and generated a form of dependency. It is also known that, following a century of steady growth, the levels of expenditure on relief continued to grow both in real terms and in relation to a rapidly growing population.[57] Taken together, the evidence presented here suggests that in the decades prior to 1834 the Old Poor Law was increasingly encompassing varied practices, and that levels of support and access to care were increasingly uncertain. Regional distinctions were certainly present, as were distinctions defined by urbanization, gender and age, but perhaps the most relevant distinction increasingly focused on the division between the settled poor and Britain's 'comers and goers'.

The 1824 Vagrancy Act is still in force. It forms the legal foundations for stop and search, and for the arrest and criminalization of beggars and rough sleepers. It creates a catch-all category of the unacceptable that the authorities still rely on and that seems brutally focused on new immigrants and old minorities. It is worthwhile being reminded that the apparent intolerance at the heart of this system was in some measure an intolerance of social welfare as a whole.

---

[57] For a recent recalculation of the long-term evolution of expenditure under the Old Poor Law, see B. Waddell, 'The rise of the parish welfare state in England, *c*.1600–1800', *Past & Present*, ccliii (2021), 151–94.

Interlude 3

Elizabeth Malbon (c.1743–1801)

Dianne Shenton

Elizabeth Warrington married the coal miner George Malbon at St Bartholomew, Wednesbury, Staffordshire, in 1763.[1] In 1775 George was 'killed by a Fall of Coals' and buried in Wednesbury.[2]

Now widowed, Elizabeth applied for parish relief for herself and her four children. Wednesbury's parish officials were keen to establish whether the Malbon family was chargeable to the parish. At an examination, the format of which would have been similar to that outlined in Chapter 3, Elizabeth was required to give evidence of her marriage, household and husband's place of settlement. Judgment was given that the family should be removed and a removal order issued.[3]

> To the Constable or Officer of the Peace of the Parish of Wednesbury, Staffs. to receive and convey, and to the Overseers of the Poor of Butterton, Staffs. to receive and obey Elizabeth Malborn [*sic*], widow with 4 children as Rogues and Vagabonds. And upon examination of said Elizabeth Malbon taken before J. Slaney J.P. upon oath, she says that her place of settlement and the said 4 children is Butterton. To convey them to Butterton and deliver them to the Church Wardens etc. according to Law. Dated 16 Aug 1775.

Several members of the Malbon family had been resident in Butterton-in-the-Moors since the appointment of a John Malbon as perpetual curate and teacher *c*.1697, but there was no evidence of George having been born there. The parish of Butterton-in-the-Moors, therefore, refused to accept Elizabeth and her children and they remained in Wednesbury. Even though the removal failed, it shows how the process of settlement

---

[1] SRO, D4383/1/21, St Bartholomew, Wednesbury, George Malbon and Elizabeth Warrington, 23 May 1763.

[2] SRO, D4383/1/5, St Bartholomew, Wednesbury, 2 Apr. 1775.

[3] SRO, QSB, 1775 M/171, Rogues' and vagabonds' passes.

could potentially deliver a family to a parish with which they had only the flimsiest of connections.

As there is another Butterton in Staffordshire, which is not a parish in its own right, there is a possibility that Elizabeth's husband was the George Malbon who was baptized at St Margaret's, Wolstanton, on 23 January 1730/1. After this date, however, there are no further references in the Wolstanton records to George Malbon and there is no extant evidence of Wednesbury having contacted the officials of Wolstanton to enquire as to whether it was George Malbon's place of settlement.

Elizabeth's first known request for assistance occurred at a critical moment in her life cycle but did not end once her children had reached adulthood. It may be that Elizabeth's offspring, who all remained in the Wednesbury area, were able to provide for their mother most of the time but, subject to occasional periods of want, they could not provide the support their mother needed throughout. Intermittent pension payments over the next twenty-six years, usually for eight shillings, culminated in the parish paying 1s for ale for her funeral (Figure 3.7).[4] She was buried at St Bartholomew's, Wednesbury, on 12 July 1801.

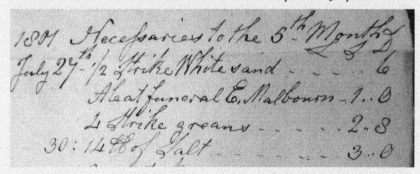

Figure 3.7 Extract of an Overseers' Voucher for Wednesbury, Staffordshire, showing ale for E. Malbourn's (*sic*) funeral, D4383/6/1/9//177, 'A list of Necessaries for the 5th Month', 27 July 1801

---

[4] For example, SRO, D4383/6/1/9/3/116, Bills entered in the parish book, 28 June 1790; D4383/6/1/9/3/177, 'A list of Necessaries for the 5th Month', 27 July 1801.

II. Providers and enablers and their critics

4. Women, business and the Old Poor Law

Peter Collinge

Widowed in 1817 and with no children to whom she could turn for support or assistance, forty-nine-year-old Elizabeth Dawes (1768–1852) of Lichfield, Staffordshire, could easily have been one of those seemingly ubiquitous women who populated early nineteenth-century towns, surviving on the margins, occasionally reliant on parish relief. Instead, upon her husband's death she inherited his goods and property and was appointed sole executrix of his will.[1] Between then and 1842 she operated independently as a grocer and tea-dealer, and supplied St Mary's workhouse.[2] Far from the trope of a widow in retail existing on a meagre income, her town centre address in St John Street provides an indication of Dawes's status and prosperity. She employed a shop assistant, and by 1841, her household consisted of herself, her niece and a servant, the latter freeing up time for Dawes to focus on her enterprise.[3] In 1851, Dawes, aged eighty-three, was registered as an annuitant.[4] She was not exceptional but representative of many women in business identified in overseers' vouchers.

This chapter presents a new perspective on women and their relationship with parish welfare under the Old Poor Law. Instead of focusing on women as the recipients of relief, it focuses on women as suppliers and conductors of business and their wider agency in commercial environments. Overseers' vouchers from Brampton, Cumberland and Lichfield, Staffordshire, are used as embarkation points to draw businesswomen and retail and Poor Law

---

[1] SRO, P/C/11, Benjamin Dawes, 1 Sept. 1817.

[2] W. Parson and T. Bradshaw, *Staffordshire General and Commercial Directory* (Manchester, 1818), p. 186; J. Pigot and Co., *National Commercial Directory for 1828–1829* (Manchester, 1828), part 2, p. 717; W. White, *History, Gazetteer and Directory of Staffordshire* (Sheffield, 1834), p. 161; J. Pigot and Co., *National Commercial Directory* (Manchester, 1842), p. 30; SRO, LD20/6/6, Lichfield, St Mary, Overseers' vouchers, E. Dawes, 6 Oct. 1823.

[3] SRO, LD20/6/6, E. Dawes, June–Sept. 1825; The National Archives (TNA, HO107/1008/3, 1841 census; J. Hughes, 'Elizabeth Dawes (1769–1852), grocer, Lichfield, Staffordshire', <thepoorlaw.org/elizabeth-dawes-1769-1852-grocer-lichfield-staffordshire> [accessed 26 July 2021].

[4] TNA, HO107/2014, 1851 census.

P. Collinge, 'Women, business and the Old Poor Law' in *Providing for the Poor: The Old Poor Law, 1750–1834*, ed. P. Collinge and L. Falcini (London, 2022), pp. 107–132. License: CC BY-NC-ND 4.0.

history together to reveal 'a petit-bourgeois world from which historians and social commentators have traditionally shied away'.[5] The vouchers are used in conjunction with trade directories, newspapers, parish registers, probate documents, census returns and grocers' ledgers. Following an overview of the number of businesswomen in Brampton and Lichfield, case studies show how women conducted business with parish authorities and their connections to wider networks. The case studies explore the channels through which goods reached the poor, frequency of contact with parish authorities, access to commercial intelligence, product ranges and pricing, and business transfers. Despite diverse economic interests, commonalities in approach and long-standing trading connections between businesswomen and individual parishes are revealed. Many of these survived changes in personal circumstances and those wrought by the 1834 Poor Law Amendment Act. It is recognized from the outset, however, that in supplying parishes women were never anything more than a numerical minority. In 1828 only ten out of 126 businesses engaged by St Mary's, Lichfield, were headed by women, with a further twelve signing receipts in outwardly 'male' enterprises.[6]

Increasing choice, shop display and levels of service are recurrent themes in research on late Georgian patterns of consumption.[7] Research by Nancy Cox, Claire Walsh, Helen Berry and Jon Stobart et al., often concentrating on metropolitan or expanding industrial towns, has analysed shop design, layout, advertising and sales techniques.[8] The focus on luxury goods, 'exotic' items and the repeat spending power of the middle ranks has added significantly to interpretations and understandings of urban retail practices. What was happening in small market towns and villages has received less

---

[5] H. Barker, 'A grocer's tale: gender, family and class in early-nineteenth century Manchester', *Gender and History*, xxi (2009), 34–57, at 341.

[6] Overlapping bills mean that some people are unidentifiable.

[7] P. D. Glennie and N. J. Thrift, 'Consumers, identities and consumption spaces in early-modern England', *Environment and Planning A*, xxviii (1996), 25–45; H. C. Mui and L. Mui, *Shops and Shopkeeping in Eighteenth Century England* (London, 1989); J. Stobart and A. Hann, 'Retailing revolution in the eighteenth century? Evidence from north-west England', *Business History*, xlvi (2004), 171–94.

[8] H. Berry, 'Polite consumption: shopping in eighteenth-century England', *Transactions of the Royal Historical Society*, xii (2002), 375–94; N. Cox, *The Complete Tradesman: A Study of Retailing, 1550–1820* (Aldershot, 2000); C. Walsh, 'Shop design and the display of goods in eighteenth-century London', *Journal of Design History*, viii (1995), 157–76; J. Stobart, '"So agreeable and suitable a place": the character, use and provisioning of a late eighteenth-century villa', *Journal for Eighteenth-Century Studies*, xxxix (2016), 89–102; J. Stobart, 'Selling (through) politeness', *Cultural and Social History*, v (2008), 309–28; J. Stobart, A. Hann and V. Morgan, *Spaces of Consumption: Leisure and Shopping in the English Town, c.1680–1830* (London, 2007).

attention.[9] Consequently, as Ian Mitchell noted, most retailers 'remain in relative obscurity, often no more than a name in a trade directory or other listing', and, as Stobart remarked, 'It remains unclear how far such modes of shopping extended down the social scale.'[10] How these and other small businesses operated frequently remains a matter of conjecture.[11] Douglas Brown's analysis of supply networks to London's mid-nineteenth-century workhouses contributes significantly to scholarship on poor relief after 1834, but research on where goods were purchased from and the manner in which they were acquired under the Old Poor Law, and on the businesses and their owners is limited.[12] The role of women in such provision and the interplay of work and social activity are particularly obscure.

Although it has long been accepted that very many women worked in family enterprises, in partnerships and as sole traders, particularly in retail, the roles they adopted and the extent of their engagement if their names were not above the door, listed in trade directories or stated in newspaper advertisements are more debatable.[13] Often, specific and shifting contributions are reduced to generalization: women worked alongside male family members but withdrew when circumstances permitted. Leonore Davidoff and Catherine Hall noted the important financial contributions made by women to business ventures and ultimately their declining significance during the nineteenth century.[14] Pamela Sharpe concurred, while recognizing the diverse effects of capitalism and industrial development on women; declining infant mortality rates and increased life expectancy resulted in the survival of more sons and increased childcare responsibilities for women.[15] All this left less room for formal female

---

[9] Exceptions include J. Stobart and L. Bailey, 'Retail revolution and the village shop, c.1660–1860', *The Economic History Review*, lxxi (2018), 393–417.

[10] J. Stobart, *Sugar and Spice: Grocers and Groceries in Provincial England, 1630–1830* (Oxford, 2013), p. 14; I. Mitchell, *Tradition and Innovation in English Retailing, 1700–1850: Narratives of Consumption* (Aldershot, 2014), p. 59.

[11] D. Kent, 'Small businessmen and their credit transactions in early nineteenth-century Britain', *Business History*, xxxvi (1994), 47–64, at 47; Stobart, *Sugar and Spice*, p. 66.

[12] D. Brown, 'Supplying London's workhouses in the mid-nineteenth century', *The London Journal*, xli (2016), 36–59.

[13] I. Pinchbeck, *Women Workers and the Industrial Revolution: 1750–1850* (London, 1981), pp. 293–5; Mui and Mui, *Shops and Shopkeeping*, pp. 148, 158–9, 204–5; A. C. Kay, 'Retailing, respectability and the independent woman in nineteenth-century London', in *Women, Business and Finance in Nineteenth-century Europe*, ed. R. Beachy, B. Craig and A. Owens (Oxford, 2006), pp. 152–66, at p. 152.

[14] L. Davidoff and C. Hall, *Family Fortunes: Men and Women of the English Middle Class, 1780–1850*, 2nd edn (Abingdon, 2002), pp. 272–315.

[15] P. Sharpe, 'Gender in the European economy: female merchants and family businesses in the British Isles, 1600–1850', *Social History*, xxxiv (2001), 283–306, at 283.

business activity. Important studies by Hannah Barker, Nicola Phillips and Amy Louise Erickson, however, point increasingly at continuity and the complexity of agency exhibited by businesswomen.[16] Analysis of overseers' vouchers builds on this research to reveal the 'fluid nature of gender roles in relation to work' and the consistent, active involvement of women in business rather than decline and withdrawal.[17]

Women and business in Brampton and Lichfield

The market town of Brampton and the cathedral city of Lichfield shared a number of similarities. Both settlements had moderately rising populations. By 1831, Brampton contained 3,345 people and Lichfield 6,360.[18] Each had good overland transport links, with regular services to larger towns and ports: Brampton with Newcastle upon Tyne, Carlisle and Whitehaven; and Lichfield with Birmingham, Nottingham and Liverpool. Passenger services from each town ran daily to London.[19] Both places had schools, almshouses, town or guild halls, the established church and Dissenting chapels, markets and fairs.[20] Retail premises often incorporated small-scale production. Brampton's fortunes rested primarily on agriculture, textiles and brewing. Lichfield, the seat of the diocese of Lichfield and Coventry, had 'excellent local trade' but was 'not remarkable for its manufactures'.[21] Both settlements had their share of the poor. For the periods covered by the vouchers, neither has corresponding overseers' accounts, although an indication of the levels of indoor, outdoor and casual relief are provided in the 1803 parliamentary returns (Table 4.1).

Official sources and trade directories often conceal female involvement in business.[22] Despite their deficiencies, however, trade directory entries for

---

[16] H. Barker, *Family and Business during the Industrial Revolution* (Oxford, 2017); H. Barker, *The Business of Women: Female Enterprise and Urban Development in Northern England, 1760–1830* (Oxford, 2006); N. Phillips, *Women in Business, 1700–1850* (Woodbridge, 2006); A. L. Erickson, 'Married women's occupations in eighteenth–century London', *Continuity & Change*, xxiii (2008), 267–307; A. L. Erickson 'Eleanor Mosley and other milliners in the city of London companies, 1700–1750', *History Workshop Journal*, lxxi (2011), 147–72.

[17] H. Barker, 'Women and work', in *Women's History: Britain, 1700–1850: An Introduction*, ed. H. Barker and E. Challus (Abingdon, 2005), pp. 124–51, at p. 133.

[18] 'Brampton, Cumberland' <http://www.workhouses.org.uk/Brampton> [accessed 17 Dec. 2019]; *The Victoria History of the County of Staffordshire* (London, 1908), i. 329.

[19] Pigot and Co., *National Commercial Directory for 1828–9* (Manchester, 1828), i. 65; White, *Directory Staffordshire* (1834), p. 162.

[20] Pigot, *Directory*, i, 65; ii, 714; W. Parson and W. White, *History, Directory and Gazetteer of Cumberland and Westmorland* (Leeds, 1829), pp. 413–14.

[21] Parson and White, *Directory Cumberland*, p. 412; Pigot, *Directory*, i. 65; ii. 714.

[22] Pigot's *Directory for 1828–9* and the 1841 census obscure Ann Jobberns's role in a

Table 4.1 Cost of poor relief in Brampton and Lichfield, 1803

	Brampton (township, part of parish)	Lichfield, St Mary parish
Poor rate	£408 16s 2d	£1291 5s 1d
Money expended out of house	£111 11s 1d	£757 3s 9d
Money expended in house	£140 0s 0d	£405 2s 11¼d
Law	£67 10s 0d	£21 19s 8d
No. relieved outdoor	13	83
No. relieved indoor	28	42
No. of children relieved outdoor	15	59
No. of casual poor relieved	6	63
No. of non-parishioners relieved	63	49

Source: *Abstract of Answers and Returns relative to the Expence and Maintenance of the Poor* (Parl. Papers 1803–4 [C. 175], xiii), pp. 78–9, 474–5.

Brampton and Lichfield do establish the minimum number and proportion of men and women in business and their occupations. Pigot's directory for 1828–9 listed 205 people in Brampton (6.13 per cent of the 1831 population) as having an occupation: 176 men and twenty-nine women (14.15 per cent of business owners).[23] For Lichfield, of the 416 business owners listed (6.5 per cent of the population), women constituted 9.9 per cent (forty-one).[24] Adding to a growing body of research on the vibrancy of retail in market towns and a counterpoint to the fluidity of rapidly industrializing centres as places where women found greater commercial freedom, the Brampton and Lichfield figures are higher than those for Manchester, where businesswomen constituted 7.6 per cent of directory entries in 1828.[25] The range of trading opportunities open for women, however, was significantly smaller than it

---

Lichfield bakery: TNA, HO107/1008/3, 1841 census; White, *Directory Staffordshire* (1834), p. 156; SRO, LD20/6/6, Thomas and Ann Jobberns, 4 Mar. 1828; LD20/6/7, Ann Jobberns, 7 Apr. 1835.

[23] Pigot, *Directory*, i. 65–6.

[24] Pigot, *Directory*, ii. 715–17.

[25] J. Stobart, 'Gentlemen and shopkeepers: supplying the country house in eighteenth-century England', *The Economic History Review*, lxiv (2011), 885–904, at 901; Barker, *Business of Women*, pp. 7–9, 56. C. van Lieshout noted that women owned 27–30 per cent of all businesses between 1851 and 1911: 'Portrait of a lady: the female entrepreneur in England and Wales, 1851–1911', | LSE Business Review (17 May 2019) <https://blogs.lse.ac.uk/businessreview/2019/05/17/portrait-of-a-lady-the-female-entrepreneur-in-england-and-wales-1851-1911> [accessed 15 Apr. 2021].

Table 4.2 Business owners in Brampton and Lichfield in
Pigot's *National Commercial Directory for 1828–9*

Business category	Brampton No. of women	Brampton No. of men	Lichfield No. of women	Lichfield No. of men
Academies, schools and teachers	2	4	9*	6
Builders	0	0	2	9
Butchers	0	0	1	10
Chemists	1	1	0	5
Confectioners	0	0	1	2
Hairdressers and perfumers	0	0	2	7
Libraries	0	1	1	1
Maltsters	0	0	1	21
Millers	1	7	0	0
Milliners and dressmakers	3	0	11	0
Shoemakers and dealers	0	10	1	15
Shopkeepers, tea-dealers and grocers	11	32	5	21
Straw-hat makers	5	0	1	1
Tailors	0	4	2	12
Taverns, inns and public houses	5	32	4	47
Woollen mill proprietors	1	0	0	0
Total	29	91	41	157

* Includes two establishments listed as 'Misses'.

was for men: just eight occupations in Brampton compared to forty-three for men and fifteen against eighty in Lichfield (Table 4.2). Only millinery and dressmaking were demonstrably female but clusters in other 'traditional' female sectors including food, drink and education are evident.

Evidence from vouchers

Overseers' vouchers were retained as part of wider moves to make those in public office more accountable.[26] The evidence they contain opens windows

---

[26] S. P. Walker, 'Expense, social and moral control: accounting and the administration of the Old Poor Law in England and Wales', *Journal of Accounting and Public Policy*, xxiii (2004), 85–127, at 92–3, 98–9, 101–3.

onto ordinary experiences and encounters, and into businesses and trading networks. Through them, the Poor Law becomes visible in action on a daily basis. The coverage of the 356 vouchers (1759–1842) for Brampton is sporadic.[27] The 3,000 vouchers for St Mary's, Lichfield (1822–38), are more comprehensive in terms of the number and range of suppliers.

Vouchers deal with the legal flow of goods and services, but the reach of the informal economy also needs to be acknowledged.[28] The vouchers do not reveal whether overseers supplemented legitimate orders with more informal transactions for which bills were not produced, or disguised such purchases with bland itemization such as 'expenses laid out'. Despite reports of regular seizures of 'illicit importations' of beverages and tobacco, contraband goods, 'clandestine malt' and adulterated pepper, and subsequent prosecutions, little could prevent the purchase of goods from legitimate businesses whose stock potentially derived from greyer markets.[29] In addition to illegal imports, between dock, customs officer, merchant, agent, wholesaler, customer and ultimate consumer, much was cut, adulterated, thinned or watered down.[30] Grocer Daniel Dickinson of Workington advertised 'dust' tea, 'miserable' cocoa and adulterants including alum and copperas alongside more expensive ranges.[31] Overseers sometimes purchased legitimate, though low quality, goods including malt dust, thirds flour and alum.[32]

Much like male business owners, female business owners engaged in activities ranging from occasionally signing receipts, drawing up bills and collecting money to full enterprise management and near-daily contact with the Poor Law. From the vouchers it is possible to distinguish between part-time contributions and more fully engaged agency stretching over a period of years; and to identify changing demographic structures within small businesses, shifting relationships between individual enterprises and parish overseers, and the sustained 'contribution made by women to the formal economy'.[33] They reveal the wide participation of lower middle-ranking women in business at

---

[27] CAS, PR60/21/13/1–8, Brampton, Overseers' vouchers, 1759–1842.

[28] B. Lemire, *Global Trade and the Transformation of Consumer Cultures: The Material World Remade, c.1500–1820* (Cambridge, 2018), pp. 138–42.

[29] Seventeen dealers in illegal whisky were convicted in Carlisle in 1824: *Carlisle Patriot*, 10 July 1824, p. 3; 12 Dec. 1818, p. 3; 17 June 1820, p. 3; 18 Jan. 1823, p. 2.

[30] Lemire, *Global Trade*, p. 220.

[31] CAS, DSEN/12/Box 240/4/2, Daniel Dickinson, Curwen Street, Workington, 1800.

[32] SRO, D3891/6/36/4, Robert Wood, 24 Dec. 1830; D3891/6/42/130, Robert Wood, 21 May 1834; D3891/6/34/4/9, Fole Mills, 18 June 1829; D1149/6/2/1/6/2–3, Thomas Wood.

[33] S. Haggerty, 'Women, work and the consumer revolution: Liverpool in the late-eighteenth century', in *A Nation of Shopkeepers: Five Centuries of British Retailing*, ed. J. Benson and L. Ugolini (London, 2003), pp. 106–26, at p. 106.

a newly granular level. In numerous instances the sources allow for networks (defined by Sheryllynne Haggerty as 'a group or groups of people that form associations with the explicit or implicit expectation of mutual long-term benefit') and supply and distribution chains to be established from supplier to shopkeeper to consumer.[34] From them, stories of community and commerce highlight mundane and personal preoccupations. With implications for notions of polite shopping and constructs of customer loyalty, it is also evident that parish representatives shopped in multiple establishments for the same goods while retailers and service providers simultaneously supplied wealthier customers and those in receipt of relief. What providers recognized was that the value in supplying the poor extended beyond immediate financial remuneration. It incorporated a more broadly held view exemplified by physician Anthony Fothergill: 'If you set apart 2 hours every day in prescribing for paupers they will not fail to spread your fame, and bring in opulent farmers and by degrees the neighbour[in]g gentry'.[35]

Overseers' vouchers point to a diverse picture of women in business. Five groups are discernible: those women already known through directories and newspaper advertisements; those recorded as business owners in voucher headings but not listed elsewhere; those running businesses recorded under male names; those assisting in male-owned businesses; and those assisting in female-owned businesses. In Brampton eleven businesswomen are identifiable, seven of whom appear in directories between 1797 and 1829: grocers Mary Routledge, Sarah Oliver and Ann Lawson; milliners and dressmakers Jane Fleming, Jane Clark, Janet Smith and Ann or Jane Bell (the *Universal British Directory* lists only a Mrs Bell while there are vouchers for both).[36] Women in the vouchers but with no directory entry include grocer Jane Davidson; dressmaker Ann Stephens; and Jane Scott, who was paid for funeral expenses.[37]

---

[34] S. Haggerty, *'Merely for Money'? Business Culture in the British Atlantic, 1750–1815* (Liverpool, 2014), p. 163.

[35] With thanks to Alannah Tomkins for this reference: C. Lawrence, P. Lucier and C. C. Booth (eds), *'Take Time by the Forelock': The Letters of Anthony Fothergill to James Woodforde, 1789–1813* (London, 1997), p. 63.

[36] CAS, PR60/21/13/5/87, Mary Routledge, 14 Oct.–2 Dec. 1819; PR60/21/13/5/112, Sarah Oliver, 21 Dec. 1818; PR60/21/13/5/66–7, Ann Lawson, 24 Sept. 1819; PR60/21/13/5/75, Jane Fleming, 13 Oct. 1819; PR60/21/13/3/48, Jane Clark, 27 Apr. 1795; PR60/21/13/2/47, Janet Smith, 15 Oct. 1782; PR60/21/13/2/20, Ann Bell, 3 Aug. 1780; PR60/21/13/2/12, Jane Bell, c.1780; P. Barfoot and J. Wilkes, *Universal British Directory* (5 vols, London, 1790–7), v, appendix, p. 28; F. Jollie, *Jollies Cumberland Guide and Directory* (Carlisle, 1811), p. xxiii; Pigot, *Directory*, i. 65–6; Parson and White, *Directory Cumberland*, pp. 417–19.

[37] CAS, PR60/21/13/5/101, Jane Davidson, 20 Jan.–1 Apr. 1819; PR60/21/13/8/18, Ann Stephens, 17 Oct. [no year]; PR60/21/13/2/55, Jane Scott, 8 Jan. 1783.

Of the seventy-nine women engaged in enterprise named in vouchers submitted to St Mary's, Lichfield, between 1821 and 1834, only sixteen appear in directories between 1818 and 1850. Forty-six women signing receipts on behalf of others were found in nine occupational sectors, with two sectors accounting for over 60 per cent: seventeen in food and drink; and twelve in shops and dealing. Regularity in signing on behalf of others varied significantly between individual enterprises, illustrating habitual involvement for some and the propensity for others to dip in and out of business. As there was no set day when accounts were settled either by the parish or by individual concerns, variations in signing may also reflect who was available at any given time. Coal dealer Mary Sutherns signed ten out of twelve bills between 1823 and 1826 whereas Sarah Holland acknowledged the receipt of money owed to her husband for shaving and cutting the hair of workhouse inmates in just five of twenty-seven bills submitted between 1822 and 1833.[38] Superficially, the thirty-three women who headed businesses occupied traditional economic roles, twenty-four of whom were found in three sectors: shops and dealing, clothing and food and drink. Behind these headline figures, however, a more varied pattern emerges. The women worked in multiple trades: hairdressers, grocers, straw hatters, bakers, flour dealers, nurserymen, shoemakers and dealers, midwives, carriers, coffin-makers, dressmakers, drapers, stay-makers, washerwomen, braziers, innkeepers, beer retailers and spirit merchants. Seven women worked in the butchery trade, three as owners and four as assistants. Six traded in coal; Alice Adie and Elizabeth Wood worked in plumbing and glazing, Mary Danks and Mary Acton in blacksmithing and Mary Naden in building and bricklaying, drawing up bills and signing receipts. The range of businesses was still significantly narrower than for men, but included women engaged in traditionally 'male' enterprises, a situation not peculiar to England.[39]

Supplying the parish

It might be tempting to follow a familiar trope and to hold that the women in the vouchers had been thrust into a working environment of which they were largely ignorant, through demographic misfortune, and that they exited business at the earliest opportunity. Such examples do exist and, while routes into business varied, the women identified in Brampton and Lichfield came largely from existing trading families. They were expected

---

[38] SRO, LD20/6/6, John Sutherns, 2 July 1823; Benjamin Holland, 1 Oct. 1822.

[39] V. Piette, 'Belgium's tradeswomen', in *Women, Business and Finance in Nineteenth-Century Europe*, ed. Beachy, Craig and Owens, pp. 126–38, at p. 130; O. Hufton, *The Prospect before Her: A History of Women in Western Europe, 1500–1800* (London, 1995), pp. 150, 158–9.

to contribute to the business, learn how to manage both it and the vagaries of the commercial environment, and be equipped to take over or establish new enterprises when circumstances shifted.[40] As a minimum, nearly half the female-run enterprises identified in Lichfield's vouchers came through inheritance. At least eight women had succeeded to 'male' enterprises before the vouchers begin in 1822. Between then and 1831, a further six did so; at least two, butcher Mary Allsop and grocer Elizabeth Budd did so after the vouchers cease.[41]

Early nineteenth-century businesswomen are often depicted as entering commercial arenas to supplement family incomes in transitional or critical periods, operating in temporary capacities until businesses were sold or liquidated, or until men were old enough to take over, whereupon the women withdrew.[42] This sequence of events did happen but the vouchers provide evidence of more sustained business involvement. Coal dealer Mary Francis acknowledged the receipt of money in seven out of thirteen bills submitted by George Francis between 1827 and August 1830 and ten bills between December 1830 and February 1832, when her name alone is found in the vouchers.[43] It was not uncommon for businesses to be inherited by widows, for daughters to inherit in preference to sons and for such businesses to remain in female hands for many years, sometimes with male assistance.[44] The vouchers show women in each stage of the life cycle engaged in business and, in widowhood, extending their economic undertakings from being assistants and keepers of accounts to becoming owner-managers who employed others.[45] Even when acting in temporary capacities and to ensure business survival, stock, customers, orders, accounts, correspondence, advertising, staff, premises and rent all had to be attended to.

The business longevity of women evident in the vouchers cannot be explained by lucrative parish contracts. Like the majority of men in business,

---

[40] H. Barker and M. Ishizu, 'Wealth-holding and investment', in Barker, *Family and Business*, pp. 38–9.

[41] *Post Office Directory of Birmingham, Staffordshire and Worcestershire* (London, 1850), pp. 276, 278. Of 33 male-owned bakers', butchers' and grocers' shops listed in 1818, 15 were still listed in 1834, 11 had disappeared and 7 were operating under the same surnames but with different forenames. Of these, six had been inherited by males: Parson and Bradshaw, *Staffordshire Directory*, pp. 184–6; White, *Directory Staffordshire* (1834), pp. 156–61.

[42] Piette, 'Belgium's tradeswomen', p. 127; T. Ericsson, 'Limited opportunities: female retailing opportunities in nineteenth-century Sweden', in *Women, Business and Finance*, ed. Beachy, Craig and Owens, pp. 139–52, at p. 142.

[43] SRO, LD20/6/6, Francis, 12 Jan. 1827; LD20/6/7/409, Mary Francis, 10 Feb. 1832.

[44] Barker, *Family and Business*, p. 39.

[45] Piette, 'Belgium's tradeswomen', pp. 127–9.

such connections generated only modest returns.[46] Although contact could be regular, relatively few bills link individual enterprises to parish authorities. In Lichfield, the trading links of Ann Keen (1771–1853) of Market Street to the overseers of St Mary's appear weak (based on surviving bills) but potentially functioned as 'bridges to wider systems of supply' increasing information networks and business opportunities.[47] Covering thirty individual transactions for men's, women's and children's ready-made shoes, Ann Keen submitted just ten bills totalling £10 9s 2d between August 1822 and January 1829.[48] This continuity with parochial authority and the details in the vouchers, however, flesh out Keen's simple listing in trade directories from 1818 to 1851.[49] The daughter of ironmonger and grocer William Keen, Ann never married. She trained her niece, Catherine Keen, to draw up bills, take payment and run a business.[50] In 1823, Catherine married tobacconist Moses Smith of Newcastle-under-Lyme and continued the enterprise after his death in 1831 while also bringing up two children.[51] Catherine's place in the shoe shop was taken over by J. Beattie (c.1825–7) and then by another assistant known only as 'WB' (c.1828–9).[52] As with other long-term business owners with family backgrounds in trade, Keen found that supplying the parish of St Mary's did not offer substantial remuneration. There was, however, perhaps something more important; a regular settling of accounts in full, usually within three weeks of the last item on a bill. There were other benefits too. Social capital accumulated through parish connections, including the conferring of respectability and recognition of a business's stability.

Following a practice that ran across all social classes, neither Lichfield's nor Brampton's overseers relied on any single supplier. Those purchasing on behalf of the poor, however, did so almost exclusively within the immediate locality while those of middling status and above purchased in local, regional and metropolitan centres.[53] In Brampton, meat purchased

---

[46] Brown, 'Supplying London's workhouses', 36–59.

[47] Stobart, *Sugar and Spice*, pp. 77–9: Haggerty, '*Merely for Money*', pp. 107, 166.

[48] SRO, LD20/6/6, Ann Keen, 14 Aug. 1822; 1 Jan. 1829.

[49] Parson and Bradshaw, *Staffordshire Directory*, pp. 165, 175, 184; W. White, *History, Gazetteer and Directory of Staffordshire*, 2nd edn (Sheffield, 1851), p. 522.

[50] SRO, D20/1/11, Lichfield St Mary, Parish register, 30 June 1823; LD20/6/6, Ann Keen, 14 Aug. 1822.

[51] SRO, BC/11, Will of Moses Smith of Hanley, Staffordshire, proved 7 March 1832; White, *Directory Staffordshire* (1834), pp. 157, 569.

[52] SRO, LD20/6/6, Ann Keen, [1825]; 7 Apr. 1827; 4 Sept. 1828; 1 Jan. 1829.

[53] Stobart, 'Gentlemen and shopkeepers', pp. 885–904; Stobart and Bailey, 'Village shop', 408.

by the parish came from male butchers, while groceries came from Mary Routledge, Sarah Oliver, Jane Davidson and Ann Lawson.[54] This might imply a gendered division of suppliers but both sexes were actively involved in the town's butchery and grocery trades. Nor should it be assumed that female responsibility for domestic food provision led to their knowledge, skills and experience being 'transferred almost without question to their public roles'.[55] Undoubtedly, domestic kitchen activity imparted knowledge of groceries, their storage and uses, but being able to store, sort, cut, clean, grind, mix and weigh products bought wholesale meant that the grocery trade was unlikely to be taken up by someone with little or no experience.[56] Moreover, to be successful necessitated operating within 'a complex network of support' and favourable market conditions.[57] These were not always forthcoming and could easily be disrupted by war, storms at sea, harvest failures and issues surrounding debt and credit.[58] All could be compounded by small customer bases. In Brampton, Mary Graham had twenty-seven customers, Joseph Forster forty-six, Elizabeth Sewell fifty-seven and Isaac Bird 178.[59] As grocers were three times more likely than bakers and four times more likely than butchers to suffer financial misfortune, it is not surprising that between 1812 and 1822 at least three grocers in Brampton succumbed: Thomas Millar, Isaac Bird (although he continued trading) and George Bell.[60]

The issues of Poor Law supplies, business practice and family strategy are brought into close alignment through the partial biographies of three Brampton women. Previous experience enabled many widows to assume

---

[54] CAS, PR60/21/13/5/1, John Halliburton, Jan. 1811; PR60/21/13/5/70, William Tinling, 4 Dec. 1819; PR60/21/13/5/46, Thomas Parker, 6 Nov. 1818–26 May 1819; PR60/21/13/5/87, Mary Routledge, 14 Oct.–2 Dec. 1819; PR60/21/13/5/73, Sarah Oliver, 22 Dec. 1818–10 May 1819; PR60/21/13/5/101, Jane Davidson, 20 Jan.–1 Apr. 1819, PR60/21/13/5/66–7, Ann Lawson, 24 Sept. 1819.

[55] J. Howells, '"By her labour": working wives in a Victorian provincial city', in *New Directions in Local History since Hoskins*, ed. C. Dyer, A. Hopper, E. Lord and N. Tringham (Hatfield, 2011), pp. 143–58, at p. 155.

[56] Stobart, *Sugar and Spice*, p. 147.

[57] Cox, *Complete Tradesman*, pp. 163, 184.

[58] Stobart, *Sugar and Spice*, pp. 48–9.

[59] Only credit purchases are recorded: CAS, DCLP/8/38–9, Isaac Bird, Brampton, Ledger and day book, 1817–19; DCLP/8/28, Elizabeth Sewell, Brampton, Ledger, 1817–20; DCLP/8/48, Mary Graham, Brampton, Ledger, 1821; DCL P/8/47, Joseph Forster, Brampton, Ledger, 1819–31.

[60] J. Hoppitt, *Risk and Failure in English Business, 1700–1800* (Cambridge, 1987), pp. 93–5; *London Gazette*, 15 Aug. 1812, p. 992; 24 May 1817, p. 1220; 10 Aug. 1822, p. 1327.

control of enterprises following their husbands' deaths, even where no specific instructions were detailed in formal documents.[61] The grocery inherited by Mary Routledge (née Calvert) in 1815 was on Front Street alongside grocer Joseph Forster, printer Robert James, chemist Elizabeth Townley and milliner Rachael James.[62] Robert Routledge's will made no stipulation regarding the continuation or disposal of the business. An enfranchisement deed of 1810 transferring shop premises to 'Robert Routledge of Brampton, grocer, and Mary his wife', however, indicates that prior arrangements may have been made, with Mary considered best placed to continue the business because of her existing 'intimate and active involvement' in it.[63] Mary was in frequent contact with the parish authorities. In a representative voucher of 1819, covering fifty days, purchases amounting to £5 5s 1½d were made on thirty-four separate occasions.[64] Regular purchases, nearly always in small amounts (except salt), helped to reduce the spoilage of potentially slow-moving stock. Beyond the act of securing provisions, the frequency of visits also suggests that shopping expeditions offered opportunities for sociability and information exchange, both of which engendered business continuity and trust.

Female control of the enterprise was no short-lived affair. Mary Routledge's position was not relinquished when her sons were old enough to take over. In 1815 the Routledges' offspring ranged in age from three to eighteen. In time, Robert the younger became a tax supervisor, William a cleric, George the founder of the eponymous publishing house and John a high constable and relieving officer, while Mary married the son of a cabinet-maker.[65] It was, therefore, daughters Margaret (1799–1880) and Ann (1807–81) who inherited the grocery on their mother's death (c.1845). They remained in business at the same address until at least 1873, employing a female servant in the census years of 1861, 1871 and 1881.[66] The minimum

---

[61] Barker and Ishizu, 'Wealth-holding and investment', pp. 34–8.

[62] Parson and White, *Directory Cumberland*, pp. 417, 418; D. J. W. Mawson, 'Brampton in the 1790s', *Transactions of the Cumberland and Westmorland Antiquarian and Archaeological Society*, lxxiii (1973), 299–316, at 299.

[63] CAS, PROB/1815/W317, Robert Routledge, 1815; DHN/C/166/11, Howard family of Naworth, Enfranchisement deed: Hardhurst, Troddermain for Robert Routledge of Brampton, grocer and Mary his wife, 20 Dec. 1810; Barker and Ishizu, 'Wealth-holding and investment', p. 39.

[64] CAS, PR60/21/13/5/87, Mary Routledge, 3 Dec. 1819.

[65] *Carlisle Journal*, 18 July 1818, p. 3; 21 Jan. 1837, p. 2; 11 Dec. 1841, p. 1; 25 June 1861, p. 4; 18 Dec. 1888, p. 2; South West Heritage Trust, 2891A/PR/1/8, Cotleigh, Devon, Parish burials, 1 Apr. 1875.

[66] TNA, RG 9/3907, 1861 Census; RG 10/5209, 1871 Census; RG 11/5149, 1881 Census; *Post*

life-span of the enterprise in female hands, therefore, was fifty-eight years and testament to their ability to manage stock, meet changing customer demands, keep regular accounts and control the balance between credit and ready money. The Routledge grocery contrasts with more usual depictions of spinsters or widows eking out a 'marginal existence in small, short-lived retail businesses'.[67] Indeed, the income generated enabled the daughters to contribute to a memorial fund, to retire on annuities and to each leave an estate valued in excess of £800.[68]

Mary Routledge supplied the parish of Brampton at the same time as Sarah Oliver (1780–1832), whose grocery business flourished between 1811 and 1825.[69] In 1808, cotton manufacturer Henry Brough Oliver was declared bankrupt and died soon after, leaving Sarah with six dependent children.[70] Resolving Henry's affairs took much time. Dividends were paid in 1811 but in 1826 a notice in the *London Gazette* called his creditors to a meeting to 'determine upon the best mode of proceeding as to a certain sum of money, lately become due to the said Bankrupt's estate'.[71] Sarah may have been engaged in an enterprise separate to that of her husband while he was still alive, but her first recorded appearance in business is in an 1811 trade directory.[72] Her surviving bills evidence active account management: separate ruled columns record purchase dates, items, weights and prices, with 'carried forward' and 'brought over' amounts duly noted; a final total; and the dates accounts were settled together with Oliver's signature. Like Routledge's bills, there is little to suggest that the overseers purchased groceries on particular days, for example, to coincide with markets. Until she transferred her business to Scotch Street, Carlisle, Oliver, like Routledge, was also in regular contact with the parish overseers. In the 139 days between 22 December 1818 and 10 May 1819 purchases totalling £16 13s 5d were made by Brampton's overseers on seventy separate occasions.[73] After moving to Carlisle, Oliver acted as agent to the London Genuine Tea

---

Office Directory of Cumberland and Westmorland (London, 1873), p. 817.

[67] R. Beachy, B. Craig and A. Owens, 'Introduction', in *Women, Business and Finance*, ed. Beachy, Craig and Owens, pp. 1–19, at p. 6.

[68] *Carlisle Patriot*, 22 Mar. 1872, p. 1; TNA, RG 11/5159, 1881 Census; National Probate Calendar (1858–1966), 30 Nov. 1881, 6 Dec. 1881.

[69] *Carlisle Patriot*, 27 Oct. 1832, p. 3.

[70] *Tradesman; or, Commercial Magazine*, i (July–Dec. 1808), 271; *London Gazette*, 26 Nov. 1811, p. 2301; *The Monthly Magazine*, xxvi (1808), 492.

[71] *Carlisle Journal*, 7 Dec. 1811, p. 3; *London Gazette*, 25 Feb. 1826, p. 437.

[72] Jollie, *Cumberland Guide and Directory*, p. xxiii.

[73] CAS, PR60/21/13/5/73, Sarah Oliver, 22 Dec. 1818–10 May 1819.

Company between 1822 and 1825. The company supplied 'unadulterated' tea, coffee and chocolate for ready money only. In the *Cumberland Pacquet* Oliver's name appears among the general list of agents supplying the northwest of England.[74] In the *Carlisle Patriot*, however, Oliver's name, in a larger font above those of other agents, helped to distinguish her business in a crowded marketplace; Pigot's directory for 1828–9 listed thirty-four grocers and tea dealers and 111 dealers in sundries in Carlisle.[75] None of the Olivers' children followed their parents into the grocery or textile manufacturing trades, although Elizabeth and Jane became milliners and dressmakers and Sarah a straw bonnet-maker. Arguably, they could have drawn on their mother's commercial experience and may have received training in her enterprise. Another daughter, Mary, married ironmonger Richard Hind.[76] Richard Oliver trained as a doctor before becoming medical superintendent of Bicton Heath Lunatic Asylum, near Shrewsbury.[77] Sarah Oliver died in 1832, aged fifty-two.[78]

The business activity of grocer Jane Davidson (1748–1827) emerged initially through overseers' vouchers and subsequent volunteer research.[79] Although neither she nor her husband appear in directories, nor advertised in newspapers, the business operated until 1827 when the *Carlisle Patriot* announced Jane Davidson's death.[80] Robert Davidson (1742–1816), a widower, married Jane Lovet in Carlisle in September 1779. When he died, only three of their eight children were mentioned in his will. An inventory valued his household furniture at £33 and swine at £2 10s. No mention was made of any business, stock-in-trade or book debts, but his personal estate and its administration devolved to his wife 'to be by her freely enjoyed without restraint'.[81] One guinea was left to his eldest son, John, by his first marriage and five pounds to his son, Thomas, by his second. Only after his wife's decease were two of his daughters by Jane to share

---

[74] *Cumberland Pacquet*, 22 Oct. 1822, p. 3

[75] *Carlisle Patriot*, 17 Dec. 1825, p. 1; Pigot, *Directory*, i. 70–2; Stobart, *Sugar and Spice*, p. 149.

[76] Pigot, *Directory*, i. 71; Parson and White, *Directory Cumberland*, pp. 165, 166; *Carlisle Journal*, 1 Nov. 1834, p. 3; 13 Feb. 1836, p. 3.

[77] TNA, HO107/1992, 1851 Census.

[78] *Carlisle Patriot*, 27 Oct. 1832, p. 3.

[79] J. Hughes, 'Jane Davidson (1748–1827), grocer, Brampton, Cumberland' <https://thepoorlaw.org/jane-davidson-1748-1863-grocer-brampton-cumberland> [accessed 18 May 2021].

[80] *Carlisle Journal*, 20 Jan. 1827, p. 3.

[81] CAS, PROB/1816/W1462A, Robert Davidson, 9 Sept. 1816.

what remained of his effects. Both were already married by the time their father died, Mary to grocer George Hadden and Jane to provision dealer Thomas Hobson. Like others similarly positioned, Robert's death was the moment for Jane Davidson to decide whether she wished to continue in an enterprise in which she might already have been involved or to dispose of it as a going concern.[82]

Between them, Routledge, Oliver and Davidson supplied Brampton's parochial authorities with imported items including tea, coffee, sugar, pepper, tobacco and snuff; and domestic items including candles, soap, starch, barley and flour.[83] These purchases confirm Stobart's view that by the nineteenth century imported groceries had gone 'from being novelties or expensive luxuries ... to central elements of the British diet'.[84] Workhouse inmates, however, had little say in what was purchased on their behalf, so, rather than ascribing the attraction of such items to 'emulative consumption', it would be more appropriate to state that the imported items were purchased because they were relatively cheap, or for their stimulant capabilities, the nourishment they offered, their ability to make monotonous fare more appetizing, or as rewards or medicine.[85] Spices, sugar and treacle added flavour to otherwise bland hasty puddings, broths, and oatmeal porridge made with beer or milk – staple foods of Brampton's workhouse inmates and the labouring poor alike.[86] As evidence of rewards or medicine, Oliver's bills itemize tea and sugar for tailors, spinners and the sick.[87]

Cooperation among retailers mattered just as much as competition. To stock their shops, Oliver and Davidson purchased goods from wholesale and retail grocer and spirit merchant Isaac Bird. His premises, 'situated in the most eligible part' of Brampton, consisted of 'a very commodious shop and dwelling house, and large warehouse'.[88] Among his customers were thirteen male and eight female grocers.[89] Davidson made three purchases

---

[82] Hufton, *Prospect before Her*, p. 229.

[83] CAS, PR60/21/13/5/87, Mary Routledge, 3 Dec. 1819; PR60/21/13/5/73, Sarah Oliver, 22 Dec. 1818–10 May 1819; PR60/21/13/5/101, Jane Davidson, 20 Jan.–6 Apr. 1819.

[84] Stobart, *Sugar and Spice*, p. 1; see also Kay, 'Retailing, respectability', p. 162.

[85] Lemire, *Global Trade*, pp. 179–80; Stobart, *Sugar and Spice*, pp. 7–9.

[86] CAS, PR/60/21/13/8/1, Food and clothing Brampton workhouse, *c.*1765; F. M. Eden, *The State of the Poor: A History of the Labouring Classes in England* (3 vols, London, 1797), i. 60; ii. 58.

[87] CAS, PR60/21/13/5/124, Sarah Oliver, 8 Jan. 1819.

[88] *Carlisle Patriot*, 28 June 1817, p. 1.

[89] CAS, DCLP/8/38, Bird, Ledger, 1817–19; DCLP/8/39, Bird, Day book, 1817–19.

consisting of tea, sugar and tobacco between October 1818 and February 1819. From May 1818 to June 1819 Oliver's purchases, made on thirteen separate occasions, included three types of sugar; two of tobacco; cheese, currants and tea, amounting to £18 2s 9d.[90] One order in May 1818 was followed by three in June, two in August, one in December, one each in March and May 1819, and four in June. Oliver settled her account in cash and once in tobacco. The narrow range of goods and irregular purchasing patterns in Bird's ledgers indicate that both women resorted to him to supplement stock ordered from their more regular suppliers. This was standard practice: their fellow grocer Joseph Forster used seventy-six different suppliers between 1815 and 1817.[91]

Brampton's vouchers show little variation over time in what was purchased by the overseers, irrespective of the supplier. Neither the range of goods, the quality of shop fittings, levels of display, nor customer service enticed the overseers into purchasing a wider range of goods. What was purchased by Brampton's overseers, however, was consistent with the range of products stocked by other grocers in the town. Indeed, the goods were identical in name and either identical or near identical in price to the flour, soap, starch, blue, candles, tobacco, barley, tea, coffee and sugar sold by Joseph Forster, Isaac Bird, Mary Graham and Elizabeth Sewell to their non-pauper customers.[92]

Of the many women who ran small enterprises from their homes, sharing the space with family activity, little is known. The women furnishing Lichfield's Poor Law authorities, however, occupied premises that separated public from domestic spaces. Attesting to their visibility and acceptability within trading communities, all the businesswomen associated with St Mary's, Lichfield, occupied centrally located premises alongside prominent tradesmen.[93] Many of them were also publicly active in other settings. Butcher Grace Brown, grocer Ann Walker and victualler Jane Godwin were among a cluster of twenty-seven business owners with premises in Sandford Street near the workhouse. Of these, twelve, including blacksmiths,

---

[90] CAS, DCLP/8/39, Bird, Day book, 1817–19, 27 May, 9 June, 2 Oct., and 24 Dec. 1818; 5 Mar., 4 and 13 Feb., and 29 June 1819; DCLP/8/38, Bird, Ledger, 1817–19, p. 94.

[91] CAS, DX5/1/1–118, Bills and receipts of Joseph Foster, 1815–17; DX5/1/2/1–4, William Routledge's accounts with Joseph Foster, 1815–17; DX5/3/1–14, Accounts from J. and W. Armstrong, carriers for Joseph Foster, 1815–17; DX5/1/5–7, Miscellaneous receipts for Joseph Foster, 1814–17; Abraham Dent made use of around 190 suppliers: T. S. Willan, *An Eighteenth-Century Shopkeeper: Abraham Dent of Kirkby Stephen* (Manchester, 1970), p. 28.

[92] CAS, DCL P/8/47, Forster, Ledger, 1819–31; DCLP/8/38, Bird, Ledger, 1817–19; DCLP/8/28, Sewell, Ledger, 1817–20; DCLP/8/48, Graham, Ledger, 1821.

[93] Stobart, *Sugar and Spice*, p. 92.

maltsters and coopers, conducted business with the overseers in 1828. All three women worked in established family enterprises, Godwin alongside her husband and Brown and Walker with their husbands and sons. There was no attempt by the parish to abandon these commercial relationships when their husbands died because the businesses were now being run by their widows. Close proximity to the workhouse may have been a factor in their ongoing business relationships, together with their ability to meet the regular requirements of the parish.

Jane Godwin, like Julia Wilkinson of Penrith (see Interlude 4), was an innkeeper.[94] One of nine women out of fifty-five victuallers listed in the 1834 directory under 'Hotels, inns & taverns', Godwin (1770–1852), became landlady of the 'well-known and old-established', 'large and convenient' Turk's Head, with its 'spacious yard, coach house, extensive stabling and piggeries', following the death of her husband James (1775–1822).[95] She submitted regular bills to the overseers from 1822 until 1835.[96] In a characteristic bill between 10 May 1829 and 23 March 1831, St Mary's overseers made purchases from Godwin on 107 separate occasions, totalling £4 4s 2d. All purchases were for the supply of ale except one for gin and two of barm for bread-making.[97] Parish business occupied only part of Godwin's time. In addition to managing the Turk's Head, Godwin was the lessee of a house, garden and piggery and owned another public house, a farm, land, house and gardens, all of which she let.[98] It was as an owner and occupier that Godwin's name appeared in a petition opposed to the construction of the Stafford–Rugby railway.[99] Her name and those of Lichfield's mayor, aldermen, burgesses and charity trustees, however, had been used without consent. The issue reached Parliament, where it was made clear that Godwin and the others did support the scheme.[100] The significance, is not whether Godwin supported the railway or not, but that her name carried sufficient weight for those opposing the scheme to use it and for her to be one of the

---

[94] See Interlude 4 (M. Dean, 'The Wilkinsons and the Griffin Inn, Penrith') after this chapter.

[95] Parson and Bradshaw, *Staffordshire Directory*, p. 172; White, *Directory Staffordshire* (1834), p. 159; *Staffordshire Advertiser*, 29 Aug. 1835, p. 1.

[96] SRO, LD20/6/6, Jane Godwin, 30 Dec. 1822; LD20/6/7/181, Jane Godwin, 2 Apr. 1831.

[97] SRO, LD20/6/7/181, Jane Godwin, 2 Apr. 1831.

[98] SRO, B/A/15/422, Lichfield, St Michael, Tithe award, 1845; B/A/15/562, Lichfield, St Mary, Tithe award, 1848.

[99] *Staffordshire Advertiser*, 5 May 1838, p. 2; 23 Jan. 1841, p. 2.

[100] J. H. Barrow (ed.), *The Mirror of Parliament* (London, 1839), ii. 1673; J. Herapath, *The Railway Magazine*, vi (London, 1839), p. 284.

few named individuals in the parliamentary petition. After quitting the Turk's Head around 1835, Godwin moved first to Queen Street and then to Dam Street, where by 1851 she was living off independent means with her daughter and two granddaughters.[101]

Between 1822 and 1832 St Mary's overseers purchased similar goods from at least thirteen grocers supplemented by produce from the workhouse garden.[102] This reduced the risk of failures in supply lines, over-reliance on one supplier or the inability of one individual to supply the regular quantities required by the parish.[103] These were important considerations when feeding workhouse inmates thrice daily. Ann Walker (1772–1832) worked alongside her husband, Richard (1770–1827).[104] Using the knowledge gained, including drawing up bills, she could assess the creditworthiness of customers and extend credit or refrain from doing so accordingly.[105] Ann took control of the business, assisted by her son, also named Richard (d.1838), after her husband's death, when the bills record 'settled the above for Ann Walker', or 'settled this account for Ann Walker'. Supplying the workhouse with sugar, tea, tobacco, snuff, black pepper, sugar, cardamom, ginger, salt, oatmeal, starch and flour, the Walkers stocked an almost identical range of goods at the same or near-identical prices to those of their competitors, including Thomas Woodward.[106] Except for flour by the sack and salt and oatmeal by the stone, nearly all goods were supplied in small quantities. Following her husband's death and revealing Ann's continued access to markets and timely commercial information, the range of goods did not diminish, and prices remained comparable to her male competitors. Between 28 June and 19 September 1828 a total of sixty-eight items were purchased on forty-five occasions costing fractionally over £5 18s.[107] The most frequently purchased items were sugar (sixteen times) and tea (thirteen), followed by salt (six) and snuff (four). Starch, pepper and potash were each ordered three times; vinegar, blue, flour, tobacco and oatmeal, twice each, but there were also

---

[101] TNA, HO107/1008/3, 1841 Census; HO107/2014, 1851 Census.

[102] P. Collinge, '"He shall have care of the garden, its cultivation and produce": workhouse gardens and gardening, 1780–1835', *Journal for Eighteenth-Century Studies*, xliv (2021), 21–39. White listed 33 grocers, shopkeepers and tea dealers in 1834: White, *Directory Staffordshire* (1834), pp. 158, 160–1.

[103] Brown, 'Supplying London's workhouses', 48, 51.

[104] SRO, LD20/6/6, Richard Walker, 2 July 1823; D27/1/9, St Michael, Burial register, 29 Apr. 1827; 19 Dec. 1832.

[105] M. Finn, *The Character of Credit: Personal Debt in English Culture, 1740–1914* (Cambridge, 2003), p. 97.

[106] SRO, LD20/6/6, Thomas Woodward, 6 Oct. 1825.

[107] SRO, LD20/6/6, Ann Walker, 19 Sept. 1828.

single purchases of bread, pipes, mustard, ginger, cardamom, coffee, treacle and a bath brick. Repeat purchases and settlement of accounts established reciprocal trust. Walker's regular contact with the parish replicated that of Thomas Woodward who, between 2 July and 6 October 1825, supplied St Mary's with a total of fifty-seven items on twenty-three separate occasions.[108] Ultimately, whether male or female, parochial officers overwhelmingly relied on traders they knew, because they were consistent in their supply of goods and demonstrated effective business management.

John (1790–1833) and Grace (née Smiles) Brown (1780–1876) supplied meat to St Mary's overseers during the 1820s and 1830s. For most of the time, the enterprise was in John's name. From the vouchers, Grace's involvement appears initially to be casual and part-time, fluctuating according to family circumstances and its ability to employ male and female servants.[109] As such, it corresponds to accounts of female participation in the workplace more broadly but obscures her long-term involvement. She signed receipts on behalf of her husband, took over after his death and worked in the business alongside her sons George (b.1812), John Samuel (b.1815) and William (1817–47).[110] She first appeared in a trade directory in 1835.[111] In 1841, she and John Samuel were recorded in the census as butchers, and in the same year she thanked the 'nobility, clergy, gentry and inhabitants of Lichfield' for the favours conferred upon her since her husband's death, announcing that the business would now be carried on in conjunction with John Samuel Brown; the announcement ended with 'Grace Brown and Son'.[112] The following year the Browns advertised for an apprentice.[113] Long-term business involvement turned into sole ownership and then into a partnership. The butchery trade, however, was not Brown's only source of income. Indicating her status as one of Lichfield's wealthier citizens, she also leased five parcels of land and owned two houses, which she let.[114] Brown's property portfolio enabled her to exercise a specific civic right. Despite female disenfranchisement in

---

[108] SRO, LD20/6/6, Thomas Woodward, 6 Oct. 1825.

[109] TNA, HO107/1008/3, 1841 Census.

[110] SRO, LD20/6/6, John Brown, 27 June 1824; LD20/6/7/60, Grace Brown, July 1830; LD20/6/7, Grace Brown, 20 Jan. 1836.

[111] Pigot and Co., *National Commercial Directory, Derby–South Wales* (Manchester, 1835), p. 417.

[112] TNA, HO107/1008/3, 1841 Census; *Staffordshire Advertiser*, 16 Jan. 1841, p. 2.

[113] *Staffordshire Advertiser*, 11 June 1842, p. 2.

[114] SRO, B/A/15/422, Lichfield, St Michael, Tithe award, 1845; B/A/15/562, Lichfield, St Mary, Tithe award, 1848. See also D. Eastwood, 'Rethinking the debates on the Poor Law in early nineteenth-century England', *Utilitas*, vi (1994), 97–116, at 107.

the Great Reform and Municipal Corporations Acts of the 1830s, in 1843 she cast four votes (out of a maximum entitlement of six stipulated in the Sturges Bourne reforms) in a contested election for the assistant overseer of St Chad's.[115] Of twenty-four other women also eligible to vote (compared to 395 men), twenty-two did so. By 1851, Brown had returned to Windley, Derbyshire, where she had been born. There, as head of the household and assisted by her son George, she farmed 100 acres, and employed five labourers and two live-in servants.[116] She was still listed as a farmer in 1861 but by 1871 had become an annuitant.[117] At her death, aged ninety-six, she was living once again in Lichfield with her son John Samuel.[118]

Close geographic proximity to St Mary's workhouse was significant to those who supplied it. Out of 126 suppliers recorded in 1828, seventy-nine lived in twelve streets, fifty-nine of whom lived in just five: Sandford Street, Bird Street, Market Street, Boar Street and Tamworth Street. One such supplier was widow Ann Hill (1748–1833), a butcher and the landlady of The Scales, Market Street.[119] With her name heading the vouchers throughout, all bills were drawn up by her and, apart from some settled by her sons William and James, she acknowledged receipt of the money.[120] As with Grace Brown, the admission of sons into the business did not result in Hill's withdrawal from it. They worked within a business that Ann Hill controlled. Her directory entry as a butcher in addition to that of victualler in 1828 merely confirmed an occupation she was already engaged in. Like all butchers' bills submitted to St Mary's, those sent by Ann Hill were short, usually listing between two and four items. In a sample of ten bills settled quarterly between April 1823 and June 1827, Hill delivered 992¾ pounds of beef, five legs and five shins of beef, one leg of veal, one unspecified amount of mutton and nine gallons of beer wort.[121] The combined cost amounted to £25 1s 2d.

Property auctions held at The Scales offered Hill opportunities for information exchange, the gathering of commercial intelligence and

---

[115] SRO, D15/4/11/9, 'W. Gorton's Notes at 1841 Parliamentary Revision Courts', with polls for assistant overseer of poor, St Chad's parish, 1843 and 1848; S. Richardson, *The Political Worlds of Women: Gender and Politics in Nineteenth-Century Britain* (Abingdon, 2013), pp. 100–2.

[116] TNA, HO107/2144, 1851 Census.

[117] TNA, RG9/2507, 1861 Census; RG10/3578, 1871 Census.

[118] TNA, RG10/2915, 1871 Census; SRO, D29/ADD/6, St Chad, Lichfield, Parish register, 23 March 1876.

[119] SRO, LD20/6/6, Ann Hill, 29 June 1824; *Staffordshire Advertiser*, 17 Dec. 1814, p. 3; Parson and Bradshaw, *Staffordshire Directory*, p. 173; Pigot, *Directory*, ii. 716.

[120] SRO, LD20/6/6, Ann Hill, 25 Jan. 1828; LD20/6/7/231, Ann Hill, 18 July 1831.

[121] SRO, LD20/6/6, Ann Hill, 1 Apr. 1824–28 June 1827.

social activity.[122] These and other links embedded her further in Lichfield's commercial life. One was the credit network of shoemaker Francis Willdey. At his death in 1824, Willdey owed nearly £300 to forty-one people including £29 17s 7d to Hill, the second highest amount after the £48 3s 11d Willdey owed his brother-in-law.[123] This was a large amount, considering that no individual bill submitted by Hill to St Mary's overseers' exceeded four pounds, but should not be taken as evidence of Hill having been exploited by a male trader; she owed Willdey a comparable £29 1s 6d. Another network to which Hill belonged, as did Ann Keen, James Godwin and John Brown, was Lichfield's Association for the Prosecution of Felons.[124] The Association's ninety-four male and six female members sought to protect their businesses and property through financial assistance and to uphold the law for the wider community. At the same time, subscribers accrued social capital.[125] For Hill, membership also brought custom: in 1816 the society's annual meeting was held at The Scales. The sociability attached to such events 'kept business and information flowing in a world where economic and social values were becoming a matter of exchange'.[126]

Business orientated, literate, numerate and at times politically active, Lichfield's businesswomen were able to participate in its commercial environment because, as Haggerty argued in a different context, there was a 'relatively homogeneous, commonly understood and conformed-to business culture' in which gender mattered less than a trustworthy reputation.[127] As the acknowledged successors to established businesses well regarded for reliable delivery (evidenced in the vouchers), their civic engagement and localism instilled business confidence further. They were, after all, as likely to meet St Mary's parish officers in the street as in their business premises.

Contracts and prices
The simple listing of items in grocers' bills submitted to overseers rarely gives any indication of variety or quality. Standard goods, however, carried almost identical prices irrespective of the supplier, male or female. Two ounces of tea

---

[122] *Staffordshire Advertiser*, 17 Dec. 1814, p. 3.

[123] SRO, LD15/12/72, Creditors of the late Francis Willdey, undated.

[124] *Lichfield Mercury*, 29 Nov. 1816, p. 1.

[125] M. Koyama, 'Prosecution associations in Industrial Revolution England: private providers of public goods?', *The Journal of Legal Studies*, xlii (2012), 95–130, at 115.

[126] J. Mee and C. W. Smith, 'Georgian fascination with conversation' (2018) <www.york.ac.uk/news-and-events/news/2018/research/georgian-fascination-with-conversation> [accessed 10 Feb. 2021].

[127] Haggerty, *'Merely for Money'*, p. 26.

and one a quarter pound of sugar in Lichfield cost 5*d*; half a pound of black pepper 2*s*; and six pounds of treacle 2*s* 6*d*.[128] Price consistency is indicative of the use of contracts, a keen awareness of competitors' prices, collusion or arrangement.[129] Awarding contracts through competitive tendering was widespread before it became a requirement in the Poor Law Amendment Act.[130] Prior to 1834 in Brampton, John Ewart submitted a bill along with a tender for goods; in Dalston, Cumberland, Matthew Routledge tendered for oatmeal, barley, butter and straw, while the overseers of Kingswinford, Staffordshire, sought tenders for flour, butcher's meat and 'malt and hops of the best quality'.[131] Where contracting was in place, both before and after the 1834 Poor Law Amendment Act, female and male suppliers had to conform to the same processes. Usually this meant suppliers brought samples and tenders to the overseers in person and provided sureties. In the immediate aftermath of the new law, Brampton's and Lichfield's overseers did not use the opportunity to exclude women from supplying parishes, even though food and drink could have been supplied wholly through male traders. By continuing to purchase from men and women (in 1835 Ann Jobberns supplied flour and Grace Brown beef to St Mary's), overseers were keen to be seen to be spreading their patronage among the more substantial traders who stocked the right mix of goods, while also returning money to those who funded the Poor Law.[132] The use of more than one supplier also enabled parish officials to keep abreast of changing commercial information where, in instances of 'poor quality', non-sanctioned price increases or failure to deliver, they could respond by switching suppliers.[133] No trader could afford to be complacent.

Making use of multiple suppliers for the same goods raises questions about the significance of customer loyalty in late Georgian England. Many private shoppers patronized retail outlets based on price, quality, variety, display and level of service, aspects that have garnered much attention

---

[128] SRO, LD20/6/6, John Budd, 31 Mar. 1825; Thomas Woodward, 6 Oct. 1825; Richard Walker, 5 July 1826; Ann Walker, 28 June 1828.

[129] Brown, 'Supplying London's workhouses', 54.

[130] Edmonton, Middlesex, *Morning Advertiser*, 18 June 1807, p. 1; Oxford, *Oxford University and City Herald*, 30 Aug. 1817, p. 3; Liverpool, *Liverpool Mercury*, 17 July 1818, p. 3; Kendal, *Westmorland Gazette*, 19 Jan. 1833, p. 1; Kingswinford, *Aris's Birmingham Gazette*, 20 May 1833, p. 1.

[131] CAS, PR60/2/13/60, John Ewart, 14 Apr. 1796; SPC/63/6, Matthew Routledge, 1827; *Aris's Birmingham Gazette*, 20 May 1833, p. 1.

[132] Brown, 'Supplying London's workhouses', 37; SRO, LD20/6/7, Ann Jobberns, 6 July 1835; Grace Brown, 20 Jan. 1836.

[133] Stobart, *Sugar and Spice*, pp. 84–5.

from historians of consumption practices.[134] Similarly, those tasked with purchasing for institutions adopted a strategy in which lowest cost was not always the determining factor and, conversely, offering the lowest prices was no guarantee of securing business against the competition. The awarding of local contracts and orders took account of a variety of issues. Not the least of these was the need to balance the self-interest of ratepayers (who constituted the membership of vestries) against the moral responsibility many felt towards those who were unable to help themselves or who faced critical transitions in circumstances.[135] Vestries and overseers, therefore, used their discretion to find community-based solutions to the national issue of poverty. They were fully cognizant that by supporting local enterprises they were reducing the number of potential occasions when and the number of people who might otherwise seek parish relief.[136] Women (especially widows) could be particularly problematic in this respect; while some had 'money and assets', others, poverty-stricken and without male support, might 'make demands on the public purse'.[137] In response, some leeway could be extended to businesses inherited by widows.[138] In Brampton, Oliver and Routledge occasionally charged the overseers a ½*d* or 1*d* more than Isaac Bird and Joseph Forster charged their non-pauper customers for goods of the same name and weight. Although price variations could be the result of competition, inflation, or irregular or scarce supplies, it could also be interpreted as evidence of the relative inability of women to secure the best prices because they lacked access to current commercial information.[139] Additional outlay not absorbed by reducing profit margins would compel businesswomen to pass such costs on. Most of the prices charged by Oliver and Routledge, however, were identical or near identical to those of their male counterparts, which makes it reasonable to assume that overall they had access to the same commercial information as men. If overseers chose to reject fractionally higher supply costs on occasion, an independent ratepaying family could easily become a dependent non-paying

---

[134] Walsh, 'Shop design', 157–76; A. Hann and J. Stobart, 'Sites of consumption: the display of goods in provincial shops in eighteenth-century England', *Cultural and Social History*, ii (2005), 165–87.

[135] R. Pearson 'Knowing one's place: perceptions of community in the industrial suburbs of Leeds, 1790–1890', *Journal of Social History*, xxvii (1993), 221–44, at 228.

[136] Brown, 'Supplying London's workhouses', 54–5.

[137] Hufton, *Prospect before Her*, p. 221.

[138] The appointment of assistant overseers, discussed by Tomkins in Chapter 5 in this volume, also suggests a proactive response to the possibility of poverty.

[139] Haggerty, 'Women, work and the consumer revolution', pp. 116–17.

one, exacerbating further fragile community finances and relationships.[140] Accepting occasionally higher prices was thus a pragmatic response to a transitional stage in the relationship between businesswomen and parish overseers. Workhouses still needed regular supplies, and widows, especially those with dependent children, needed an income.

Conclusion

For those in search of casual relief, welfare provision was often short-term and the response of parochial officers appears frequently to have been reactive.[141] From the supply perspective, however, especially in parishes with workhouses, there were more predictable costs. In response, vestries and traders developed a system that anticipated requirements while also being alive to changing circumstances. Through the lens of overseers' vouchers, it is apparent that the Old Poor Law influenced what traders produced, stocked and retailed. The regular, consistent purchase of goods, often in small quantities, is also evident in Elizabeth Spencer's chapter on clothing. The active participation of businesswomen in this system points to an environment of economic cohesion in which women were doing far more than struggling along with little or no assistance to eke out a sparse living. Those who also purchased goods from fellow tradespeople, as Oliver, Davidson and Hill did, strengthened their positions, in the process becoming fully integrated into distribution and provision networks.[142] Negotiating the line between providing for themselves and their families and being required to maintain creditworthiness, they adapted and extended their entrepreneurial activities, maintained their independence and forged identities beyond the domestic. In doing so, they also extended the meaning of female business ownership beyond the purely physical and the legal to become familiar and essential figures in their communities.

Although some of the women supplying parishes ultimately divested themselves of their enterprises, the inheritance of business, property and/ or investments saw none of those cited here retreat into rentier-funded retirement in the immediate aftermath of bereavement. Only in very old age did Elizabeth Dawes and Grace Brown withdraw from business; Davidson, Hill and Keen all died in harness. Jane Godwin, however, was

---

[140] One-fifth of ratepayers were likely to receive poor relief at some stage: S. Williams, *Poverty, Gender and Life-Cycle under the English Poor Law, 1760–1834* (Woodbridge, 2011), pp. 79, 162–3.

[141] S. King, *Poverty and Welfare in England, 1700–1850: A Regional Perspective* (Manchester, 2000), p. 5.

[142] Cox, *Complete Tradesman*, p. 179.

the exception. After trading on her own for thirteen years, she enjoyed an independent income for the next seventeen. Through family, assistants, co-partners or servants, the children of Routledge, Davidson and Oliver, Brown, Hill, Walker and Godwin all benefited from the training, experience, employment, income, security or support provided by their mothers' business endeavours. They, in turn, inherited enterprises, established their own, married local traders or moved into the professions.

Despite their sometimes piecemeal nature, overseers' vouchers have provided the opportunity to see beyond the simple listing of businesswomen in trade directories and to consider how women conducted business. Long-term survivors established, maintained and renewed business and social contacts and adopted solid working practices. In all the enterprises, newspaper advertising was the exception rather than the rule, but pricing structures and product ranges matched those of male traders, showing that women had access to timely commercial information. Indeed, numbers aside, there was often little to distinguish female traders and their businesses from their male counterparts in terms of the goods and services provided, prices charged and individual levels of engagement with parish authorities.

Interlude 4

The Wilkinsons and the Griffin Inn, Penrith

Margaret Dean

Licensed premises were the locations of much parish business (see the Preface, Introduction and Chapter 4). In Penrith, the Griffin, a large coaching inn containing kitchens, parlour, dining rooms, lodgings,

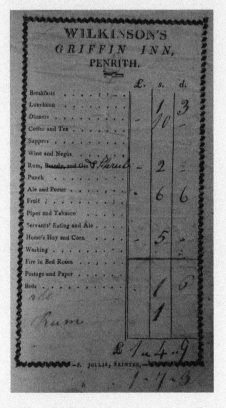

Figure 4.1 Pre-printed bill for expenses at the Griffin Inn, Penrith, submitted to the overseers of Threlkeld, c.1800, CAS, SPC 21/8/11/13

cellars, brewhouse and stables, was such a place.[1] A pre-printed bill for board and lodging submitted to the overseers of Threlkeld shows that, alongside accommodation, the inn offered breakfasts, luncheons, dinners and suppers, beers, wines and spirits, pipes, tobacco, washing, and corn and hay for horses (Figure 4.1).

From at least the 1790s the Griffin was run by the Wilkinson family. John Wilkinson married Julia Harrison (1768–1824) at Greystoke in 1789. They had six children, four of whom survived into adulthood. After John's death in 1801, Julia settled his estate and the lease of the Griffin was offered for a term of nine years.[2] In 1811, however, Jollie's directory listed Julia Wilkinson as the innkeeper of the Griffin.[3] She appears to have been the only female proprietor of the inn before it ceased trading at the end of the nineteenth century.[4]

As well as running the inn, Julia administered the estate of her father after he died in 1818. Applications regarding the letting of his house and thirty acres in Greystoke were to be submitted to her at the Griffin.[5] The following year, local newspapers reported that Julia Wilkinson, 'late of the Griffin', had married Isaac Hodgson of London at a ceremony in Greystoke. Hodgson was a slop merchant, a trader providing clothes and bedding to sailors.[6] Despite the announcement, no such marriage had taken place. The *Carlisle Patriot* issued a retraction, claiming it to be the 'invention of some wiseacre' whom they wished to detect and expose.[7]

Julia died in 1824.[8] The Griffin remained in the Wilkinson family but was again offered for lease.[9] None of Julia Wilkinson's children followed her into the licensed trade. Her eldest son, Harrison (1790–

---

[1] For further details see M. Dean, 'Wilkinson's Griffin Inn, Penrith', The Poor Law <https://thepoorlaw.org/wilkinsons-griffin-inn-penrith> [accessed 13 Apr. 2021]. The blog post is made available under a Creative Commons Attribution-NonCommercial 4.0 International License (CC BY-NC 4.0); *Cumberland Pacquet and Ware's Whitehaven Advertiser*, 8 June 1779, p. 1.

[2] *Carlisle Journal*, 17 Jan. 1801, p. 1; 7 Feb. 1801, p. 1.

[3] Jollie, *Cumberland Guide and Directory*, p. xxxi.

[4] *Cumberland and Westmorland Herald*, 11 Mar. 1893, p. 4.

[5] *Cumberland Pacquet and Ware's Whitehaven Advertiser*, 8 Sept. 1818, p. 3.

[6] *Carlisle Patriot*, 31 July 1819, p. 3; *Cumberland Pacquet*, 3 Aug. 1819, p. 3.

[7] *Carlisle Patriot*, 14 Aug. 1819, p. 3.

[8] CAS, PR5/11, Greystoke, St Andrew, Burial register, 1813–90.

[9] *Carlisle Patriot*, 17 Dec. 1825, p. 1.

1830), joined the Royal Navy before settling as a surgeon in Hounslow, Middlesex.[10] In his will he instructed his trustees to divide the majority of his estate between his siblings Thomas (1797–1860), Mary (1791–1848) and Ann (1800–1865).[11] The Griffin made up part of his estate. Dorothy, the eldest daughter of his sister Mary, was the beneficiary of the profits arising from the Griffin Inn.

---

[10] *London County Directory* (1811), p. 1566.

[11] TNA, PROB11/1792/175, Will of Harrison Wilkinson of Hounslow, Middlesex, 3 Nov. 1831.

5. The overseers' assistant: taking a parish salary, 1800–1834

Alannah Tomkins

The people of Dalston parish in Cumberland took an atypical decision on the death of their assistant overseer in 1847, when they chose to memorialize him: James Finlinson's headstone was put up by his Odd Fellows lodge in recognition of his 'valuable services' as an assistant overseer of 'many years', stretching back to the period of the Old Poor Law. Finlinson was thereby made prominent among a largely unsung group of men who applied for and secured work as permanent, perpetual or assistant overseers.[1]

Parishes under the Old Poor Law recruited salaried overseers in an ad hoc fashion up to the permissive legislation of 1819, and more consistently thereafter. The thinking behind the employment of salaried overseers was relatively simple: the appointments were 'designed to allow parishes to restrict relief' and, in broad terms, the legislative reform that permitted these posts was successful.[2] A combination of select vestries and assistant overseers did tend to reduce the amounts spent on relief, despite the occasional doubt or demurral.[3] Elected overseers would have been forgiven for seeing additional advantages in employing a paid assistant, for the post-holders personally rather than for the ratepayers of the parish. The volume of Poor Law business generated by a populous parish could be vast, whereas parishes covering thousands of acres risked involving overseers in substantial travel.[4] To these considerations might also be added the advantage for parish administrations of requesting certain skills from assistants, which could be

---

[1] J. Wilson, *Monumental Inscriptions of the Church Churchyard and Cemetery of S. Michael's Dalston* (Dalston, 1890), p. 79; Finlinson was not, however, unique: see the monumental inscription at Hillingdon, St John the Baptist, for William Reid, assistant overseer, who died in 1829, at Find my Past <https://www.findmypast.co.uk> [accessed 8 Sept. 2020]. See also Interlude 5 (W. Bundred, 'The parochial career of James Finlinson (1783–1847)' after this chapter.

[2] S. Shave, *Pauper Policies: Poor Law Practice in England, 1780–1850* (Manchester, 2017), p. 111.

[3] W. E. Taunton, *Hints towards an Attempt to Reduce the Poor Rate* (Oxford, 1819), p. 9.

[4] Shave, *Pauper Policies*, p. 121. For the huge annual costs in 1830s Birmingham see C. Upton, *The Birmingham Parish Workhouse 1730–1840* (Hatfield, 2019), p. 99.

A. Tomkins, 'The overseers' assistant: taking a parish salary, 1800–1834' in *Providing for the Poor: The Old Poor Law, 1750–1834*, ed. P. Collinge and L. Falcini (London, 2022), pp. 137–163. License: CC BY-NC-ND 4.0.

variable or absent among the elected overseers.[5] A paid, permanent man might be more alert to the circumstances of the resident poor, and attuned to the encroachments of mobile paupers (for whom, see Chapter 3). Finally, it is possible to surmise (if not to prove) that the benefit of a salaried overseer to the annually elected men was their capacity to deflect personal criticism following decisions about poor relief that offended or upset either the ratepayers or the poor claimants.[6] It was the assistant's fault if the rates rose, or if a specific case of poverty went unrelieved – or it could be made to seem so. A Sussex observer sympathetic to the plight of the poor pointed in this direction when she noted: 'I know a Guardian of the Poor who is generally allowed to be the most hard-hearted person in his parish: and on *this* account the Farmers are desirous of making *his* office perpetual.'[7] Assistant overseers are thus important for our understanding of the Poor Law as a system both of welfare and of social control, rather than simply as a feature of statutory performance in a given location.

Relatively little is known about this group's occupational background, social position or life experience beyond the office. The Poor Law Commission of 1834 made a number of assumptions about the occupational antecedents of assistant overseers (schoolteachers, tradesmen, farmers) and was generally favourable in its verdict. Much-repeated claims of their intelligence and zeal were leavened with cautions about their control by committee and lightly sprinkled with anecdotes of errant employees' fraud.[8] The 'Small Bills' project has offered a new evidential pathway to view the salaried assistant overseer and unpacked partial biographies for the men (they were all men), their working lives and their relieving activity

---

[5] Specifically, beyond functional literacy; applicants could allude to their familiarity with keeping accounts.

[6] It was, of course, possible for elected annual overseers to be informally salaried, but none were found for the three counties studied here. For an example in Derbyshire see Derbyshire Record Office, D845A/PO1, Mappleton, Overseers' accounts, 1796–1834, giving a salary of £5 5s to annual overseers between at least 1805 and 1832. I am indebted to Dianne Shenton for this reference.

[7] S. Markham, *A Testimony of her Times: Based on Penelope Hind's diaries and Correspondence, 1787–1838* (Wilton, 1990), p. 109 (emphasis original).

[8] *Report from His Majesty's Commissioners for Inquiring into the Administration and Practical Operation of the Poor Laws* (Parl. Papers 1834 [C. 44]), throughout, given tentative confirmation by T. Sokoll, *Essex Pauper Letters, 1731–1837* (Oxford, 2006), p. 23, which sees parishes with assistant overseers as being more likely to retain letters, both phenomena being consonant with improvements in administration. M. Pratt, *Winchelsea Poor Law Records, 1790–1834* (Lewes, 2011), pp. xx–xxi, credits the scope of his own research to Charles Arnett, assistant overseer in Winchelsea, who retained incoming correspondence more systematically than either his predecessors or his successors.

within the three counties of Cumbria (incorporating the historic counties of Cumberland and Westmorland and parts of Lancashire and Yorkshire), East Sussex and Staffordshire.

This chapter will provide three perspectives on this group: first, it will survey the short but not generally merry existence of the office under the Old Poor Law in England before its reincarnation under the New Poor Law; second, it will analyse the multiple applications sent in response to one specific job advertisement in County Durham in 1831; and, third, it will offer a series of insights into men employed across the three counties of Cumbria, East Sussex and Staffordshire, in parishes where there are surviving Poor Law vouchers, and some conclusions about the causes and consequences of taking a parish wage. The central finding of this work is that assistant overseers, while not paupers, were men with financial difficulties of their own. As such it corresponds to the findings in Chapters 2 (by Elizabeth Spencer) and 4 (by Peter Collinge) in this book on the discretion of parish vestries to award work to those who might have been deemed 'at risk' of requiring poor relief.

This investigation is important because, despite a number of histories about the professions per se, and some specifically about administrators, our knowledge of parish staffing remains rudimentary.[9] Mark Goldie has judged that the holding of parish office before the eighteenth century extended across a broad social spectrum without generating further enquiry.[10] The drive of 'history from below' has been firmly in favour of the paupers over the ratepayers, and those in the middle who provisioned or ran the Poor Law were sidelined. The lone exception among the many early nineteenth-century assistant overseers is Stephen Garnett of Kirkby Lonsdale, chiefly of interest as the recipient of pauper letters.[11] David Eastwood suggested rather grandly in 1994 that the statutory permission to appoint assistant overseers facilitated the creation of a Poor Law civil service, but this contention has not subsequently been tested.[12] The recent work of Samantha Shave has redirected research to the importance of law, policy and implementation in conditioning the way parish relief played out in a specific context, and has looked at the uptake of Sturges Bourne's Acts specifically in Wessex

---

[9] P. Corfield, *Power and the Professions in Britain, 1700–1850* (London, 1999); D. Eastwood, *Governing Rural England: Tradition and Transformation in Local Government, 1780–1840* (Oxford, 1994).

[10] M. Goldie, 'The unacknowledged republic: office holding in early modern England', in *The Politics of the Excluded, c.1500–1850*, ed. T. Harris (London, 2001), pp. 153–94, at p. 163.

[11] J. S. Taylor, 'Voices in the crowd: The Kirkby Lonsdale township letters, 1809–36', in *Chronicling Poverty: The Voices and Strategies of the English Poor*, ed. T. Hitchcock, P. King and P. Sharpe (Basingstoke, 1996), pp. 109–26, at pp. 110–11.

[12] Eastwood, *Governing Rural England*.

including the employment of assistant overseers.[13] This latest research has provided an additional historiographical spur to the task of looking again at permanent overseers, albeit asking personal rather than policy-based questions. The evidence of the 'Small Bills' project suggests that a civil service did not emerge in any organized sense before 1834 and that its beginnings were faltering indeed.

By way of comparison, historiography is no more attentive to the Poor Law's operational staff than it is to administrators. Salaried workhouse governors predated assistant overseers by decades, but there is very little discrete work on them either.[14] They are mentioned dismissively as contractors or not at all.[15] Physicians and surgeons who dealt with the poor for a set fee have attracted more attention from medical historians, for the role of a parish contract in securing a professional reputation.[16] Such medical men have not been considered in the round of parish employees, perhaps because neither historians nor the modern medical profession can countenance viewing them as mere contractors on a par with others who took annual parish pay.[17] The history of parish staff including but not privileging medicine has yet to be written.

It is generally held that assistant overseers were appointed in the years immediately following legislation but with patchy appearances across England. This is unsurprising given the variety of organizational forms adopted by parishes and townships for the delivery of poor relief, varying

---

[13] Shave, *Pauper Policies*.

[14] For a recent honourable exception see S. Ottaway, ' "A very bad presidente in the house": Workhouse masters, care, and discipline in the eighteenth-century workhouse', *Journal of Social History* 54 (2021), 1091–1119. Workhouse employees were considered for the 18th-century Birmingham workhouse, suggesting among other things that an assistant overseer who became a workhouse master was moving up a parish career ladder: Upton, *Birmingham Parish Workhouse*, pp. 114–33.

[15] S. Webb and B. Webb, *English Poor Law History*, i, *The Old Poor Law* (London, 1963), set the tone for the treatment of Poor Law employees, with occasional details subsequently illuminating the landscape. The workhouse master of Terling at the end of the 18th century was poor himself, and narrowly avoided being removed when he failed to produce a settlement certificate, an echo of what was to follow for assistant overseers: S. R. Ottaway, *The Decline of Life: Old Age in Eighteenth-Century England* (Cambridge, 2004), p. 231.

[16] A. Digby, *Making a Medical Living: Doctors and Patients in the English Market for Medicine, 1720–1911* (Cambridge, 1994); I. Loudon, *Medical Care and the General Practitioner, 1750–1850* (Oxford, 1986); S. King, *Sickness, Medical Welfare, and the English Poor, 1750–1834* (Manchester, 2018); A. Tomkins, 'Who were his peers? The social and professional milieu of the provincial surgeon-apothecary in the late eighteenth century', *Journal of Social History*, xliv (2011), 915–35.

[17] Although see Interlude 6 (J. Kisz, 'Abel Rooker (1787–1867), surgeon') in this volume.

by region, settlement type or economic context. Samantha Shave has reminded researchers that the snapshot views offered by Parliamentary Papers probably concealed a good deal of adoption of the relevant Sturges Bourne Act, dropping of assistant overseers in the light of experience, and even, it must be supposed, the readoption of salaried officers.[18] What can be said from an analysis of these parochial returns is that between 6 and 29 per cent of all parish or similar authorities with responsibility for poor relief reported making use of assistants between 1821 and 1824. At the county level, the vast majority fell into the range of between 11 and 22 per cent, and all three counties studied here were found in this subset: 16 per cent of places in Sussex (the eastern and western parts of the county were combined at this period) employed assistants, as did 22 per cent of places in both Cumberland and Staffordshire.[19] This suggests that, despite the variation in approaches to relief management, there was a measure of alignment between geographically diverse English places over the perceived utility of employing paid overseers. There is one local caveat, however, in relation to Cumberland. This was a county where parishes made heavy use of contractors, and routinely farmed the poor (as flagged in the Introduction to this volume). Therefore, it is interesting to note that, even in a region characterized by parochial delegation, the use of assistant overseers was not out of line with the national picture.

Parish experiences: employers and employees

Assistant overseers experienced their first unsanctioned jobs in parishes around the country during the eighteenth and early nineteenth centuries.[20] Their appointments were possibly well intentioned, and indeed had been proposed by Richard Burn on the grounds that elected overseers were rarely

---

[18] Shave, *Pauper Policies*, pp. 118–20.

[19] Westmorland, part of modern Cumbria, fell outside this pattern, with just 9 per cent of places using a salaried assistant. Data on the number of parishes, townships and other places responding to parliamentary inquiries from 1813 to 1818 have been taken from *Abridgement of the Abstract of the Answers and Returns made pursuant to an Act, passed in the Fifty-fifth Year of His Majesty King George the Third, Intitules 'AN ACT for procuring Returns relative to the Expense and Maintenance of the Poor in England; and also relative to the Highways' so far as relates to THE POOR* (Parl. Papers 1818), while counts of assistant overseers per county have been taken from *Report from the Select Committee on Poor Rate Returns* (Parl. Papers 1821, 1824).

[20] From Chew Magna in Somerset to Northowram in Yorkshire; Shave, *Pauper Policies*, p. 115; Painswick in Gloucestershire: see W. J. Sheils, *History of the County of Gloucester* (Oxford, 1976), pp. xi, 79–80; *Report … into the Administration and Practical Operation of the Poor Laws*.

'adequate to the performance ... [since] ... no man chuses to serve for nothing'.[21] John Saint in Wednesbury (Staffordshire), and John Wannup in Greystoke (Cumbria) secured work as paid overseers in 1784 and 1809 respectively, and doubtless there were men whose paid work as parish clerks or in other roles effectually regarded some of the money as compensation for dealing with the Poor Law.[22] Nonetheless, like many illegitimate beginnings, the employment specifically of paid overseers was technically forbidden, by a test case at King's Bench in 1785, and could carry a significant social or financial cost.[23] Madeley in Staffordshire, for example, appointed James Halmarack in May 1816 on a dangerously low salary of £5 per year. The parish became displeased with his services and tried to disown him three years later. Halmarack was asked to return all parish money, at which point he informed the vestry that he was an undischarged bankrupt and no longer had control of any of his former resources.[24] This was quite true: James Halmarack the elder of Madeley, retailer of wine and spirits, was later reported bankrupt in the *London Gazette*.[25] Madeley sought legal advice, but was told there was no remedy, as the original appointment was not lawful.[26] Legal counsel rather piously observed that a salaried overseer 'may now be appointed by 59 Geo 3.c.12 f. 7', which must have been tremendously reassuring to the vestry of Madeley facing an accounting shortfall of £200.[27]

---

[21] R. Burn, *The History of the Poor Laws with Observations* (London, 1764), pp. 214–15; Gilbert's Act also diminished the role played by elected overseers, from similar concerns; L. Ryland-Epton, 'Social policy, welfare innovation, and governance in England: the creation and implementation of Gilbert's Act 1782' (unpublished Open University PhD thesis, 2020), p. 231.

[22] J. F. Ede, *History of Wednesbury* (Wednesbury, 1962), p. 166; CAS, PR5/43, Greystoke, Poor account book, 1740–1812, minute of 26 Apr. 1809. The noted Sussex diarist Thomas Turner, for example, was paid as parish clerk in some of the same years he acted as overseer.

[23] F. Const, *Decisions of the Court of King's Bench upon the Laws relating to the Poor* 1 (London, 1793), pp. 277–9; J. B. Bird, *The Laws respecting Parish Matters* (London, 1799), p. 50.

[24] Unsalaried overseers could also fall bankrupt or be declared insolvent, but with less damaging consequences for their home parish: see 'Isaac Lightfoot, overseer, attorney, and bankrupt, Wigton' <https://thepoorlaw.org/isaac-lightfoot-overseer-attorney-and-bankrupt-wigton> [accessed 8 Sept. 2020].

[25] *London Gazette*, 13 Oct. 1821, p. 2042. This assistant overseer is not to be confused with James Halmarack the younger of Newcastle-under-Lyme, draper, whose own bankruptcy was reported in the *Gazette*, 1813–21.

[26] SRO, D3412/5/698, Madeley, Parish case paper relating to an assistant overseer, 1819.

[27] The requirement of magistrates to investigate men's financial indemnity after 1819 did not rule out the men's financial collapse (Shave, *Pauper Policies*, p. 114). For assistant overseers discharged as insolvent debtors or committing suicide in debtor's prison see, respectively, *Liverpool Mercury*, 4 July 1834, p. 2, and *Jackson's Oxford Journal*, 1 Feb. 1834, p. 2.

Traces of assistant overseers before 1819 are piecemeal, but evidences of these employees after the Act of 1819 are geographically widespread and easy to find within and beyond the parishes of the 'Small Bill's project.[28] For instance, parishes up and down the country tried to manage their new employees by inventing an 1820s equivalent of the job description and person specification, and by comparing notes. In Kent, the parish of Wrotham St George went about the task methodically, devising a list of expectations for appointments from 1829 onwards. This included a requirement for meticulous investigation of every pauper household, and

> the character which he [the pauper head of household] bears with his master, or any respectable persons in the neighbourhood, for industry, honesty, sobriety and economy … that he [the assistant overseer] may be able to discriminate between the deserving and undeserving poor.[29]

Similarly, Ticehurst in Sussex wanted a married man without encumbrance to collect the rates, list the poor, manage the workhouse, attend petty sessions and present fortnightly accounts to the select vestry.[30] Ticehurst's security against fraud rested on the appointee offering £500 security against default, putting the post beyond the personal means of many.[31] Applicants would have needed wealthy and trusting friends. Sussex parishes in general developed printed 'warrants' outlining the totality of tasks for assistant overseers (virtually everything formerly undertaken by their annually elected predecessors), with statutory permissions being cited for each activity.[32] At the opposite end of the country, the churchwardens of Penrith wrote to their fellow vestrymen in other north-western parishes for details of 'the duties, usefulness and salaries' of 'permanent' overseers. Carlisle St Mary parish had a ready-trained man in the person of John Routledge, the

---

[28] A survey of the online catalogues of thirty-three English county archives offices in 2019 revealed indications of rich data.

[29] Kent Archives, P406/18/9, Wrotham St George, A sketch of the duties performed by the assistant overseer, 1829; E. Melling (ed.), *Kentish Sources*, iv, *The Poor* (Maidstone, 1964), pp. 184–5, for the duties of the assistant overseer at Cranbrook; Shave, *Pauper Policies*, p. 124.

[30] ESRO, PAR492/37/46, Ticehurst, Duty of an assistant overseer, [presumed 1821].

[31] Bonds and sureties were adopted elsewhere too, e.g., Gloucester Archives, P244/OV/7/3 (Painswick's miscellaneous overseers' records include a bond for the execution of duties of assistant overseer, 1832); Surrey Archives, 853/2/1 (Walton-on-Thames's overseers' bond for Matthew Steele as assistant overseer to the value of £200, 1828); Kent Archives, P4/18/5, Aldington St Martin (bond from Thomas Ayres as assistant overseer, 1825).

[32] ESRO, PAR 361/37/49(1–3), Hastings All Saints, Mr John Lulham's warrants as assistant overseer, 1825–7. See also the exceptionally detailed document in Pratt, *Winchelsea Poor Law*, pp. 339–43.

manager of their workhouse, who in 1822 or 1823 was given an extra £10 a year to be permanent overseer as well (making £40 in all, with workhouse residence). Significantly, Routledge did not collect the rates: elected overseers paid the rate income into a bank account and Routledge could draw down money only to the exact value of bills approved by the vestry.[33] Aside from this, he had 'the whole of the business to transact which attaches to this Office', including visiting the poor at home, granting temporary relief to new applicants, handling all aspects of bastardy cases, inquiring about settlements, answering letters, paying the weekly poor and producing memorandums for the attention of vestry meetings. The tight financial rein restraining Routledge was deemed 'a compleat check', resulting in 'a great saving to the Parish'.[34]

Applicants for posts, in their turn, were compelled to draw up letters of application, which they did very cursorily in places where they were already well known. John Longley's application for the job in Hastings in 1828 comprised a single line, to the effect that 'if it meets your approbation' he would fill the post for one year for £50, but then he was already the surveyor to the town's improvement commissioners.[35] Joseph Jobs, who went for the same post, effected a similar impression of distance, if with more prose, writing in the third person:

> provided they [the vestry] would feel disposed to humour him with that department he will execute the Parochial Duties in the best manner in his power and refers them to his letter on that subject presented at the last election for his qualifications and ability to act.

Neither Longley nor Jobs was appointed, as the post went to the man already in the role. Where an applicant was previously unknown to the vestry, there was reason to be more fulsome in a written application. There was a vacancy for an assistant overseer three times in Wrotham St George in Kent in 1830–3, and one or two letters on each occasion made astute enquiries or offered evidence of candidates' own previous experience and reliability.[36]

A feature of recruitment that was repeated across the country was the expectation that an attentive administrator could be retained for very modest

---

[33] Policy varied between different locations, as parishes came to opposite conclusions about the best deployment of assistant overseers. In Birmingham, early assistants (1782) *only* collected the rates and played no role in distributing money to the poor: Upton, *Birmingham Parish Workhouse*, p. 87.

[34] CAS, PR100StA/97, Penrith St Andrew, Workhouse papers, 1770–1826.

[35] ESRO, DH/B/140/70, Hastings, Application for permission to widen the road, 1825.

[36] Kent Archives, P406/18/16, Wrotham St George, Applications for the post of assistant overseer, 1830–3.

financial inducement. Assistant overseers were not well paid, particularly if they were expected to make parish work their only occupation. The Poor Law Commission reported that salaries usually fell in the range of £20 to £80 per annum, and research on Cumbria, East Sussex and Staffordshire suggests that £80 was at the upper end of payment by provincial parishes.[37] This placed assistant overseers in the same income bracket with watchmen, lower-level government employees and teachers.[38]

The level of remuneration in different parishes was not obviously calibrated by features of the locality or historic expectations about the extent of relieving work. The salaries of paid overseers across all three project counties post-1800 were examined for any remote relationship they might bear to the acreage of the parish, the population as reported in censuses, and typical annual spending on poor relief. No commonalities or correlations were found other than the tendency of the salary to fall somewhere between 1 per cent and 5 per cent of total annual expenditure. There was no regional complexion discernible in the decision to pay assistants generously or otherwise, since higher-spending parishes could be found in all three counties.

Low and inconsistent calculations about salaries made it unsurprising if men like John Routledge (mentioned earlier) combined parish appointments, or that the lauded James Finlinson (in addition to his service as assistant overseer) was surveyor of the highways and governor of the Dalston workhouse. At Tamworth in Staffordshire the accumulation of titles enabled the same man to act as assistant overseer, governor of the workhouse, vestry clerk and police constable of the borough.[39] Such duplication entitled post-holders to claim they were devoting all of their work time to the parish, town or (pre-1834) union while assembling a viable annual income above that of their clients (the labouring poor). Unfortunately, it also opened them up to pressure to accept lower salaries overall: Thomas Baker of Lichfield was persuaded to take a pay cut from £50 per year to £40 when he became governor of the workhouse (which duty came with accommodation).[40]

Possession of multiple roles raises the prospect that assistant overseers

[37] *Report ... into the Administration and Practical Operation of the Poor Laws.* London parishes offered salaries of £100 or above.

[38] J. G. Williamson, 'The structure of pay in Britain, 1710–1911', *Research in Economic History*, vii (1982), 1–54.

[39] *Report ... into the Administration and Practical Operation of the Poor Laws.*

[40] SRO, LD 20/6/9, Lichfield St Mary, Vestry minutes, 7 Apr. 1830. I am indebted to Janet Kisz for this information.

might themselves have employed deputies on still lower salaries that were again unprotected by legal recognition. If tempted to do so, they would have been mimicking their counterparts in government service, albeit lacking the opportunity to offer subordinates promotion or progress on an established career ladder.[41] Were the less appealing aspects of parish, town, borough and county work repeatedly devolved? Such delegation would not be captured in overseers' vouchers, so the 'Small Bills' project provides no proof of this practice, yet the possibility must be acknowledged.

When in post and on task, the men were potentially guided by advice literature such as John Ashdowne's *Churchwardens' and Overseers' Guide and Director*, which was purchased by the parish of Lichfield St Mary.[42] Such guides had been published from the seventeenth century. Burn's *Justice of the Peace, and Parish Officer*, published from 1755, became a standard in the field, but advice needed updating in light of the Sturges Bourne Acts.[43] Steven King has argued that these works offered 'a sort of do-it-yourself version of standardisation' in the absence of uniformity imposed by the state.[44] Assistants were bound to all of the same responsibilities as elected overseers, with the additional reassurance that if the duration of their appointment was unspecified it was presumed to be annual. This therefore conferred a legal settlement in the parish where they worked and, if the parish was wealthy, it might have been an added attraction for employees whose own finances were precarious.[45] Printed guides were generally written by lawyers, who framed them to allow parish officers 'to discharge their multifarious duties with credit and safety' to themselves and their communities.[46] Even so, lacunae abounded: James Bird's *Laws respecting Parish Matters* was updated to cover new provisions for select vestries under 59 Geo III, c 12, but the 1828 edition was still (falsely) emphatic that overseers were not entitled to pay assistants.[47]

Parishes' reactions to their employees' emerging track record were generally

---

[41] J. Brewer, *The Sinews of Power: War, Money and the English State, 1688–1783* (New York, 1989), pp. 69–70, 79.

[42] J. Ashdowne, *Churchwardens' and Overseers' Guide and Director*, 5th edn (London, 1824).

[43] R. Burn, *The Justice of the Peace, and Parish Officer* (London, 1755). Greystoke parish, Cumbria, bought a copy of Burn's manual and kept it in the vestry room to be permanently available for consultation: CAS, PR5/43, Greystoke, Poor account book, 1740–1812, minute of 11 Mar. 1809.

[44] S. King, *Writing the Lives of the English Poor, 1750s–1830s* (Montreal, 2019), p. 130.

[45] J. Steer, *Parish Law: Being a Digest of the Law* (London, 1830), pp. 442–3.

[46] J. Shaw, *The Parochial Lawyer* (London, 1829), p. iii.

[47] J. B. Bird, *The Laws respecting Parish Matters*, 8th edn (London, 1828), pp. 57, 141–52.

at odds with those of the paupers because the latter responded with suspicion and active resentment to 'permanent' overseers 'as the "face" of the dreaded new system'.[48] Salaried overseers provided a tangible fracture point between the 'natural' authority of those in a markedly higher social position and the delegated authority of an employee without any of the visual markers of power. Assistant overseers did not sport badges of office or carry staffs/wands in the manner of beadles. Consequently, animosity between paupers and salaried relieving officers was foreseen, characterized speculatively as 'continual warfare' as early as 1815 and led to instances of physical assault in the early 1820s.[49] There must, of course, have been many assistant overseers who were *not* subjected to threats or injury; yet among the project counties East Sussex provides clear examples. The town of Winchelsea appointed Charles Arnett as assistant overseer and master of the workhouse in 1823, and by 1824 he was in need of legal protection from his fellow townspeople: Richard Edwards had threatened him so that 'he goes in danger of his life'; William Morris (a poor labourer) had abused him and had to be bound over; and in the following year Isaac Hearnden (not a pauper but a parish supplier of miscellaneous goods) had spat in his face. Matters reached a head in November 1825 when a group of five men allegedly threatened to 'kick my arse' and menaced Arnett with other verbal abuse and by throwing stones.[50] Arnett's successor in Winchelsea, David Laurence, seems to have had a less turbulent relationship with the townspeople.[51]

Triggers for such conflicts are easy to find. Assistant overseers became targets for their intrusive scrutiny of household incomes and for withholding relief, since one of the key justifications for employing them was an expectation that costs would be cut.[52] Vestry permission to make enquiries about pauper livelihoods and demeanour seemed to sanction officious and intrusive behaviour. Cultural norms around church attendance or sobriety were enforced, while others, such as keeping animals, might be denied as a condition of relief.[53] Occasionally assistant overseers drastically

---

[48] Shave, *Pauper Policies*, p. 138.

[49] J. S. Duncan, *Collections relative to Systematic Relief of the Poor* (Bath, 1815), p. 163. See Cornwall Archives, QS/1/10/366 and QS/1/10/528, for examples of Cornish assistant overseers being threatened or assaulted in 1822 and 1824.

[50] Pratt, *Winchelsea Poor Law*, pp. 2–5.

[51] Pratt, *Winchelsea Poor Law*, pp. 68, 234–5; see also the threats to murder John Colebrook, assistant overseer of Rogate: West Sussex Record Office, QR/W729, Chichester, Quarter sessions roll, Oct. 1823.

[52] Shave, *Pauper Policies*, pp. 126–7.

[53] Shave, *Pauper Policies*, pp. 128–9.

exceeded their authority and were guilty of interpersonal brutality that patently did not fall within the remit of their job and that fell outside of the law, discriminating between the deserving and the undeserving poor. In Horsham an assistant overseer, in collaboration with other parish officers, forcibly cut a pauper woman's hair and was found guilty of a violent assault (damages of £60 were awarded to the pauper).[54] The vulnerability of poor women was further exploited in the same decade when an assistant overseer at Wilsden Chapel attempted rape.[55]

Sussex and other south-eastern counties came to the fore when assistant overseers were explicitly targeted in the disturbances attributed to Captain Swing.[56] William Cobbett specifically identified assistant overseers in his rousing speeches in Sussex in October, and reprisals against resented assistants in the locality were probably inevitable. In November 1830, for example, the poor of Ringmer called loudly for the removal of permanent overseers, while in Brede the 'flinty-hearted' assistant overseer Thomas Abell was dragged in a cart by women to the edge of the parish as part of more general disorder.[57] A comparison of disturbances listed as 'workhouse riots' by Hobsbawm and Rudé with a search of digitized newspapers for parish staff as targets for 'Swing' yields a minimum of nine incidents menacing specifically *assistant* overseers in November and December 1830, chiefly across Sussex, Kent and Hampshire.[58] Beyond Swing's heartland, aggression directed at assistant overseers came from individuals or small groups with grievances, and fanned out from the Swing counties. Reuben Hill, who was employed by Dursley parish in Gloucestershire, for example, was attacked in May 1831 by John and Henry Smith, who were found guilty of beating him and fined £3. What is more, in line with research by Carl Griffin,

---

[54] *The Standard*, 27 Mar. 1830, p. 4. For hair-cutting as both a matter of institutional hygiene and a strategy for control see A. Withey, *Concerning Beards: Facial Hair, Health and Practice in England, c.1650–1900* (London, 2021), pp. 187–206.

[55] *Examiner*, 16 July 1826, p. 13.

[56] E. Hobsbawm and G. Rudé, *Captain Swing* (London, 1969), p. 104 and *passim*; M. Matthews, *Captain Swing in Sussex and Kent* (Hastings, 2006), pp. 58–61; Markham, *Testimony*, pp. 177–88.

[57] *Cobbett's Weekly Political Register*, 30 Oct. 1830, p. 591, and 13 Nov. 1830, p. 725; Hobsbawm and Rudé, *Captain Swing*, pp. 90, 105; *Bristol Mercury*, 30 Nov. 1830, p. 3; *Standard*, 30 Nov. 1830, p. 3; R. Wells, 'Poor-law reform in the rural south-east: the impact of the "Sturges Bourne Acts" during the agricultural depression, 1815-1835', *Southern History*, xxiii (2001), 52–115.

[58] Eight more incidents specified overseers without identifying them as permanent or assistant overseers; this is without counting workhouse masters as targets or other examples of parish disturbance where staff were not mentioned in the newspapers.

The overseers' assistant: taking a parish salary, 1800–1834

Figure 5.1 Advertisement for an Assistant Overseer, Greystoke, 1835. Cumbria Archive Centre, Carlisle

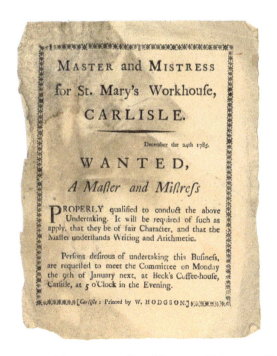

Figure 5.2 Advertisement for a Master and Mistress of St Mary's Workhouse, Carlisle, 1785. Carlisle Library

hostility could outlast the period of Swing: at Dymchurch in Kent the assistant overseer John Goodwin was not safe in 1833, when two labourers had to be bound on recognizance to keep the peace towards him.[59] Cowfold in western Sussex saw violence as late as 1834.[60] Evidently, salaried overseers and their assistants were a focus for parishioners' discontent in a way that elected overseers or a select vestry were not.

Swing made for a volatile denouement to the experiences of the first generation of assistant overseers, officials who were given a somewhat different set of responsibilities under the Poor Law Amendment Act of 1834.[61] The much-vaunted efficiency of assistant overseers emerging from the rural and urban queries in Parliamentary enquiries is problematized by these geographically widespread accounts, but not so much by isolated frauds. Rather, in line with Cobbett's contemporary analysis, the impersonality of a salaried overseer weakened any ties of obligation on both sides: devolved paternalism was short on moral responsibility, and arguably paupers and other parishioners jibbed at compliance with dispassionate relief from salaried hands or responded with greater resentment to a refusal of relief. There may have been further subtleties of response if the assistant had been appointed from within or outside the parish, depending on whether the resident poor were more wary of or antagonistic towards someone already known to them or a stranger.

Who were the aspiring bureaucrats who secured these jobs, jobs that surely proved a mixed blessing both in advance (given the typical scale of remuneration) and often in progress? Letters of application have the potential to provide potted histories of the men who sought employment as an assistant overseer, and the Small Bills counties contain examples of these just after the passage of the New Poor Law. Greystoke in Cumbria recruited an assistant in 1835 and received letters of application from five men, two of whom offered references or a very brief resumé.[62] The advertisement for this post survives in the vouchers (Figure 5.1).

The modest evolution in advertisements for parish posts can be seen in a comparison of the handbill of 1835 to a handbill fifty years earlier (Figure 5.2).[63] The need for writing competency is specifically requested in 1785, if

---

[59] C. J. Griffin, 'Swing, swing redivivus, or something after swing? On the death throes of a protest movement, December 1830–December 1833', *International Review of Social History*, liv (2009), 459–97; Kent Archives, RM/JQr21/56, Romney Marsh, Quarter sessions roll, 1832–3.

[60] West Sussex Archives, QR/W771, Petworth, Quarter sessions roll, 1834, fo. 194.

[61] 4 & 5 Will IV, c 76.

[62] CAS, PR5/53, Greystoke St Andrew, File of vouchers, 1829–35.

[63] CAS, PR5/53, Greystoke St Andrew, File of vouchers, 1829–35; Carlisle Library, Jackson Collection, M174 [no item no.], Carlisle, 1785.

not necessarily demonstrable at the in-person meeting in a coffee house, whereas written 'sealed proposals' are the basis of application in 1835. Anyone in the habit of seeking parochial office, therefore, would have found the layout and format of such advertisements instantly recognizable: position, duties and contact information were joined by an emphasis on 'properly qualified' persons. A further collection of letters for the period of the Old Poor Law, albeit beyond the project counties but one neighbouring Cumbria, is rich in indicative evidence.

The appeal of a salaried post: the unwitting significance of Lamesley, County Durham

On 21 May 1831 the *Newcastle Courant* and other newspapers for the northeast of England carried a job advertisement for an assistant overseer to serve the chapelry of Lamesley, near Gateshead (population 1,910 in the same year).[64] The appointee was expected to conform to some stringent conditions of employment. In exchange for £60 per year, the man must live in the chapelry, follow no other occupation and offer security to the value of £200 against the risk of financial losses in office. Candidates were given notice that an election would be held on 10 June 1831 at 3 p.m.

In advertising widely, Lamesley was merely doing what a number of parishes thought wise: the chances of securing the best candidate were improved if knowledge was circulated beyond the existing residents.[65] What was unusual in this case was the number of responders to the opportunity, and the retention of the letters in the parish collection (when most of the other sources for the history of poor relief in Lamesley do not survive).[66] Thirty-one men replied to the advertisement by writing to the Reverend John Collinson, and the sixty-five pieces of correspondence in the collection include testimonials from multiple supporters and occasional withdrawals from the contest.

The applicants had a variety of occupational backgrounds, fulfilling some of the later assumptions of the Poor Law Commission. Five were either current or former farmers or schoolteachers. A range of additional trades were cited (grocer, draper, ironmonger), as were roles in industrial concerns (including a colliery and a pottery works). More surprising was the

---

[64] *Comparative Account of the Population of Great Britain, 1801, 1811, 1821 and 1831* (Parl. Papers 1831).

[65] Hayton advertised for an assistant overseer in the same year: CAS, PR 102/112/24, Voucher of July 1831. For parishes seeking contractors rather than officials see Shave, *Pauper Policies*, p. 156.

[66] Durham County Record Office (DCRO), EP/LAM 7/174–240, Letters of application for the post of assistant overseer, 1831.

geographical pull of the post. Men wrote from across the north of England (but not from Scotland), including from Westmorland and Liverpool.

The letter writers displayed a varying awareness of the skills they would require and of their preparation for the job. John Elliott, the son of a clergyman, confessed frankly to being 'somewhat unacquainted with the minutia required'.[67] Seven men alluded to familiarity with parish office work, most successfully in the case of William Wren who won the election.[68] Wren lived close by in Ravensworth and had previously served as the overseer of Winlaton in exceptionally challenging circumstances. The removal of a big employer from Winlaton, moreover one that had offered superannuation for former workers, flooded the vestry with requests for relief in 1816 at the same time as the onset of a post-war economic slump. The poor rate quickly rose from 4*s* 6*d* to 16*s* 6*d*: Wren had been the man to navigate these difficulties to the select vestry's 'Intire satisfaction' (quoted from the Winlaton vestry's testimonial rather than a self-assessment from Wren).[69] Even the son of the contractor of the poor in Sunderland, otherwise a strong candidate, could not compete with Wren's track record.[70]

The testimonials sent to accompany applications offered a range of positive adjectives to promote their preferred candidates. The men were described most frequently as either industrious or active, while other popular claims were assurances of honesty and sobriety. A clergyman recommended his own butler, where the latter came with the surprising addition of personal wealth based on rental income from houses in Leeds.[71] A minority of referees were diffident. The perpetual curate of Hartlepool admitted he had 'not much personal intercourse' with the applicant Robert Proctor and offered rather cold comfort to the electors of Lamesley: 'I will not say that a sad series of reverses might not occasionally make him improvident, but not so as to detract from his general worth.'[72] The Reverend Collinson, as the recipient of this mixed postbag, added his own caveat to one letter that Joseph Miller may indeed be sober, honest and industrious, but he could not confirm that he was therefore qualified for office.[73]

---

[67] DCRO, EP/LAM 7/186.

[68] Specific experience in Poor Law roles was also persuasive elsewhere: Upton, *Birmingham Parish Workhouse*, p. 130.

[69] DCRO, EP/LAM 7/238, 240; see also E. MacKenzie, *An Historical, Topographical, and Descriptive View of the County Palatine of Durham* (Newcastle upon Tyne, 1834), i. 195–6.

[70] DCRO, EP/LAM 7/217–18, 220–1, 224, 226.

[71] DCRO, EP/LAM 7/187.

[72] DCRO, EP/LAM 7/185.

[73] DCRO, EP/LAM 7/214.

The letters from the candidates also reveal aspects of the appointing process, involving not only the election but also prior canvassing. Thomas Wilkinson wrote first of all to apply, and then to thank the vestry at Lamesley for their kind reception 'in my canvass through your chapelry'.[74] Another applicant thought it pointless to continue with his application when he would have to canvas as 'a stranger in your neighbourhood', while a third wished his canvas had begun sooner. Jonathan Cooke asked Collinson rather pointedly for assurances that the job had not been promised to a local man before the advertisement (as it had been in Hastings in 1828), behaviour that he considered ungenteel.[75] A canvas for election as an assistant overseer after 1834 was expected, but by that time the guardians themselves were compelled to stand for election. It is clear that the hot contest in Lamesley had not been anticipated by all the applicants, since a sixth of them offered the names of no references and no letters of support, raising the question of how typical this episode was under the Old Poor Law. Was this an unusual one-off scramble for a salary or well-documented testimony to a widely held assumption that parish office was an attractive employment?[76]

The most notable aspect of this collection of letters, however, is the unguarded way in which some of the men and their referees alluded to desperation for employment. That they needed the work was advanced as persuasive rather than avoided as an inhibitor of success. George Pearson gave a summary of his adult career, interrupted by ill health which had forced him to become a teacher 'as an occupation rather than to make a living by it, there being over many schools [in his Westmorland parish] before I began'. His salary had formerly been more than double that advertised by Lamesley, but 'such is the competition for situations and so numerous are applicants' that he had already applied, without success, for posts with the 'best recommendations'.[77] He reluctantly withdrew his candidacy when he realized that his small chance of election as a 'stranger' would not warrant the expense of attending the election.[78] Major Nicholas Bird of the North Shields and Tyneside volunteer force alluded to his 'reduced situation' (one of his referees was the duke of Richmond), whereas John Elliott referred to

---

[74] DCRO, EP/LAM 7/208.

[75] DCRO, EP/LAM 7/182. Joseph Robinson's application was conditional on the situation not having already been bestowed: see DCRO, EP/LAM 7/195.

[76] There was an election for a workhouse governor in Cheltenham (a Gilbert Act institution) in 1828, where candidates advertised election pledges: Ryland-Epton, 'Social policy', p. 181.

[77] DCRO, EP/LAM 7/188.

[78] DCRO, EP/LAM 7/229.

his 'disastrous' economic reverses and family responsibilities (hardly a wise admission when aiming for a position where finances and their application were crucial).[79] Joseph Robinson, a fifty-year-old schoolmaster, withdrew from the contest with the histrionic protest 'situated as I am at present I certainly would have grasped like a drowndling [sic] person at every thread that even shadowed my success'.[80] Referees could adopt a similarly confessional mode in revealing the economic fragility of their candidates, as having known better days or suffering necessitous circumstances.[81]

Yet even employment at Lamesley came at a cost: a relatively modest salary and a prohibition against any simultaneous occupation proved less tempting on closer inspection, particularly among those living at a distance. George Pringle travelled to Lamesley to make enquiries about the post and then wavered when it came to surrendering his existing employment, admitting somewhat naively that 'Mrs Pringle thinks the exchange unprofitable'.[82] John Brown of Sedgefield was more candid: he thought the salary was insufficient 'to allow a Man to appear decent and support a family' and regretted that the money on offer was not more liberal.[83] Perhaps he hoped that such a response would encourage the vestry to offer more, with an underlying warning that, unless they did so, they risked appointing an inappropriate candidate.

The tenor of this correspondence yields three key insights into the situation of would-be assistant overseers in the north-east of England in 1831. First, there was a demand – unmet by other employers – for relatively secure, salaried employment among men of both professional and trading backgrounds. Candidates were seeking the same kind of social safety net that was offered by government service in customs, excise and elsewhere in state bureaucracy.[84] Second, the occupations of the men who were initially attracted by the post were quite diverse and by no means confined to farming or education. Third, a subset of the applicants freely admitted to struggling with their personal finances as an argument in favour of their recruitment. Rebuilding fortunes was a motive for seeking and holding parish office, as it was in the search for even more marginal payment (for bell-ringing, bearing coffins or killing vermin).

---

[79] DCRO, EP/LAM 7/186 and 192.
[80] DCRO, EP/LAM 7/233.
[81] DCRO, EP/LAM 7/191 and 228.
[82] DCRO, EP/LAM 7/223.
[83] DCRO, EP/LAM 7/232.
[84] Brewer, *Sinews of Power*, pp. 66, 79.

Table 5.1 Assistant overseers appointed to selected parishes in Cumbria, Staffordshire and Sussex after 1800[90]

Name	Location	Born	Appointed (annual salary)	Died	Other
Thomas Abell	Sussex, Brede (formerly Ninfield)	c.1777	By 1829–35 (Ninfield 1825–8) (salary not found)	1835	Farmer; victim of rioting 1830; estate worth under £300
Charles Arnett	Sussex, Winchelsea	1791	1823–7 (£15–£20)	1857	Schoolmaster; removed for improper conduct; reappointed by Bexhill
Thomas Baker	Staffordshire, Lichfield	1776	1826 to at least 1830 (£50–£40)	1834	Wheelwright
John Beard	Staffs., Whittington	c.1766	c.1826 (salary not found)	1839	Tailor
Solomon Bevill	Sussex, Hastings St Clements	c.1750	1828–1833 (£50)	1834	Controller of the port of Hastings and/or privateer
Richard Brown	Cumbria, Hayton	c.1776	By 1830 (£16)	[many possible]	Farmer
Thomas Burn	Greystoke, Cumbria	c.1776	By 1821 to at least 1834 (salary not found)	1850	Farmer
William Buttery	Cumbria, Wigton	c.1786	1822 (£12)	1853/4	Shopkeeper in 1841; assistant overseer in 1851
Patrick Cormick	Staffs., Aldridge	c.1762	1815–20 (salary not found)	1827	Farmer
Robert Argles Durrant	Sussex, Ringmer	c.1757	By 1804 to 1823 (£35–£40 from c.1811)	1823	Maltster; the subject of a notice to creditors 1811; assistant overseer to Patcham 1813

John Finch	Sussex, Ringmer	[many possible]	1824–34 (salary not found)	Possibly Uckfield 1850	Also vestry clerk, governor of poor house and surveyor of the highways
James Finlinson	Cumbria, Dalston	c.1786	By 1828–at least 1838 (£25–£30 in 1828)	c. 1847	Also governor of the workhouse, included in salary
Stephen Garnett	Cumbria, Kirkby Lonsdale	c.1763	By 1809 (£10)	1840	Grocer, seedsman and auctioneer
Joseph Lancaster	Cumbria, Wigton	c.1771?	1819 (£8)	[many possible]	Shopkeeper
David Laurence	Sussex, Winchelsea	c.1784	1828–1830s (£10 at first)	1848	Carpenter
William Leek	Staffs., Lichfield	c.1769	By 1834 (salary not found)	1836	Joiner
Samuel Lyon	Staffs., Alrewas	c.1808	By 1833–5 (£30)	1869	Teacher, then clerk to Staffordshire county court
Thomas Martin	Cumbria, Dalston	c.1759	By 1816 to 1820s (£25)	1826	Innkeeper and other pursuits
Thomas Norris	Staffs., Uttoxeter	c.1787	By 1826 to 1830s (£42)	1848	Gentleman; later relieving officer to the Uttoxeter union
Joseph Reynolds	Staffs., Aldridge	1791	1820–2 (£25)	1860	Farmer, beer-house keeper, butcher
Edward Tester	Sussex, East Hoathly	c.1788	1833 (salary not found)	1869	Farmer
John Wannup	Cumbria, Greystoke	1773?	1809 (£3 10s)	1821?	Agent for the duke of Norfolk
John Wetton	Staffs., Colwich	1769	Before 1815 to at least 1834 (salary not found)	1855	Tailor
John Wilson	Cumbria, Brampton	c.1778	By 1816–at least 1830 (salary not found, but tenders invited 1833)	[many possible]	Agricultural labourer in 1851, possibly

Partial biographies for assistant overseers

A broad-brush survey of parish employees throughout England and the snapshot of applicants for a single post in the north-east provide new knowledge about the candidates for a parish salary. Even so, the men remain silhouetted against their parishes or captured in passing rather than being seen in detail as individuals. This is where the methodology of the 'Small Bills' project can shine. The repeated appearance of assistant overseers in vouchers across not just months but years makes them more visible than the neediest pauper and illuminates their administrative practices or financial competencies.

At least twenty-four men from the three project counties were appointed as assistant overseers under the Old Poor Law after 1800, in parishes with surviving vouchers. Concrete evidence of their actions in parish office, plus old-fashioned genealogy, naturally proffer a better-defined impression of their experience throughout life compared to just that at the time of appointment. The biographies that follow are of necessity patchy. They are, however, able to shed light on men's families, working lives and financial fortunes.

The lives of assistant overseers began in the 1750s, when the men destined for office were born. One of the earliest confirmed baptisms was for Robert Argles Durrant who lived at Wellingham in Ringmer all his life.[85] He was the son of William Durrant and his second wife, Rebecca, and had at least three brothers and four sisters who survived to adulthood.[86] A maltster by trade, potentially a very lucrative business but one that was taxed heavily by the government, he married for the second time relatively late in life, aged approximately forty-five, and had a son of the same name.[87] The precise terms of his parish appointment are unknown, yet he seems to have served continuously as one of the two overseers of Ringmer from at least 1804 until his death in 1823.[88] It is not yet clear when he became salaried but his permanence in office significantly predated the permissive statute.

Lifetime residence in one location enabled multiple points of connectivity with his neighbours: it is not surprising that Durrant and his wife witnessed the will of a yeoman farmer in Wellingham in 1806.[89] More

---

[85] I am indebted to John Kay for extensive details of Durrant's genealogy and parish employment.

[86] ESRO, AMS384, Copy admission, surrender and admission, manor of Ringmer, 1784.

[87] See marriage of 27 Mar. 1802 and baptism of 15 Apr. 1805, both Ringmer, at Find my Past <http://www.findmypast.co.uk> [accessed 8 Sept. 2020]. This is the source for all baptisms, marriages and burials cited.

[88] See burial of 29 Dec. 1823, Ringmer.

[89] ESRO, AMS433, Copy of will of Thomas Bannister, proved 15 Sept. 1815.

germane to his experience in post is the evidence of his financial troubles in 1811, and his continued appointment by Ringmer and at least one other parish as an assistant overseer thereafter. Durrant became insolvent and was presumably imprisoned for debt, as newspaper notices to his creditors urged their attendance at the relevant meeting 'in order that Mr Durrant may return to his family'.[91] The accoutrements of his malting business were sold in May 1811 to satisfy his creditors, so Durrant needed salaried employment and seemingly received it in parish office. The parish may first have paid him a salary of £35 in March 1811, which would presumably have been defrayed immediately to support him on leaving prison. Sadly for Ringmer, Durrant was not a scrupulous custodian of parish finances: on his death he was indebted by £217 to the Poor Law funds (a debt his wife vigorously disputed).[92] Ann Durrant was perhaps more reliable with money than her husband, given that she became a 'master' maltster in her own right and seemingly ran the business successfully for over twenty years.[93]

As in the case of Durrant, information about belonging can be interleaved with clues to prosperity (or otherwise) to fill out a man's biography. Patrick Cormick may not have been born in the parish of Aldridge in Staffordshire but he was living there at the time of his marriage to Dorothy Fowell in 1796.[94] The couple had no children – Dorothy, forty-one when they

[90] TNA, HO107, Censuses of 1841 and 1851; General Register Office, Death certificates of 8 Oct. 1848 (Norris) and 20 Apr. 1850 (Burn); CAS, PR 60/118, Brampton, Printed advertisement for meeting to receive proposals for the maintenance of the poor, 1833–4; PR36/119, Wigton, Vestry minute book, 1735–1885, 9 Dec. 1819 and 24 May 1822; PR 102/114/4/1, Hayton, Overseers' vouchers, and SPC 44/2/25–6, Dalston, Overseers' accounts, 1816–36; SRO, D783/2/3/9i, Alrewas, Overseers' printed accounts, year ending 1834; Baptisms of 17 May 1807, 1 May 1808, 4 June 1809, and 22 Aug. 1811 in St Chad, Lichfield; Burials of 6 Feb. 1805 and 21 July 1836 in Lichfield St Chad; Baptisms of 26 June 1822 and 17 Mar. 1824 in Uttoxeter; ESRO, PAR 461/35/2/1, Letter from William Goddard to R. A. Durrant, 1804, and PAR 461/37/4/9, Ringmer, Printed justices' order, 1813; Burial of 1869, Whitton Cemetery, Birmingham; *Carlisle Journal*, 22 Oct. 1803 (for which reference I am grateful to Margaret Dean); *Sussex Weekly Advertiser*, 25 March. 1811, p. 2; Pratt, *Winchelsea Poor Law*, pp. 1–9, 306; W. White, *History, Gazetteer and Directory of Staffordshire* (Sheffield, 1834), p. 629; J. Pigot and Co., *Pigot and Co.'s National Commercial Directory ... Stafford* (1835), p. 391; Taylor, 'Voices in the crowd', p. 110. Wigton had appointed its first assistant overseer before 1800. John Rook was retained in 1792 on an annual salary of £9, which indicates that remuneration in the parish went down over time: T. W. Carrick, *The History of Wigton* (Carlisle, 1949), p. 44.

[91] *Sussex Weekly Advertiser*, 1 Apr. 1811, p. 2.

[92] ESRO, PAR461/31/3/1, Ringmer, Overseers of the poor vouchers to account, 1781–1849.

[93] TNA, HO107, 1841 and 1851 censuses, Ringmer. I am indebted to John Kay for information about Ann Worrall Durrant (née Flinders).

[94] See marriage of 8 July 1796 at Hints St Bartholomew, Staffordshire.

married, was older than Patrick – and they were quite poor.[95] Patrick was listed as a farmer in 1818, but left no will at his death in 1827.[96] Even so, like Durrant, he secured the job before it was sanctioned by statute. His successor in post eventually enjoyed very different marital and financial circumstances from Cormick. Joseph Reynolds (born in Warwickshire) was probably a farmer during his incumbency as assistant overseer in Aldridge from 1820 to 1822.[97] He was a younger man than most of his professional peers, aged just twenty-nine at his first appointment, and remarried as a widower in 1830. He certainly could have counted as having encumbrances after his second marriage, which saw the birth of seven children (including one set of twins). He prospered, became a farmer of fifty acres by 1851 and died in 1860.[98] Samuel Lyon was even younger than Reynolds, and possibly travelled further in terms of social mobility if he did not reach the same heights of prosperity. He was recorded as illegitimate at his baptism, yet became clerk to the Staffordshire county court.[99]

Other assistant overseers defy much identification beyond the vouchers, but the vouchers themselves can be unpacked and (with luck) set alongside additional shreds. John Wilson was an active overseer, whether salaried or not, in the parish of Brampton in Cumberland. Vouchers survive for his work in 1816, when among other things he receipted payment for plants for the workhouse garden.[100] He was subsequently appointed assistant overseer, and in that capacity was prosecuted for embezzlement in 1830, aged fifty-two; he was acquitted on a technicality.[101] It is unfortunate that he cannot be traced decisively in other parish records, given the ubiquity of his first and surnames, but if he is the man who appears in Brampton in the 1851 census (born in approximately the right year) he was a native of Cumberland but in occupational terms merely an agricultural labourer by that point (i.e., in his early seventies).[102]

Thomas Abell, who had been so humiliated by the rioters at Brede in 1830, was not a Sussex man. He was probably born in Leicestershire in 1780 or 1781, and married Grace Phillips at Duffield in Derbyshire in 1801.[103]

[95] For Dorothy's age, see burial of 19 Feb. 1851, Aldridge.
[96] See burial of 18 July 1827, Aldridge.
[97] See baptisms of 1 Mar. 1817 and 25 Dec. 1818, both Aldridge.
[98] TNA, HO107, 1841 and 1851 censuses; IR27/334, Index to death duty registers, 1860.
[99] Baptism of 1 May 1808, Lichfield St Chad; TNA, HO107, Census of 1851.
[100] CAS, PR60/21/13/5, Brampton, Vouchers and papers of overseers of the poor, 1759–1849.
[101] *Newcastle Courant*, 28 Aug. 1830, p. 2.
[102] TNA, HO107, 1851 census.
[103] Possible baptisms of 16 May 1780 at Sutton Cheney or 16 Apr. 1781 at Grimston, both

The couple moved to Thomas's home county of Leicestershire where four daughters were born at Shepshed between 1802 and 1810.[104] The family then recedes from view until Thomas is found working as the overseer of Ninfield in eastern Sussex from 1825, raising the question of whether the family moved specifically to take up parish work, or whether migration came first and the attraction of a parish salary subsequently.[105] Parish policy in Ninfield had long been attentive to setting the poor to work, so even if Abell did not already possess experience of work schemes he was effectually trained in implementing them. The poor of Ninfield workhouse were systematically allocated to different parish landowners and received 'pay' from their allotted employers which was used to offset parish expenditure on the house.[106] Abell obtained the salaried post in Brede in about 1829 and allegedly set the poor to work in punishing and degrading ways. His regime apparently included compelling paupers to drag a cart loaded with wood to a wharf some miles distant, explaining the manner of his rough handling and enforced journey in the same parish cart in late 1830.[107] Abell worked as assistant overseer in Brede until the year of his death, despite his ignominious cart ride and his report to the Poor Law Commission that 'his life would not be safe' if he tried to reduce the relief bill.[108] It may be inferred that he ran some sort of smallholding alongside his parish work, as he was described as a 'yeoman' at the time his estate was administered, but it was a fairly small smallholding as his estate was worth less than £300.[109]

Occupational uncertainty about Abell can be set against occupational complexity for at least two other men. Thomas Martin of Dalston in Cumberland was a man of multiple pursuits, according to the occupational labels he gave himself or that were attributed to him. His will identifies him as an innkeeper, but at the time of his children's baptisms he was variously a cotton manufacturer or joiner, as well as a publican.[110] In the 1810s he became

Leicestershire; marriage of 25 May 1801, Duffield, Derbyshire.

[104] See baptisms of 28 Mar. 1802, 19 May 1805 and 20 July 1810, all Shepshed.

[105] The confidence that the Leicestershire Thomas Abel was also the East Sussex Thomas Abel is based on both being certainly married to a woman called Grace.

[106] ESRO, PAR430/12/1/1, Ninfield, Vestry book, 1821–3; PAR430/31/1/3–4, Ninfield, Pauper ledgers, 1821–7; PAR430/31/3/1–3, Ninfield, Workhouse work books, 1825–7; PAR430/31/7/1, Ninfield, Overseers' notebook, 1828–9.

[107] *Morning Post*, 11 Nov. 1830, p. 4.

[108] *Report … into the Administration and Practical Operation of the Poor Laws*, appendix A, p. 201.

[109] ESRO, PBT1/3/22/222B, Thomas Abell of Brede, yeoman, grant of administration, 1836.

[110] See baptisms of 1 July 1787, 5 July 1789 and 7 Jan. 1802, all in Dalston and all giving different occupations; CAS, PROB/1826/W246, Will of Thomas Martin, innkeeper of Dalston.

assistant overseer, manager of the vagrant office and then workhouse master, but in the published Dalston parish registers he is alleged to have been an amateur architect, credited with building the King's Arms inn, and devising the architectural plans for the first church restoration in 1818. In 1822 he took on all the poor-relief work of the parish, including all disbursements to the poor, for an annual payment of £880.[111] This eclectic paternal activity saw Martin's children placed in professional or otherwise hopeful careers, without yielding the family long-term success. Martin's estate was worth less than £200 when he died in 1826, and his sons died relatively soon after him in the 1830s.[112] In contrast, Charles Arnett (who inspired such a negative response in Winchelsea) was mostly a frustrated educator with a patchy career. He was a schoolmaster near Rye before landing the job of assistant overseer, and after his departure from office (under a cloud) he tried a number of ventures that did not quite succeed. He was briefly an innkeeper at Tenterden in Kent, then ran a carrier service that failed. He removed to France where he tried to establish a school in Calais (which was stymied), became a bookkeeper and temporarily a lace manufacturer before he attempted to open a school for English children in France (which seemed to have operated).[113]

Arnett's experience points up the scope for sequential employments in different sectors, and in most cases it can only be assumed that (owing to the low level of salaries) men had access to other forms of personal or household income to make ends meet at the same time that they were in post as assistant overseers. Alternatively, this diversification (to use a twenty-first-century concept) could be construed as quite astute if it allowed men to avoid reliance on any one income stream. In contrast, for at least seven of the twenty-four men, there was a clear life-cycle aspect to their parish work because they sought or retained the posts after the age of sixty and worked to near their deaths or died in post.[114] William Leek of Lichfield in Staffordshire took on the job aged approximately sixty-five, and died two years later in one of the city workhouses (presumably as the governor

---

[111] J. Wilson (ed.), *The Parish Registers of Dalston Cumberland*, ii, *1679–1812* (Dalston, 1895); *Carlisle Patriot*, 4 July 1818, p. 1.

[112] Wilson, *Monumental Inscriptions*, p. 101.

[113] Pratt, *Winchelsea Poor Law*, pp. xx–xxi.

[114] The only existing shred of evidence to compare with this relates to elected overseers in late 17th-century Aldenham in Hertfordshire, where the majority were under forty years old: W. Newman-Brown, 'The receipt of poor relief and family situation: Aldenham Hertfordshire 1630–90', in *Land, Kinship and Life-Cycle*, ed. R. M. Smith (Cambridge, 1984), pp. 405–422, at pp. 420–2. 'Some' of the Birmingham assistant overseers were said to be old men in 1834, without specific data being given: Upton, *Birmingham Parish Workhouse*, p. 87.

rather than as a pauper).[115] These men were using a reliable parish income to support their declining years. Did the workload permit semi-retirement, or did financial necessity and the narrowing of other work options channel older men into overseer roles?

Among younger, fitter men office-holding and local responsibility could become a habit. William Buttery of Wigton in Cumbria was a home-grown assistant overseer. He was born in the parish in approximately 1786, was appointed to his post in 1822 and proved his worth through long service. He became an assistant overseer after 1834 too and was listed as an assistant overseer in 1851.[116] Similarly, Thomas Norris, assistant overseer of Uttoxeter in Staffordshire under both the Old and the New Poor Law, further demonstrated that personnel could span different administrations. Uttoxeter probably still operated its poor-relief provision under Gilbert's Act (adopted in 1800) and, as Louise Ryland-Epton has argued, there was 'a good deal of continuity in personnel if not in ethos' across former Gilbert regimes into the post-1834 era.[117] Norris is unique in one respect, however, in that he is the only man not also associated with another occupation as well as assistant overseer, despite being approximately thirty-nine years old at the time of his first parish appointment. At the births of his children before 1826 he was identified as a gentleman, and after 1826 as an overseer of the poor (on one occasion as a guardian of the poor, indicating Uttoxeter's continued adherence to Gilbert's Act) or relieving officer until the time of his death.[118] This example takes us further towards a conclusion that could have been reached from the potted biographies of other men, and that is most palpable for Norris: the post of assistant overseer was filled by men whose fortunes were in decline. A salary of whatever level (Norris received £42 per year in 1830, for example) was an assured income for a household anticipating or experiencing fragility.

Conclusion

Bryan Keith-Lucas argued in 1980 that the Acts that permitted the appointment of assistant overseers and the formation of select vestries emerged in part from a desire to take the relief of the poor 'out of the

---

[115] See burial of 21 July 1836 at Lichfield St Chad.

[116] TNA, HO107, 1851 census.

[117] SRO, Q/SB/1800 E/88, Agreement by the inhabitants of Uttoxeter to adopt the provisions of the Act for the Better Relief and Employment of the Poor, 22 Geo III (1800); Ryland-Epton, 'Social policy', p. 251.

[118] See baptisms of 26 June 1822, 17 Mar. 1824, 7 Apr. 1826, 25 Oct. 1828 and 23 Oct. 1830, all Uttoxeter; Steer, *Parish Law*, p. 443.

hands of the poor themselves'.[119] Policy implementation in this respect was undermined by an unforeseen trend among men who secured the work. Assistant overseers under the Old Poor Law were men of small estate whose success in other money-making endeavours was jeopardized by their economic contexts as well as by their own shortcomings. They were typically aged forty or over, married men who understated their encumbrances, with a more complicated employment history than the headline generalizations of the Poor Law Commission could represent. Most importantly, parishes might choose to support men in precarious financial positions rather than avoid placing trust in them. The Parliamentary Poor Law Commission of 1832–4 observed incredulously that one parish had bailed out a shoemaker who was unfortunate in business by making him assistant overseer, and then re-elected him despite the disappearance of the accounts, but gave only three further references in the 8,323 pages of the report alluding to assistant overseers as 'decayed tradesman'.[120] The 'Small Bills' project gives substance to these fleeting allegations: in Ringmer and other parishes covered by the project, appointment to salaried office was effectually welfare by other means.

---

[119] B. Keith-Lucas, *The Unreformed Local Government System* (London, 1980), p. 98.

[120] *Report … into the Administration and Practical Operation of the Poor Laws*, p. 184; appendix A, pp. 68 and 117.

Interlude 5

The parochial career of James Finlinson (1783–1847)

William Bundred

The chapter on Assistant Overseers opened with the decision taken by the parish of Dalston, Cumberland, to memorialize James Finlinson. Over a lifetime dedicated to public service, Finlinson occupied a number of other parochial positions. Spanning the Old and New Poor Law these included workhouse governor, overseer, registrar of Dalston district, manager of roads, guardian of the poor and assistant registrar of the Carlisle union.[1]

The eldest of four children of yeoman James Finlinson of Houghton and Ann (Nancy) Corry, Finlinson was baptised at Bolton, Cumberland, in 1783.[2] He married Elizabeth Pape (1784–1869) in Kingston-upon-Hull. He may also have been the James Finlinson, weaver, recorded in the 1818 militia list for Cumberland.[3]

Notices illustrating Finlinson's activity appeared regularly in Carlisle's newspapers and are recorded in vestry minutes. In 1825, he and his wife were appointed respectively as governor and matron of Dalston workhouse on a salary of £14 and were also provided with a room for a loom.[4] In 1826, a new workhouse was built, and the following year Finlinson was appointed assistant overseer on a salary of £13 and keeper

---

[1] For further details see W. Bundred, 'James Finlinson', The Poor Law (2020) <https://thepoorlaw.org/james-finlinson> [accessed 13 Apr. 2021]. The blog post is made available under a Creative Commons Attribution-NonCommercial 4.0 International License (CC BY-NC 4.0).

[2] CAS, PR158/2, Bolton, Cumberland, All Saints parish register, 1714–90, 2 Mar. 1783.

[3] CAS, Q/MIL/6/2/7, Militia liable books, Cumberland ward, 1814–19.

[4] East Riding Archives and Local Studies Service, PE185/16, Hull St Mary Lowgate, Parish register, 11 May 1809.

of the workhouse for which he was paid £12.[5] In 1838, in his capacity as assistant overseer, Finlinson supported pauper Jane Hall's claim for relief. Unable to work owing to an inflammation of the chest, Hall and her nine-year-old daughter were dependent on parish relief.[6] In the same year, applications to survey and map Dalston were sent to Finlinson, in his capacity as manager of the roads.[7] In 1844, he became embroiled in a case involving a John or George Cairns of Carlisle. Cairns was charged with causing a false entry of a birth to be made by Finlinson in the Dalston parish register and of having obtained money under false pretences. Cairns claimed that his wife had given birth on 6 July at Buckabank. Finlinson registered the birth and gave Cairns two shillings. Joseph Nixon (the relieving officer for Carlisle), Margaret Bell (a midwife) and John Hodgson (a surgeon) all disputed Cairns's story attesting that Jane Cairns had given birth on 23 June and that the child had been registered at St Mary's, Carlisle; relief had also been given at the same time. Cairns, who was in an advanced stage of consumption, was committed for trial for perjury.[8]

Despite a proliferation of parish appointments, no occupation for James Finlinson is stated in the 1841 census. In 1842, he was elected as a poor law guardian, a position he also occupied in 1846.[9] He resigned as overseer in November 1844, only to be reappointed in February 1845. He died in 1847 and is buried in Dalston churchyard.

[5] CAS, SPC44/1/1, Dalton, Vestry minute book, 1825–7.
[6] *Carlisle Patriot*, 19 May 1838, p. 3.
[7] *Carlisle Journal*, 29 Dec. 1838, p. 2.
[8] *Carlisle Journal*, 20 Jul. 1844, p. 3; 10 Aug. 1844, p. 3.
[9] *Carlisle Journal*, 26 Feb 1842, p. 1; 27 Feb. 1846, p. 1.

6. Who cares? Mismanagement, neglect and suffering in the final decades of the Old Poor Laws[1]

Samantha A. Shave

the provision made in this Town for the Poor, does not preserve them from want, or even from nakedness

John Rutter[2]

the public purse of the parish was cruelly withholden

Philip Henvill[3]

Poor Law historians have focused on the 'welfare process' under the Old Poor Law over recent decades, a phrase coined by Lynn Hollen Lees and taken up by Steve Hindle.[4] This work has often focused on the 'obligation and responsibility', as Hindle puts it, negotiated between poor-relief claimants and those vested with powers to administer the Poor Laws.[5] On one side of the negotiation, parish officers such as overseers and assistant overseers, who

---

[1] I would like to thank Peter Collinge, Louise Falcini, Tim Hitchcock, Steven King and especially Tom Akehurst for their insightful suggestions and supportive comments on draft versions of this chapter. This research was generously supported by a research grant from the Marc Fitch Fund, for which I was grateful. Some of the initial research was presented at the Rural History Conference in 2019. The pamphlets can be found in digitized collections unless noted otherwise. The emphasis in the quotes selected are as in the original sources.

[2] J. Rutter, *A Brief Sketch of the State of the Poor, and of the Management of Houses of Industry; recommended to the consideration of the inhabitants of the town of Shaftesbury, and other places* (Shaftesbury, 1819), p. iv.

[3] P. Henvill, *A Brief Statement of Facts; wherein, several instances of unparalleled inhumanity, oppression, cruelty, and neglect, in the treatment of the poor in the parish of Damerham South, in the County of Wilts, are considered and exposed* (Salisbury, 1796), p. 29.

[4] L. H. Lees, *The Solidarities of Strangers: The English Poor Laws and the People, 1700–1948* (Cambridge, 1998), p. 33; S. Hindle, *On the Parish? The Micro-Politics of Poor Relief in Rural England, c.1550–1750* (Oxford, 2004), p. 363.

[5] Hindle, *On the Parish?*, p. 6.

S.A. Shave, 'Who cares? Mismanagement, neglect and suffering in the final decades of the Old Poor Law' in *Providing for the Poor: The Old Poor Law, 1750–1834*, ed. P. Collinge and L. Falcini (London, 2022), pp. 167–193. License: CC BY-NC-ND 4.0.

were regularly providing relief in money and in kind, as well as magistrates, who had a 'supervisory' role in overseeing the relief system and could overturn an overseer's decision, have received the greatest attention in this literature.[6] The concurrent focus on the micro-politics of the parish, the dynamics between those 'who had a stake in the allocation of resources in the local community' and poor relief claimants, has nuanced the dualism of 'entitlement' and 'subordination' of the relief recipient in Poor Law research.[7] Unearthing these negotiations and complications also reveals where the power sat in the distribution of relief, as the chapters in this book attest.[8] As Steven King re-emphasized, relief was 'crucially dependent upon the respective personalities of official and pauper'.[9] Yet, because of the emphasis on how poor relief was managed and negotiated on an everyday basis, the tendency has been to focus on the actions and inactions of those who had official responsibilities to administer and influence poor relief. The interests and roles of the wider community have been overlooked and, as a consequence, undervalued. This chapter aims to shed light on members of the community who were not responsible for the day-to-day provision of poor relief, but whose actions were, nevertheless, important in the administration and quality of poor relief.

Studies focused narrowly on the core relief administrators have led to little direct information about how other people, such as land agents acting

---

[6] P. Slack, *The English Poor Law, 1531–1782* (Cambridge, 1990, repr. 1995), p. 11; for more literature on magistrates see P. Dunkley, 'Paternalism, the magistracy and poor relief in England, 1795–1834', *International Review of Social History*, xxiv (1979), 371–97; P. King, 'The rights of the poor and the role of the law: the impact of pauper appeals to the summary courts, 1750–1834', in *Obligation, Entitlement and Dispute under the English Poor Laws*, ed. P. Jones and S. King (Cambridge, 2015), pp. 235–62; S. Williams, *Poverty, Gender and Life-Cycle under the English Poor Law, 1760–1834* (Woodbridge, 2011), pp. 93–4. Other parish officers included churchwardens, constables and surveyors of the highways.

[7] Hindle, *On the Parish?*, p. 363; for an introduction to the politics of the parish, see K. Wrightson, 'The politics of the parish in early modern England', in *The Experience of Authority in Early Modern England*, ed. P. Griffiths, A. Fox and S. Hindle (Basingstoke, 1996), pp. 10–46. See also D. Eastwood, 'The republic in the village: the parish and poor at Bampton, 1780–1834', *Journal of Regional and Local Studies*, xii (1992), 18–28; S. Hindle, 'Power, poor relief, and social relations in Holland Fen, c.1600–1800', *The Historical Journal*, xli (1998), 67–96; J. Healey, 'The development of poor relief in Lancashire, c.1598–1680', *The Historical Journal*, liii (2010), 551–72.

[8] This is a theme throughout the literature, such as the edited collection by Jones and King, *Obligation, Entitlement and Dispute*, and research on pauper letters, most recently S. King, *Writing the Lives of the English Poor, 1750s–1830s* (Montreal, 2019).

[9] S. King, 'Introduction: Hertfordshire in context', in *Social Welfare in Hertfordshire from 1600: A Caring County?*, ed. S. King and G. Gear (Hatfield, 2013), pp. 1–13, at p. 8.

on behalf of landowners, influenced relief under the Old Poor Law.[10] There are, though, several other overlooked groups in studies of the Old Poor Law, including religious individuals, such as the Anglican clergy, who were not part of the core parish relief administration team but nonetheless oversaw poor relief. As Frances Knight explains, the 'plight of the poor had long been a cause for Christian concern', and bishops and senior clergy were 'closely involved in the remaking of the poor law from an early date'.[11] In early workhouses, they were paid to visit the poor and sick, and more generally to instil religious observance in the institution.[12] Within the vestry, many clergy would act as the vestry chairman or assume the role of a parish officer when administrating charitable and statutory assistance.[13] When the property requirement for justices of the peace was lowered in the mid eighteenth century, John Tomlinson noted, more clergymen started to take up the role of magistrate. Indeed, in England and Wales, this increased from 11 per cent of magistrates in 1760 to just over 25 per cent in the 1830s.[14] It is little wonder, therefore, that approximately 20 per cent of the 'Rural Queries' returned to the 1832 Royal Commission on the Poor Laws were completed with the input of a member of the clergy, demonstrating their knowledge of poor-relief provision on the ground.[15] Nonconformist groups were also significantly engaged in poor relief, including Quakers who formed and managed early workhouses in Bristol and London, and who provided generous amounts of their own independently funded relief to Quaker members.[16]

This chapter seeks to examine how religious parishioners cared about cases of neglect and suffering under the Old Poor Law by examining two

---

[10] S. A. Shave, 'The land agent and the Old Poor Laws: examining the correspondence of William Spencer in Sapcote, Leicestershire', *Agricultural History Review*, lxviii (2020), 190–212, at 196.

[11] F. Knight, *The Nineteenth-Century Church and English Society* (Cambridge, 1995), p. 68.

[12] For a detailed case study see S. C. Tye, 'Religion, the SPCK and the Westminster workhouses: "re-enchanting" the eighteenth-century workhouse' (unpublished Oxford Brookes University PhD thesis, 2014).

[13] A. Warne, *Church and Society in Eighteenth-Century Devon* (Newton Abbot, 1969), p. 148.

[14] J. B. Tomlinson, 'The decline of the clerical magistracy in the nineteenth-century English Midlands', *Studies in Church History*, lvi (2020), 419–33, at 420.

[15] *Report from His Majesty's Commissioners for Inquiring into the Administration and Practical Operation of the Poor Laws* (Parl. Papers 1834 [C. 44]), appendix B.1, *Answers to the Rural Queries in Five Parts*, part 1: 'clergy' on the basis of their given title or job title (including vicar, rector, reverend, minister, curate, sub-curate, minister); my thanks to Courtney Devine for helping me to collect this data.

[16] T. V. Hitchcock, 'The English workhouse: a study of institutional poor relief in selected counties, 1696–1750' (unpublished University of Oxford DPhil thesis, 1985).

pamphlets from two authors living in two different communities with two different Christian denominations. They expose the conditions of parishioners receiving indoor relief, vulnerable individuals who were too unwell, young or infirm to undertake work topped up by outdoor relief. These sources somewhat cloud the view within Poor Law studies that poor relief could always be negotiated and contested by relief claimants and recipients. The first pamphlet, published in 1796, about the treatment of the indoor poor of the agricultural village of South Damerham, situated on the southern boundary of Wiltshire about ten miles from Salisbury, was written by Philip Henvill.[17] Henvill was a curate of South Damerham and the neighbouring parish of Martin, and had lived in South Damerham for about four years. He had then retired at some point, before coming out of retirement to write the pamphlet out of a 'strong sense of duty'.[18] Before arriving in the parish, he had studied at Oxford, held curacies in parishes within southern Hampshire and was ordained in Winchester in 1787.[19] In 1799 he published his sermons which were of interest to evangelical Christians.[20] The second pamphlet, published in 1819, was composed by John Rutter, a Quaker and local printer. A Quaker meeting was formed in his home town of Shaftesbury in Dorset in 1746. During his life he attempted to raise the quality of life of the poor in various ways and wrote on other topics including vagrancy and turnpikes.[21] While serving on a committee to assist the overseers in their 'arduous and important duties', he became 'excited by various cases of misery, and by the numerous instances of deprivations and sufferings'.[22] Together these pamphlets demonstrate that those in receipt of relief were at times severely neglected, and their only route for redress may have been the advocacy of well-meaning supporters.

The chapter has three main themes. First, it examines how these two men reported and explained the mismanagement and neglect of the poor, showing that the authors knew that a minimum standard of relief was not

---

[17] Henvill, *A Brief Statement*.

[18] Henvill, *A Brief Statement*, p. 12; quotation from p. 4.

[19] 'Henville, Philip (1783–1795)', Clergy of the Church of England Database, Person ID: 76902 <https://www.theclergydatabase.org.uk/jsp/persons/CreatePersonFrames.jsp?PersonID=76902> [accessed 4 Jan. 2021], notably listed as a curate for all of these positions; Oxford detail from 'Review of new publications', *The Gentleman's Magazine*, lxix (1799), 1061.

[20] P. Henvill, *Sermons on Practical and Important Subjects, with a preface particularly addressed to candidates for orders and the younger clergy*, i (London, 1799), advertised in supplement to *The Evangelist Magazine*, vii (London, 1799), 562.

[21] J. Stuttard, *The Turbulent Quaker of Shaftesbury: John Rutter (1796–1851)* (Gloucester, 2018), *passim* and publications on pp. 183–4; a discussion of Rutter's *A Brief Sketch* is on pp. 53–9.

[22] Rutter, *A Brief Sketch*, pp. iii–iv.

being provided. The next section outlines the authors' motivations and views of morality, and how they used these to develop critiques of the local relief regime, the parish officers implementing it, and the Old Poor Law system as a whole. These two pamphlets are then used as a lens into the micro-politics of poor relief and care from the authors' perspectives. There was a range of relationships between different groups and individuals within the parish, and these pamphlets expose how these men were combative with parish officers, yet collaborative with many others. The conclusion suggests that, to understand more about the 'welfare process' from both sides of the negotiation, further studies of more cases of neglect and suffering within the Old Poor Law system are needed, as is a greater understanding of the perspectives, actions and care of a wider community. To begin with, some local and national context is necessary, including why the indoor poor in particular received their attention.

Context

It is widely accepted that the economic and social conditions in the final decades of the Old Poor Law led the labouring poor to the vestry door, and ratepayers saw their poor-rate bills escalate. These pamphlets were published during particularly difficult years. There were significant crises when Henvill took his pamphlet to the press in 1796. Indeed, between 1794 and 1796 and between 1799 and 1801 poor harvests, limited agricultural work, higher wheat prices and a deficiency of empathy or intervention by landowners culminated in widespread hunger and food riots.[23] The end of the Napoleonic Wars pushed England into dire straits again, forming the context for Rutter's pamphlet. The rural poor struggled with yet worsening conditions and increasing societal hostility.[24] The £2 million spent on relief in England and Wales in 1783–5 had doubled by 1802–3, and doubled once again to £8 million by 1818. The average annual cost of poor relief, even when accounting for population growth, increased from four shillings per head in 1776 to thirteen shillings in 1818.[25] Both on the arable chalklands of Wiltshire, and the pastures and woodlands of Dorset, agricultural labourers and their families found it increasingly hard to make a living. From the late

---

[23] R. Wells, *Wretched Faces: Famine in Wartime England, 1763–1803* (Gloucester, 1988); more recently C. J. Griffin, *The Politics of Hunger: Protest, Poverty and Policy in England, c.1750–c.1840* (Manchester, 2020).

[24] See examples in C. J. Griffin, *Protest, Politics and Work in Rural England, 1700–1850* (Basingstoke, 2014), p. 62.

[25] B. Harris, *Origins of the British Welfare State: Society, State and Social Welfare in England and Wales, 1800–1945* (Basingstoke, 2004), p. 43.

eighteenth century the under- and unemployment of labourers in southern England was common, and those who had wages did not see them rise with the cost of grain. At the start of the nineteenth century, Wilson writes, 'subsistence living and often actual hunger for the Wiltshire agricultural labourer' were a common experience, and one shared in neighbouring rural Dorset.[26] According to the Dorset magistrate David Okeden Parry Okeden in 1830, labourers in the county were 'unappreciated', 'unrewarded' and 'in cheerless endurance of the present'.[27] The subsistence living experienced by many became increasingly tough as access to common land and piecework for women and children dwindled.[28] As a consequence, poor-relief expenditure was high. In the year 1812–13, Wiltshire spent £1 13s per head of the population relieving the poor, and Dorset 17s, when the average in England was 13s. Although the national rate declined to 10s in 1823–4, in Dorset and Wiltshire it remained slightly higher at 11s and 12s respectively.[29] While this gives us an idea of the amounts of relief given out rather than need per se, it does provide an indication of the extent of poverty in the two counties.

During this time, new relief policies and practices were being discussed, developed, implemented and abandoned at a fast pace on both national and local levels. The 'huge crop of pamphlets' addressing the Old Poor Law at this time were 'mostly written by farmers, ratepayers, and clergymen closely concerned with administration, and eager to have their proposals adopted nationally'.[30] Of course there were other outlets too, including letters, books, pieces in periodicals such as the *Annals of Agriculture*, and reports such as those produced by the Society for Bettering the Condition and Increasing the Comforts of the Poor which was established by prominent evangelical Christians in 1796.[31] The pamphlet literature in particular,

---

[26] A. R. Wilson, *Forgotten Labour: The Wiltshire Agricultural Labourer and his Environment, 4500 BC– AD 1950* (East Knoyle, 2007), p. 189; for more on the southern counties see S. A. Shave, *Pauper Policies: Poor Law Practice in England, 1780–1850* (Manchester, 2017), pp. 6–9.

[27] D. O. P. Okeden, *A Letter to the Members in Parliament, for Dorsetshire, on the Subject of Poor-Relief and Labourers' Wages*, 2nd edn (Blandford, 1830), p. 10, cited in S. A. Shave, 'The dependent poor? (Re)constructing the lives of individuals "on the parish" in rural Dorset, 1800–1832', *Rural History*, xx (2009), 67–97, at 67.

[28] On piecework in Dorset see J. Richards, 'Rethinking the makeshift economy: a case study of three market towns in Dorset on the later decades of the Old Poor Law' (unpublished University of Leicester PhD thesis, 2019).

[29] *Report from the Select Committee on Poor Rate Returns* (Parl. Papers 1824 [C. 420]), p. 11.

[30] K. D. M. Snell, *Annals of the Labouring Poor: Social Change and Agrarian England, 1660–1900* (Cambridge, 1985), p. 110.

[31] J. R. Poynter, *Society and Pauperism: English Ideas on Poor Relief, 1795–1824* (London,

however, has offered historians a rich source for understanding both the energy and nuances of Poor Law debates during years of experimentation and distress.[32] Beatrice and Sidney Webb, who first took note of the importance of pamphlets in Poor Law history, identified four successive waves of pamphlet writing from the mid-eighteenth century to 1834, 'differing one from the other in general context, and each characterised by a particular note of its time'.[33] The first focused on 'the need for superior administration', arguing that parish officials should be superseded or their powers reduced through the use of Poor Law unions, and the second on the establishment and use of humane workhouses that excluded the able-bodied poor. During the period of more intense distress, there was a focus on the rising outdoor relief costs and stress within the outdoor relief system (often blamed on allowances). A final wave from 1815, in general, argued for a more restrictive relief system.[34] In sum, King notes, such writings provided 'alternative practical and ideological models for the treatment of the poor and the administration of relief', although Snell contends that the political economic discourse in some became 'puddles' of text in which the authors 'waded through ... Smithian, Benthamite and Malthusian dogma'.[35]

Given the historiography, using pamphlets to examine local issues of poor-relief mismanagement might therefore be perceived as an unusual choice, as it is often assumed that pamphlets just contain national-level debate. However, a wealth of information about local relief provisions can be found in pamphlets such as those by Henvill and Rutter, whose writings do not seem to fit neatly into the Webbs' waves.[36] They were part of a 'strand of social commentators

1969), p. 91; J. Innes, *Inferior Politics: Social Problems and Social Policies in Eighteenth-Century Britain* (Oxford, 2009), p. 152.

[32] For a concise summary see A. Brundage, *The English Poor Laws, 1700–1930* (Basingstoke, 2002), pp. 37–60.

[33] S. Webb and B. Webb, *English Poor Law History*, i, *The Old Poor Law* (London, 1927), p. 158.

[34] Webb and Webb, *English Poor Law History*, pp. 158–9.

[35] S. King, *Poverty and Welfare in England, 1700–1850: A Regional Perspective* (Manchester, 2000), p. 32; Snell, *Annals of the Labouring Poor*, p. 110; see also Knight, *The Nineteenth-Century Church*, p. 68.

[36] It is possible to find others too, created in urban and as well as rural contexts for this period, e.g., T. Battye, *A Disclosure of Parochial Abuse, Artifice, & Peculation, in the Town of Manchester; which have been the Means of burthening the inhabitants with the present enormous parish rates: with other existing impositions of office, in a variety of facts, exhibiting the cruel and inhuman conduct of the hireling officers of the town, towards the poor* (London, 1796); H. Wake, *Abuse of the Poor-Rate!! A statement of facts, submitted to the candid and unprejudiced by the Rev. Henry Wake, A. M. Rector of Overwallop, Hants; and vicar of Mere, Wilts.*, 2nd edn (Andover, 1818), copy in the Hampshire Record Office, 15M84/Z3/61. Ballads and

and pamphlet writers' identified by Jones and King who, when they learned about deterrent indoor relief regimes, were 'disquiet and soul-searching'.[37] The aim of both Henvill and Rutter was, in the first instance, to expose the problems of the mismanagement of relief in one community and thereby bring the local mismanagement of poor relief into focus. In doing this, the authors did develop some wider points about the nature of the statutory poor-relief system, but these were secondary. A notable difference, though, between the two works relates to the matter of reform. While neither author suggested a comprehensive mode of national reform, Henvill emphasized that the Poor Laws gave parish officers too much power over poor relief provision which, when left unchecked, could lead to disastrous consequences, whereas Rutter argued for the reform of the poor relief system specifically at the local level with the implementation of a new workhouse system in Shaftesbury. This is an important distinction, which will be returned to throughout this chapter.

The lack of contextual historiography about these kinds of Poor Law pamphlets does not distract from the fact that they contain rich details of poor-relief mismanagement, neglect and suffering, and of the micro-politics of relief provision. Of course, the authors tell closely edited stories, which were meant to be read by others and were devised to change the status quo. Indeed, these particular authors sought to influence their local administrators and elites, and how they operated poor relief, and it is important to acknowledge this. It was hoped that parish documents would contextualize these two works, triangulate some of the information they contained (such as relief amounts and frequencies, and parish accommodation details), and reveal how the vestries and their members reacted to the writings. Disappointingly, there are no surviving vestry minutes for either of these two places around the time the pamphlets were published; in South Damerham this was probably a result of the deficient bookkeeping practices which were disclosed by Henvill.[38] Accessible parish surveys might have provided some information too, but they do not feature in either Fredrick Morton Eden's 1797 survey of poverty and poor relief in England and Wales, or in the Royal Commission's 'Rural Queries' of 1832.[39] Some of the minutes of the meetings of the Quakers at Shaftesbury have survived for this period,

---

broadsides also contained details of cruelty: see T. Hitchcock, 'The body in the workhouse: death, burial, and belonging in early eighteenth-century St Giles in the Fields', in *Suffering and Happiness in England, 1550–1850: Narratives and Representations: A Collection to Honour Paul Slack*, ed. M. J. Braddick and J. Innes (Oxford, 2017), pp. 153–73.

[37] P. Jones and S. King, *Pauper Voices, Public Opinion and Workhouse Reform in Mid-Victorian England: Bearing Witness* (Basingstoke, 2020), p. 7.

[38] Henvill, *A Brief Statement*, p. 46.

[39] F. M. Eden, *The State of the Poor* (3 vols, 1797, repr. 2001).

which may provide some information about their independent relief systems but these have been inaccessible during the pandemic.[40] To understand the involvement of individuals such as Henvill and Rutter in the relief of the poor, however, and why they were drawn in particular to highlight the problems with indoor relief we have to look elsewhere.

Christians held a variety of views about poor relief and relief recipients under the Old Poor Law, and it is not possible to summarize them here. Even the Anglican clergy within one county possessed a range of perspectives and approaches.[41] Some were very vocal about the complete abolition of the poor-relief system, most famously the Reverend Joseph Townsend in Wiltshire who advocated for a compulsory contributory insurance scheme.[42] The point for Poor Law historians to engage with, however, is just how keen individuals motivated by Christian values were to intervene in the provision for the poorest. Knight argues that in general, on the ground, many clergy took 'great pains to ensure that relief was administered in the best interests of the beneficiaries'.[43] They reminded parish officers of their responsibilities to provide outdoor relief, for instance, even when they had entered into unions with other parishes to provide a workhouse.[44] George Fox, the principal founder of Quakerism, explicitly encouraged meetings to collect and distribute their own monies for the poor, and membership of the Quakers was introduced in consequence of this (in 1737).[45] Local studies of how this worked in the Midlands provide more detail. Forde, in an exploration of Quakers in Derbyshire, found that 'Friends were as generous as possible' with allocating assistance in their meetings.[46] This generosity was mirrored in Staffordshire where Quaker leaders, Stuart has argued, 'acted as quasi-parish overseers', even offering money from their own pocket to be reimbursed at a later date.[47]

The support of the religious community was also important in individual statutory relief requests. King's recent work on pauper letters, identified correspondence sent by or on behalf of the non-resident poor to vestries,

---

[40] Dorset History Centre (DHC), series NQ1/L and NQ1/J.

[41] R. J. Lee, 'Encountering and managing the poor: rural society and the Anglican clergy in Norfolk, 1815–1914' (unpublished University of Leicester PhD thesis, 2003).

[42] J. Townsend, *A Dissertation on the Poor Laws, by a well-wisher to mankind* (London, 1786).

[43] Knight, *The Nineteenth-Century Church*, p. 68.

[44] Shave, *Pauper Policies*, p. 96.

[45] W. C. Braithwaite, *The Second Period of Quakerism* (London, 1919), pp. 272, 459.

[46] H. Forde, 'Derbyshire Quakers, 1650–1761' (unpublished University of Leicester PhD thesis, 1977), abstract.

[47] D. Stuart, 'The early Quaker movement in Staffordshire, 1651–1743: from open fellowship to closed sect' (unpublished University of Leicester PhD thesis, 2001), p. 274.

demonstrates that relief requests were often the work of multiple people: friends, family and neighbours, as well as the wider community, of that claimant. Figures such as 'teachers, clergymen, military men, and others' would write letters that the relief claimant signed.[48] Strikingly, 36 per cent of all letters penned by advocates 'were written by clergymen of different stripes' which, King argues, highlights the 'continuing link between welfare, advocacy, and religion'.[49] This also fits with a broader point, made by Jones and King, that the poor wanted such advocates because they 'would have expected to have been listened-to by overseers and vestry officials'.[50] After the passage of the New Poor Law, both Anglicans and Quakers acted to help the poor in significant ways. For instance, in Hampshire, the Reverend William Brock gathered evidence about the maltreatment of three young boys in events that culminated in the Droxford–Fareham union scandal of 1837–8.[51] In a similar way to other Christian groups, Quakers visited workhouses and joined boards of guardians.[52] In 1840s Lancashire, Quakers also organized their own form of relief to their membership, in the form of money, beds and bedding, so they could help them avoid entering the deterrent workhouse system in the first place.[53] These 'active bystanders' were challenging and preventing harm.

It is little wonder that, in the swiftly deteriorating conditions of the late eighteenth and early nineteenth centuries, religious people took their pen to the page. As King writes, as well as engaging in the main debates outlined by the Webbs, they could also be 'active in channelling information on alternative models of welfare'.[54] The clergy came up with ways to supply the poor with food at lower cost, and developed indoor relief systems to save the parish money.[55] Across the county they had also devised schemes to feed the poor, often using charitable subscriptions rather than statutory

[48] King, *Writing the Lives*, pp. 34–5.

[49] King, *Writing the Lives*, p. 124.

[50] S. King and P. Jones, 'Testifying for the poor: epistolary advocates and the negotiation of parochial relief in England, 1800–1834', *Journal of Social History*, xlix (2016), 784–807, at 790.

[51] S. A. Shave, '"Great inhumanity": scandal, child punishment and policymaking in the early years of the New Poor Law workhouse system', *Continuity and Change*, xxxiii (2018), 339–63, at 344.

[52] Examples in S. Stanley Holton, *Quaker Women: Personal Life, Memory and Radicalism in the Lives of Women Friends, 1780–1930* (London, 2007), pp. 216, 225.

[53] R. Watson, 'Poverty in north-east Lancashire in 1843: evidence from Quaker charity records', *Local Population Studies*, lv (1995), 28–44.

[54] King, *Poverty and Welfare*, p. 32.

[55] Shave, *Pauper Policies*, pp. 159–65.

relief funds. In 1798 the Reverend Thomas Gisborne described the practice of supplying milk to Staffordshire's poor, and the Reverend Tovey Jolliffe supplied soup throughout the winter and beef at Christmas to the poor of Skelton in Cumberland in 1820.[56] During a period of escalating poor rates, this interest could take an extreme direction: the infamous Reverends J. T. Becher and R. Lowe designed and implemented the harsh and deterrent 'anti-pauper system' in Nottinghamshire which served as inspiration for the New Poor Law.[57] Ideas to restrict poor relief had been present for some time, and many poorhouses or workhouses, even those established under the optional Gilbert's Act (1782) which were supposed to be safe havens for the most vulnerable, developed a more deterrent emphasis.[58] At the same time, parishes were putting the poor to work on roads and requiring them to seek work in return for assistance, as well as restricting relief to stabilize or reduce their poor rates. Sturges Bourne's Acts, passed in 1818 and 1819, permitted the appointment of select vestries and assistant overseers, which both reflected and legitimized harsher treatment of the poor.[59] At the end of the eighteenth century (1793), an Act was passed allowing magistrates to fine overseers and other parish officers for 'Neglect of Duty in their respective offices' after hearing a complaint made on oath.[60] While this may seem like an anomaly given the direction of legislation and practice in this period, it is an obvious indication of growing negligence towards the poor.

It was within this changing policy landscape, and hardening attitudes towards the poor, that Henvill and Rutter wrote their pamphlets. It is perhaps little wonder that they focused on the neglect of indoor relief recipients living in deteriorating housing stock. As John Broad's research has shown, the provision of accommodation for the poor became an important function of vestries during the late eighteenth and early nineteenth centuries. The early Poor Law, including the 1601 Act for the Relief of the Poor and Knatchbull's Act of 1723, 'permitted parish authorities to build or acquire a housing stock

---

[56] Rev. Thomas Gisborne, 'Extract from an account of a mode, adopted in Staffordshire, for supplying the poor with milk', in *The Reports of the Society for Bettering the Condition and Increasing the Comforts of the Poor* (London, 1798), i.129–34; *Carlisle Patriot*, 30 Dec. 1820, p. 3.

[57] D. Marshall, 'The Nottinghamshire reformers and their contribution to the New Poor Law', *The Economic History Review*, xiii (1961), 382–96.

[58] Shave, *Pauper Policies*, pp. 56–110; Shave, 'The land agent'.

[59] S. A. Shave, 'The impact of Sturges Bourne's Poor Law reforms in rural England', *The Historical Journal*, lvi (2013), 399–429, with corrigendum in *The Historical Journal*, lvii (2014), 593.

[60] 33 Geo III, c 55; Henvill himself was aware of a 'case recently determined in the Court of King's Bench' of an overseers' neglect to visit poorhouses: Henvill, *A Brief Statement*, p. 49.

from the poor rate' to provide indoor relief. This sometimes merged with charity accommodation, which, although it was used to generate money for distribution, would sometimes be let to poor individuals and families 'rent free'.[61] During the late eighteenth and early nineteenth centuries, not only was there an increasing rural population, and deepening poverty as time went on, but also rural housing became overcrowded and of poor quality.[62] This impacted on those receiving indoor relief within houses or cottages rather than in the larger purpose-built institutions that were often founded under the workhouse Acts or specially formulated local Acts. Indeed, a dwelling that may have contained just one person in the seventeenth century, Sharpe and McEwan explain, would now house several people, and the level of parish housing stock was 'subject to the decisions of parish officials who might be under pressure to put the money to other uses'.[63]

It is not too unusual to find petitions pleading for more housing in southern England. In the 1820s in Wimborne Minster (Dorset) four members of the select vestry asked the lords of the manors of Kingston Lacy and Wimborne for waste to build cottages for poor parishioners.[64] In the same decade the rector of Cliddesden (Hampshire) led a petition to Lord Portsmouth detailing that 210 poor people were housed in a total of twenty-nine cottages of poor quality, where the typhus fever was raging and causing deaths; a neighbouring parish was similarly overcrowded.[65] As illustrated by these cases, where the majority of land was held by one or few landowners ('close' parish), advocacy on behalf of the labouring poor was an important mechanism for redress.[66]

---

[61] J. Broad, 'Housing the rural poor in southern England, 1650–1850', *Agricultural History Review*, xlviii (2000), 151–70, at 157; for the use of charity and parish funds see J. Broad, 'Parish economies of welfare, 1650–1834', *The Historical Journal*, xlii (1999), 985–1006; for an urban context see A. Tomkins, *The Experience of Urban Poverty, 1723–1782: Parish, Charity and Credit* (Manchester, 2006).

[62] Broad, 'Housing the rural poor'; Broad, 'The parish poor house in the long eighteenth century', in *Accommodating Poverty: The Housing and Living Arrangements of the English Poor*, ed. J. McEwan and P. Sharpe (Basingstoke, 2011), pp. 246–62.

[63] P. Sharpe and J. McEwan, 'Introduction: Accommodating poverty: the housing and living arrangements of the English poor, c.1600–1850', in *Accommodating Poverty*, ed. McEwan and Sharpe, pp. 1–21, at p. 15.

[64] DHC, PE/WM/VE/2/2, Wimborne Minster, Select vestry order book, 31 Dec. 1822.

[65] Hampshire Record Office, 8M62/79, Petition 'To the Trustees of the Estate of the Right Honourable The Earl of Portsmouth' [The Right Honourable Lord Grantley, The Honourable Newton Fellows and John Hanson Esq., signed on behalf of the vestry by Col. Lamb J. Brooks], 1827.

[66] For more on this see B. A. Holderness, '"Open" and "close" parishes in England in the eighteenth and nineteenth centuries', *Agricultural History Review*, xx (1972), 126–39.

These pamphlets demonstrate that the same was true of deficient parish owned or rented properties for the accommodation of the most vulnerable poor, and the neglect caused to the residents. Henvill's South Damerham had a small population (529 inhabitants in 1801) and was under the control of a few individuals, in particular one controlling farmer.[67] The parish was remote. Henvill wrote that the poor 'knew not on whom to look for redress' – there was no Wiltshire magistrate 'within many miles of the parish'.[68] When Rutter wrote this pamphlet, Shaftesbury was a borough formed of St Peter, St James and Holy Trinity parishes, and in 1821 it consisted of 546 inhabited households, and a population of 2,903.[69] Shaftesbury was also under the control of a few people. The town was largely owned by Lord Grosvenor. In 1830 two parliamentary candidates were presented by Grosvenor for the town, but in a step of resistance Rutter and others proposed their own. The returning officer of the election was one of Grosvenor's agents, and concerns about election rigging (certainly a number of votes that could have secured a seat were rejected) led to unrest and property damage.[70]

Reporting and explaining mismanagement, neglect and suffering

Having explored the context of these two pamphlets, attention now turns to the first theme drawn out from their contents: how these two men reported and explained the mismanagement, neglect and suffering they came across in their local communities. Both authors relied on a reportage or exposé style, as if they were bringing something to light for the first time. Henvill's attention was actually drawn to the plight of the indoor poor in South Damerham because of what he had heard about the condition of

---

[67] 'Table of population, 1801–1951', in *The Victoria History of the County of Wiltshire*, iv (London, 1959) <https://www.british-history.ac.uk/vch/wilts/vol4/pp315-361#h3-0028> [accessed 4 Jan. 2021]; this source also confirms that South Damerham was placed in Hampshire from 1894.

[68] Henvill, *A Brief Statement*, pp. 14, 48.

[69] House of Lords, *The Sessional Papers, 1801–1833*, ccxciii (1831), *Returns relating to Parliamentary Representation* (C. 105), no. 16, *Limits, Houses, and Population of Cities, &c. in England and Wales*, p. 147. A Vision of Britain through Time, GB Historical GIS/University of Portsmouth, 'Population Statistics', 'Total Population': Shaftesbury St Peter AP/CP <http://www.visionofbritain.org.uk/unit/10458651/cube/TOT_POP>; Shaftesbury St James CP/AP <http://www.visionofbritain.org.uk/unit/10458535/cube/TOT_POP>; Shaftesbury Holy Trinity CP/AP <http://www.visionofbritain.org.uk/unit/10458389/cube/TOT_POP> [accessed 8 Jan. 2021].

[70] D. Hardiman, 'The turbulent Quaker of Shaftesbury and the riots in the Commons' (22 June 2021), Shaftesbury Gold Hill Museum <https://www.goldhillmuseum.org.uk/the-turbulent-quaker-of-shaftesbury-and-riots-in-the-commons> [accessed 30 July 2021].

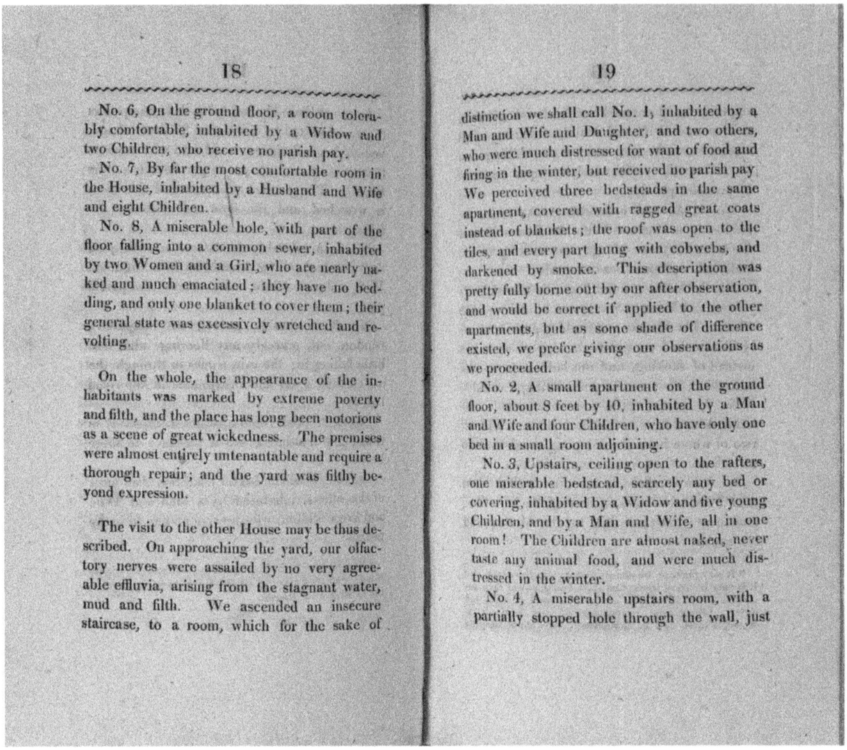

18

No. 6, On the ground floor, a room tolerably comfortable, inhabited by a Widow and two Children, who receive no parish pay.

No. 7, By far the most comfortable room in the House, inhabited by a Husband and Wife and eight Children.

No. 8, A miserable hole, with part of the floor falling into a common sewer, inhabited by two Women and a Girl, who are nearly naked and much emaciated; they have no bedding, and only one blanket to cover them; their general state was excessively wretched and revolting.

On the whole, the appearance of the inhabitants was marked by extreme poverty and filth, and the place has long been notorious as a scene of great wickedness. The premises were almost entirely untenantable and require a thorough repair; and the yard was filthy beyond expression.

The visit to the other House may be thus described. On approaching the yard, our olfactory nerves were assailed by no very agreeable effluvia, arising from the stagnant water, mud and filth. We ascended an insecure staircase, to a room, which for the sake of

19

distinction we shall call No. 1, inhabited by a Man and Wife and Daughter, and two others, who were much distressed for want of food and firing in the winter, but received no parish pay. We perceived three bedsteads in the same apartment, covered with ragged great coats instead of blankets; the roof was open to the tiles, and every part hung with cobwebs, and darkened by smoke. This description was pretty fully borne out by our after observation, and would be correct if applied to the other apartments, but as some shade of difference existed, we prefer giving our observations as we proceeded.

No. 2, A small apartment on the ground floor, about 8 feet by 10, inhabited by a Man and Wife and four Children, who have only one bed in a small room adjoining.

No. 3, Upstairs, ceiling open to the rafters, one miserable bedstead, scarcely any bed or covering, inhabited by a Widow and five young Children, and by a Man and Wife, all in one room! The Children are almost naked, never taste any animal food, and were much distressed in the winter.

No. 4, A miserable upstairs room, with a partially stopped hole through the wall, just

Figure 6.1 John Rutter, *A brief sketch of the state of the poor, and of the management of houses of industry: recommended to the consideration of the inhabitants of...Shaftesbury, and other places.* Shaftesbury, 1819, pp. 18-19.

one parishioner, Elizabeth Haskol. Haskol was '*confined to her room*' and laid upon a hard '*oaken floor*' over several years.[71] The building she resided in had missing internal doors and '*about a yard from her head*' was a large hole where a window would have been.[72] She had not been provided with a bed, sheets or blankets, and as she declined 'reports of her deplorable condition began to be rumoured through-out the parish'.[73] A woman 'sent' to visit Haskol conveyed further details, written up by Henvill in disturbing detail: 'she lay a *perfect skeleton*, her bones being *nearly through her skin*', with few coverings and '*vermin crawled about her, like bees round a hive*'.

[71] Henvill, *A Brief Statement*, p. 16.

[72] Henvill, *A Brief Statement*, p. 23.

[73] Henvill, *A Brief Statement*, p. 17.

When Henvill said he would visit Haskol himself, the woman replied that he could not because "*she has not clothes to cover her nakedness*".[74] Haskol's case was not isolated, however, and Henvill referred to several other people in distress. He heard that Anne Russel, who was pregnant and lived in the same house, was without coverings or other necessary items and was too cold to give birth.[75] He then visited the house with his wife. He exclaimed, 'Good God! What a scene of wretchedness and misery', and described some residents as having 'squalid, emaciated, countenances'.[76] The inspection was not over, though. On their return to the vicarage Elizabeth Marlow asked him to visit her unwell husband, Edward, who had been refused medical relief by the overseer.[77] The man was dying on a bedstead and lying in 'rotten' diarrhoea, in the same space where their children were expected to sleep.[78]

Rutter's style of reporting is different from Henvill's. Instead of descriptions of cases (which he thought would be 'tedious'), Rutter methodically provided notes on his observations of two houses with eight rooms each (Figure 6.1). These were his observations of 'some inhabitants of this Town'; rather thoughtfully, he decided to keep the identities of the inhabitants anonymous.[79]

Both houses were not owned by the parish per se but were rented from 'Parish Funds', and were effectively the only two 'Poor Houses' the town had.[80] Rutter did not visit these houses alone, so these were probably the notes he took while he was part of the committee mentioned earlier.[81] The first poorhouse, he wrote, had 'long been notorious as a scene of great wickedness'. He noted how the inhabitants were 'marked by extreme poverty and filth', while the building needed repairing and the yard cleaning. A pool of 'stagnant water, mud and filth' greeted them in the yard of the second house.[82] Rutter described how each of the buildings had fallen into disrepair and within his methodical lists recorded the sizes of the rooms (often small), using words such as 'wretched' and 'miserable' to describe what he saw. After observations on the second house, he discussed the remedy – a well-managed workhouse. Mirroring the

---

[74] Henvill, *A Brief Statement*, pp. 17–18.

[75] Henvill, *A Brief Statement*, p. 20; Anne Russel's name given on p. 26.

[76] Henvill, *A Brief Statement*, p. 20.

[77] Henvill, *A Brief Statement*, p. 24; Edward Marlow's name given on p. 26. The experience of the Marlows can be contrasted with the wide-ranging medical assistance provided in Darlaston: see Interlude 6 (J. Kisz, 'Abel Rooker (1787–1867), surgeon') after this chapter.

[78] Henvill, *A Brief Statement*, p. 25.

[79] Rutter, *A Brief Sketch*, p. 16.

[80] Rutter, *A Brief Sketch*, p. 17.

[81] Rutter, *A Brief Sketch*, p. 18; he uses the word 'we'.

[82] Rutter, *A Brief Sketch*, p. 18.

views of other reformers of this time, he thought that workhouses would reduce the poor rates and 'remedy the distresses of paupers'.[83]

From both of these descriptions, the authors had ideas about the minimum standards of care that could be expected. Rutter may have emphasized the structural inadequacies of the buildings, but he was clearly excited by the deficient conditions, and the lack of outdoor relief to assist the poor accommodated there. Beds were either not of good quality or of sufficient quantity, and bedclothes and clothing were inadequate. While several family groups received money or some food (primarily potatoes) from the parish, five family groups did not receive any relief in cash or kind (Figure 6.1). By noting its absence, it is clear that he expected them to be receiving something in addition to the shelter. Henvill also thought that parishioners at South Damerham were not receiving the correct standard of assistance, as evinced by his actions. After he was informed of Haskol's situation, Henvill swiftly represented her case to the overseer, requesting that she be cleaned and supplied with bedding by the end of the week. This was, apparently, fulfilled.[84]

Henvill stressed that, while the Poor Law had reinforced a liberal and benevolent spirit among the ratepaying community, there were notable problems in the ways in which the laws were being *implemented*. In his words, the 'most obvious objection, arises not, indeed, from a defect in the laws themselves, as from mal-conduct in the administration of them'.[85] There was clearly a strong sense of the injustice, and in this pamphlet there was an obvious cause. He noted that his wife said 'the Parish-Officers *ought to be dragged there*',[86] and observed that parish officers had a habit of passing the burden of an individual's need around, and that the overseers had not even visited the poorhouse, which he thought was required by law.[87] As a consequence, he claimed that they were avoiding their duty. When parish nurses were allocated to the vulnerable poor, further abuses arose. He thought that Haskol's carer had taken her allowance and eaten her food. Henvill suggested that this was due to the carer's bad character, and to her parish wages being so low, at just 6*d* a week.[88] Each case Henvill added further damaged the reputation of the parish officers. Sarah Gibbs, a widow who was provided with 4*s* per week, experienced frequent threats that such an allowance would be withdrawn '*because she had a house*'. While it was

[83] Rutter, *A Brief Sketch*, p. 40.
[84] Henvill, *A Brief Statement*, p. 18.
[85] Henvill, *A Brief Statement*, p. 6.
[86] Henvill, *A Brief Statement*, p. 22.
[87] Henvill, *A Brief Statement*, pp. 49–50.
[88] Henvill, *A Brief Statement*, pp. 50–2.

common for those in receipt of outdoor relief to give up their possessions, the cottage was her son's, and he had to attend the vestry from some distance to make the ownership clear to them.[89]

Rutter took a different path, but this was in part related to his aim of promoting a scheme for reform. The buildings had only been in this state very recently due to 'general and local causes': 'the want of adequate employment, – the high price of provisions, – the present law of settlement, – the increased depravity both of individuals and families, – *and the moral impossibility of regulation by any other means than a radical change of system*'.[90] Evidently, the economic and socio-legal contexts had exacerbated the condition of the labouring classes. Notably, he wrote that the labouring poor were 'remarkably patient under the prevalence of both general and local pressures', highlighting their endurance in such conditions.[91] Unlike Henvill, Rutter placed less blame on the inability of the parish to adapt their relief provision to meet the needs of parishioners. The 'remedy' for such 'evils', he argued, would be the provision of one well-regulated workhouse. He drew on the example of the Fordingbridge workhouse in Hampshire. The workhouses of Boldre, Hampshire, Sturminster, Dorset and St Martin-in-the-Fields in London also provided further evidence of their effectiveness; Rutter had either visited these, corresponded about them or read about them in publications. The resulting 'House of Industry' scheme was detailed in three succinct sections, focusing on the house and appendages, its internal regulation and management, and the employment of its residents.[92]

Morality and duty

As was the common view within Poor Law debates, the suffering of the poor and their need for poor relief was explicitly linked to their morality. The provision in Shaftesbury, Rutter claimed, 'generally induces habits of indolence and negligence, and frequently affords encouragement to vice of the grossest nature'.[93] Rutter's proposed remedy, to provide a well-managed, industrious institution rather than mere accommodation in rented houses without money, clothing or food, would increase both the 'moral condition and comfort of the Poor' in the community.[94] Indeed, when discussing

---

[89] Henvill, *A Brief Statement*, p. 27.
[90] Rutter, *A Brief Sketch*, pp. 20–1.
[91] Rutter, *A Brief Sketch*, p. 39.
[92] Rutter, *A Brief Sketch*, pp. 26–39.
[93] Rutter, *A Brief Sketch*, p. iv.
[94] Rutter, *A Brief Sketch*, p. v.

the new institution at Fordingbridge, Rutter exclaimed that 'immorality and profligacy daily decreased' and 'the morals of the lower classes were ... materially improved'.[95] This was evidently linked to their religious instruction, with regular attendance at services, prayers every evening, and the policing of language and behaviour, the latter of which was 'inculcated and enforced'.[96] As was the dominant discourse at this time, good morals meant good workers. Rutter noted how the poor women were being sought out as domestic servants after institutionalization.[97] The maladministration of poor relief also reflected negatively on the moral standing of all those involved in the welfare process: overseers, vestrymen and landowners should feel morally responsible for the administration and maladministration of poor relief, including medical assistance. Henvill was more direct in his criticisms than Rutter. Parish administrators were, in his view, 'unworthy of that confidence which the legislature seems to have reposed in them', and parishioners should be given '*what the law entitles him [sic] to expect*'.[98]

This led to thoughts about the operation of the entire poor-relief system. For Henvill, the Poor Laws were still 'undoubtedly good': they were part of the 'spirit of liberality and benevolence'. Foreshadowing Malthus's *Principle of Population*, Henvill noted the rise in population and the price of provisions, which should have resulted in 'revision' to the Poor Law.[99] But he also equated the failures of the Poor Law system with greed, demonstrating some class prejudice. He suggested that the yeomen of the past were different from those of the 'present day', whose lives were full of 'the luxuries, the extravagancies, and the refinements of the age'.[100] The wealthy also lacked interest in the wider community, he suggested, a point which supports the view that old paternalist structures within rural society of this time were breaking down. Rutter had a similar viewpoint, quoting directly from the periodical *Philanthropist*, which he described as 'valuable', to argue that the 'effect of the present system' is to demoralize the poor and oppress those giving relief.[101] Rutter then developed this point by drawing on extracts from a sermon by the Reverend George Richards on the Poor Law.[102] The virtue and peace that the relief system once created was now

---

[95] Rutter, *A Brief Sketch*, p. 24.

[96] Rutter, *A Brief Sketch*, p. 33.

[97] Rutter, *A Brief Sketch*, p. 24.

[98] Henvill, *A Brief Statement*, pp. 6, 56.

[99] Henvill, *A Brief Statement*, pp. 5–6.

[100] Henvill, *A Brief Statement*, p. 6.

[101] Quoted in Rutter, *A Brief Sketch*, p. 8.

[102] Rev. G. Richards, *The Immoral Effects of the Poor Laws Considered, in a sermon preached*

'almost annihilated by the operation of the Poor laws', and societal disorder, dissatisfaction and crime stemmed from the increased provision of poor relief.[103] Notably, Richards's writings had 'conflated criminality and the poor' which, as Philipson tells us, meant such writings were 'often (ill) disguised as attacks on the "undeserving poor"', typically the unemployed labourer.[104]

By extension, the authors believed that the flawed management of poor relief and the low mood of the poor brought the morality *and* the prosperity of the whole country into question. It was often argued that employing the poor in profitable work would reduce the poor rates and 'even [cause] an increase in national wealth'.[105] The Webbs identified the origin of this discourse in the work of Sir Josiah Child and late seventeenth-century philanthropic pamphlets, whence it was 'repeated generation after generation for a century and a half … buoyed up by splendid hopes, moral as well as material'.[106] Rutter followed this same path. Quoting Richards, he believed that 'Industry, the ground work of national prosperity, and of individual happiness has decreased amongst the lower classes'.[107] He asked the reader to pay an interest in the Poor Law, exclaiming that those debating them 'loudly call upon all who feel a love for their country' to help the poor.[108] A similar discourse is present in Henvill's work. He contends that the poor should be an indicator of a 'civilized and humane people', which is 'highly becoming the subjects of a great, powerful, and generous nation'.[109] He compares English poorhouses to homes in Africa, using the racist language of his time: 'That a degree of nastiness should prevail in an English Poor-House, which would be banished from the residence of a Hottentot'.[110] The idea of the civilized nation is then reflected back onto the community: an 'English Village', which for Henvill was a place of peace and rest for 'the honest, and industrious peasant' who 'may find a comfortable asylum in the place which gave him birth'.[111]

---

at the parish church of Bampton, Oxfordshire; on Monday in Whitsun week, 1818, at the Annual Meeting of the Friendly Societies of that place (London, 1818).

[103] Rutter, *A Brief Sketch*, p. 9.

[104] T. Philipson, 'The sick poor and the quest for medical relief in Oxfordshire, ca.1750–1834' (unpublished Oxford Brookes University PhD thesis, 2009), p. 132.

[105] Webb and Webb, *English Poor Law History*, p. 408.

[106] Webb and Webb, *English Poor Law History*, p. 408.

[107] Rutter, *A Brief Sketch*, pp. 8–9.

[108] Rutter, *A Brief Sketch*, p. 11.

[109] Henvill, *A Brief Statement*, p. 56.

[110] Henvill, *A Brief Statement*, p. 17.

[111] Henvill, *A Brief Statement*, pp. 55–6.

Attached to their sense of morality were the authors' feelings and their sense of duty. Rutter was 'excited by various cases of misery, and by the numerous instances of deprivations and sufferings'.[112] Henvill connected his excitement to a belief that the truth had not seen the light of day. He wrote that he did not want to 'exaggerate' details but at the same time he did not need to, as they were 'already too flagrant, and too notorious'.[113] The duty to expose the 'facts' of these cases of neglect was explicit in both accounts; for both men, their interest in the poor was seen as part of their role or duty within society. This is most obvious in Henvill's piece. The epigraph selected for the title page of the pamphlet states '"none [is] so proper as the Priest or Deacon to be an Advocate"' for the poor, that such people were 'none so fit to comfort them' and it was 'his Duty to use his best Endeavours that suitable Provision be made for them'.[114] Inside the pamphlet he mirrors this language: he has acted with 'earnest endeavour' to 'promote the interests of humanity', which is part of his role in discharging his parochial duties.[115] Henvill stressed that 'I came not to Damerham, to be taught my duty, but to *practise it*'.[116] While Henvill regarded his *own* duty as driving the publication, Rutter focused on the wider communal duty, writing 'that any reluctant feelings' we have in relation to the 'publication of such melancholy facts, are entirely removed by our sense of duty'.[117] The communal discourse features elsewhere in the pamphlet – the reforms, he urged, needed the support of all people in the community, not just the wealthy benevolent class, to help 'our suffering neighbours'.[118]

Exploring the morality and duty evident in Henvill's and Rutter's pamphlets has illuminated something about how they considered their role own within the welfare process. Henvill was a moral authority in the parishes he served through his curacy, and Rutter was a prominent vocal individual and business owner. But, in addition to the differences in their methods of reporting and explaining the mismanagement and suffering, this analysis has highlighted their very different motivations. Rutter argued for a workhouse regime, using the cases of suffering as a foundation to his argument for relief reform. Unlike Henvill, he did not seek to help a particular individual in need at that moment. He perceived and wrote about those in parish accommodation in the way

---

[112] Rutter, *A Brief Sketch*, p. iv.
[113] Henvill, *A Brief Statement*, p. 12.
[114] Henvill, *A Brief Statement*, p. 1.
[115] Henvill, *A Brief Statement*, p. 3.
[116] Henvill, *A Brief Statement*, p. 54.
[117] Rutter, *A Brief Sketch*, p. 16.
[118] Rutter, *A Brief Sketch*, p. 40.

many pamphleteers wrote about the poor at this time – as a problematic, homogeneous group that required moral and spiritual reform, which would ultimately benefit the wider community. Suffering was, he thought, to be dealt with through substantial reforms and individuals like him felt it to be their duty to campaign, to be reformers. Henvill showed more care towards the individual – he tried to understand their circumstances and neglect in more depth. His narrative, however, is more patronizing in some respects. He saw himself as an important advocate for morality and duty, and as a truth-teller, for *victims* of the system. Of course, while Henvill did provide us with a few (probably edited) words spoken by the poor, they were both very absorbed in creating a channel for their own views and positions. Each wanted their principles to be practised and reflected in their communities and beyond, at a national level. As such, they served as significant critical voices on parish poor-relief provision, as overseers of the overseers and of other parish officials, by inspecting and questioning the provision and withholding of relief.

Micro-politics

To examine Henvill and Rutter's positions in more detail we now turn to the final theme of the chapter. These pamphlets expose the micro-politics of poor relief from the perspective of the authors. When the involvement of land agents in poor relief is examined, it is apparent that there were moments of harmony as well as of conflict between land agents and parish officers, and also with the workhouse committees they had brought into existence.[119] This section draws out the complex relationships of both pamphleteers and parish officers. Notably, both Henvill and Rutter saw themselves as peripheral to the core group that was able to administer relief under law, the parish officers. That liminal position was ultimately helpful, for it enabled them to highlight the abuse within the system and to engage with other like-minded people, such as magistrates, local reformers and others interested in the welfare of the poor. These individuals provided more evidence of mismanagement, neglect and suffering, helping the authors to seek redress.

Henvill wrote about both moments of cooperation and of conflict between him and the parish officers. The moments of cooperation seem fleeting, and the overseers fell short of his expectations. For instance, Henvill managed to get the overseer to provide more relief for Haskol, and the hole in the wall was resolved.[120] Henvill had expected a new frame and window to be installed rather than light-sapping boards which, he wrote,

---

[119] Shave, 'The land agent'.
[120] Henvill, *A Brief Statement*, pp. 18, 24.

had become 'a Monument of the Brutality of a Damerham Overseer'.[121] He also noted others' frustrations with the overseers in agonizing detail and with immense passion, reflecting his own anger about their conduct. For instance, when Elizabeth Marlow asked the overseer for a doctor to be sent to her husband, Edward, Henvill reported the interactions in full. The overseer said to her that Edward was a '"*a rogue*"' and '"*nothing was the matter with him*"'.[122] Such deliberate meanness was experienced by others. One poor woman, who could not see a way of spending a bad sixpence just granted to her was told by the overseer that 'while *she kept it*, she would always *have money in her pocket!*'[123] Henvill also provided details about the treatment of Sarah Gibbs, who '*could not articulate to be understood*', illustrating the fear and intimidation that such parishioners felt when facing the vestry; apparently, Gibbs died soon after the ordeal.[124] Another widow parishioner noted how the poor would '"*tremble*"' on seeing one person in particular.[125] The frustration of the poor with the overseers of the parish mirrored his own; they not only neglected their roles but also showed signs of maladministration, from the failure to have their accounts settled (i.e. checked by a magistrate) for four to five years to keeping parish records on 'detached pieces of paper'.[126]

Henvill's frustration reached its peak after almost two years of remonstrating with the parish officers. He decided to call a vestry meeting in January 1795, when these severe cases of neglect had come to his attention and when he had noticed an increase in distress among the poor.[127] The overseer did not attend the vestry meeting, and as the parish books were in his possession it was proposed that the meeting be adjourned. If Henvill agreed to the adjournment, a farmer said, they could approach 'Mr. __' for help in providing for the poor, and if the latter did not help the farmer said that he himself would. 'Mr. __' met with Henvill the next morning and 'seemed to be somewhat convinced' of the need to help the poor; Henvill was instructed to find out what they needed, and the gentleman would purchase it. However, in a vestry meeting without Henvill, both the gentleman and farmer decided not to provide

---

[121] Henvill, *A Brief Statement*, p. 24.
[122] Henvill, *A Brief Statement*, p. 25.
[123] Henvill, *A Brief Statement*, p. 47.
[124] Henvill, *A Brief Statement*, p. 27.
[125] Henvill, *A Brief Statement*, p. 47.
[126] Henvill, *A Brief Statement*, pp. 45–6 (quoted from p. 46); the law required accounts to be signed off by a magistrate annually, and this was reinforced in 1743–4 under 17 Geo II, c 38.
[127] Henvill, *A Brief Statement*, p. 31.

anything to the poor.[128] Henvill drew his next card: threatening to inform the magistrate, possibly utilizing the 1793 Act. This resulted in various articles being provided to the poor. Although he eventually achieved what he had set out to do, Henvill then entered into a bitter battle over the timings of vestry meetings. Essentially, he thought that he should now start attending these meetings, but they would have to be held in the afternoons to allow him to take his morning services, which was also required under the 1601 Act. The vestry rejected his requests and continued to meet almost exclusively in the morning. He then warned the parish officers and secured the attention of a magistrate. Their unlawful meetings led to a summons; two were fined and one was excused due to illness.[129] Henvill explained that he was quite willing to drop this prosecution if poor parishioners were to 'be better treated', but it was to no avail. The farmer, who had misled Henvill throughout this period, was also instrumental in ensuring the parish officers ignored this deal.[130] Notably, this farmer had had his eye on Henvill from the start of his post, when he asked him to promise '*not to concern myself with parish matters*', which Henvill had interpreted as referring to 'political disputes', not the allocation of statutory poor relief.[131]

Rutter did not detail his interactions with the core relief administrators or even the committee members with whom he worked to investigate poor relief in the town. By using the term 'fellow Townsmen', he avoided naming individuals or groups. Such 'fellow Townsmen' should become acquainted with the misery he had exposed 'as a means of inducing them to devote a portion of their time, in endeavouring to remove it'.[132] Was he directing this at the parish officers or the wider vestry, at ratepayers or the whole community? It is difficult to know. The term 'fellow Townsmen' may have been used quite deliberately by Rutter; both non-conflictual and non-hierarchal, it could have reflected his Quaker faith. Maladministration was therefore distanced from any one group or person.[133] He did allude to the very divisive politics of the town, arguing that a new purpose-built workhouse would 'in a great measure' solve the 'jarring contentions of party and acrimony of opposite interests'.[134] Rutter placed Shaftesbury's circumstances

---

[128] Henvill, *A Brief Statement*, p. 33.

[129] Henvill, *A Brief Statement*, pp. 34–6.

[130] Henvill, *A Brief Statement*, p. 39.

[131] Henvill, *A Brief Statement*, p. 42.

[132] Rutter, *A Brief Sketch*, p. 16.

[133] For more examples of Rutter's approach to a wide range of social and political issues in Shaftesbury throughout his lifetime see Stuttard, *The Turbulent Quaker*.

[134] Rutter, *A Brief Sketch*, p. 39.

within a wider context: distress 'prevails in many other places, and has in great measure originated from the same causes'.[135] It would be wrong to assume that his trials and tribulations with the parish officer were not as tumultuous as Henvill's. It is likely that there were personal discussions, meetings and letters on this topic, but they were not divulged by Rutter here. Keeping on good terms, of course, was also strategic, as it was more likely to result in his ideas for reform being implemented.

In the micro-politics of relief these men appear separate from the parish officers, but are they separate from the overall vestry? Rutter's position is ambiguous from the source. His generalizing and distant tone could suggest that he was not a vestryman at the time his pamphlet was published, although he did acknowledge being part of a committee to assist the overseers, which may indicate he was, or had been, a vestryman. Nevertheless, with the wording 'townsmen' he assumed that every gentleman of standing was, or should be, concerned about the poor. The tone of Henvill's writing is very different, and what is especially revealing are two sections in his pamphlet that demonstrate clearly how he felt not being part of the vestry. First, in justifying his own 'measures' to seek redress from the magistrates, he questioned whether he had '*quarrelled with the parish*',[136] writing about how 'the parish' had obstructed relief and care toward the poor:

> If they enter into combinations, – have their previous meetings, and preconcert their plans, merely to oppose, and overthrow, whatever proposition I may make for the benefit of the Poor and of the parish, – *is it I* who quarrel *with them?* ... do they not rather "*seek a quarrel against me,*"[137]

So 'the parish' is used to mean the wider parish community, but it also used to describe its representatives – the vestry – a group with which he did not identify. This distancing is notable elsewhere. Reflecting on the writing of the pamphlet, he said that he had removed the names of individuals whom he had challenged: 'The Parties will know *their own portraits*; and the parish cannot mistake them.'[138] The term 'the parish' means the wider parish community here, while 'parties' describes the vestrymen. Henvill saw himself as separate from the vestry, the group that did not include him and moreover sought to exclude him.

These pamphlets also tell us about the relationships these men had with people outside of the vestry. Rutter spoke of how Jesse Upjohn, 'one of our

---

[135] Rutter, *A Brief Sketch*, p. v.
[136] Henvill, *A Brief Statement*, p. 36.
[137] Henvill, *A Brief Statement*, p. 37.
[138] Henvill, *A Brief Statement*, p. 53.

Townsmen', was pivotal to the workhouse at Fordingbridge.[139] His 'meritorious exertions' had improved their workhouse through a system of superintendence, which was supported by 'a Committee of the respectable inhabitants', plus magistrates and 'neighbouring Gentleman', both in spirit and with money. They had 'afforded very material support' to the new workhouse, which enabled it to become a 'success'.[140] The conditions and savings were described in detail, whereby the indoor poor now exhibited 'orderly conduct' and a 'comfortable appearance' (instead of 'insolence and misery') and the poor rates were reduced by a third.[141] While Rutter had examined Upjohn's documents about this workhouse, it is very likely the two men had met to exchange their ideas or Rutter had visited the workhouse in person.[142] The willingness of reformers such as Upjohn to pass on their knowledge and experiences was not unusual at this time, and many such men published their own pamphlets proclaiming to have found a remedy within the bounds of existing legislation.[143]

While Rutter's peripheral status allowed him to engage with poor-relief reformers, Henvill's peripheral status enabled him to engage with other people within the local community regarding the neglect of the indoor poor. An apothecary was finally sent to Edward Marlow after a delay of two days, but it was too late. Marlow was dying of the typhus fever. The apothecary who went with Henvill to the poorhouse exclaimed that in all his time visiting poorhouses he had '"*never seen any thing so bad as this [sic]*"'. Henvill's position enabled him to gather more perspectives on the condition of the indoor poor, which bolstered his own views. When he suggested to the apothecary that he might be asked for evidence to corroborate a testimony, the apothecary said that Marlow's circumstances had left '"*such an impression on his mind*"' and he '"*so often repeated them since*"'.[144] Henvill also recounted the discussions he had with the labourer Richard Cutler and his wife, who resided close to the poorhouse. Concerned about the poor treatment of Haskol in particular, they had given her food, fuel (which was shared throughout the house) and, on one occasion, a haircut to alleviate an extensive lice infestation. While this case of charity and benevolence was much admired by Henvill, it had also further

---

[139] Rutter, *A Brief Sketch*, p. 23.

[140] Rutter, *A Brief Sketch*, pp. 23–4. First quote from p. 23, other quotes from p. 24. There are other examples of this, for instance at the Uttoxeter workhouse, Staffordshire: Derbyshire Record Office, D239/Z/6, Fitzherbert of Tissington Papers, Memorandum Uttoxeter workhouse, 10 May 1782.

[141] Rutter, *A Brief Sketch*, p. 25.

[142] Shave, *Pauper Policies*, p. 155; Shave, 'The land agent', pp. 206–7.

[143] Shave, *Pauper Policies*, pp. 159–65.

[144] Henvill, *A Brief Statement*, p. 26.

evidenced the problems in the parish and given him more confidence in his own judgements.[145]

Conclusion

This chapter set out to explore the interests and roles of members of the wider community which have often been overlooked and undervalued in studies of the welfare process under the Old Poor Law. The two men in this study, Henvill and Rutter, while they did not act as parish officers and at times did not even attend the parish vestry, wanted to bring cases of mismanagement, neglect and suffering to wider attention. They were both advocates of the poor, with strong principles and values, but advocates came in different forms. Rutter was a lobbyist, playing a game of persuasion, being careful not to blame, and therefore possibly alienate, any one person or group. This was possibly a reflection of this Quaker values, but it was also part of his plan to find a solution to what he saw. While his aim was to advocate for the better treatment of the poor, he was also an advocate of reform, and he saw himself as playing a pivotal part in that reform. Henvill, on the other hand, was much more interested in the lives of those who were suffering, and was more antagonistic and confrontational with those in power. His frustration with specific individuals, the parish officers and vestry is obvious throughout his pamphlet. While both men were not parish officers themselves, and therefore did not have the legal responsibilities and powers to give and withhold poor relief, they were important individuals within the welfare process. These were self-informed advocates who investigated and reported on what they observed and experienced. They made sense of this using both local and national contextual knowledge, and protested against it using their knowledge on the Poor Law and their views of what poor relief and care should be. Their investigative and outsider positions also enabled them to befriend others, gathering their testimonies about the indoor poor and their guidance on alternative ways of providing relief.

The lack of parish records means that there is limited evidence about the actual effect these men had on the lives of the poor. From Henvill's pamphlet we learn that he had some immediate successes with individual cases and saw improvements in the general provision of poor relief in the six months prior to its publication.[146] The impact of Rutter's pamphlet is quite unknown. By 1832, Okeden, in his role as assistant commissioner for the Royal Commission, reported that only six to eight workhouses were in operation in Dorset and

---

[145] Henvill, *A Brief Statement*, pp. 28–30.
[146] Henvill, *A Brief Statement*, p. 48.

that use of them as workhouses 'seems almost abandoned'.[147] A new workhouse was unlikely to have been established in Shaftesbury until 1840, when the town hosted a large new union workhouse under the New Poor Law for nineteen parishes. While waiting for it to be built, the board of guardians housed the indoor poor in parish accommodation elsewhere, not in Shaftesbury, providing further evidence that little changed.[148] Of course, to assume that the only function of their efforts was to help the poorest would probably be naive. They may have wanted affirmation and praise and, while we cannot be privy to their conversations, there were reviewers who were willing to offer it.[149] They may have wanted recognition for their efforts and may have elaborated on their observations and experiences to gain a wider readership. This we do not know. Indeed, their publications sold outside their immediate communities: Henvill's was sold in Salisbury, Winchester and London, and Rutter's to 'neighbouring booksellers'.[150] While this was all possible, writing about cases of parish neglect and cruelty may have encouraged others elsewhere to question similar conditions within their own communities.

These pamphlets clearly say more about their authors and their motivations, actions and perspectives than about those whom they were trying to help. Nevertheless, they also provide us with a rare lens on the experiences of the most vulnerable poor under the Old Poor Law, living in substandard accommodation often without additional relief. The indoor poor in these communities were often too unwell to obtain help. They were out of sight, unlike their outdoor counterparts, and so they could be easily ignored by their patrons. The case of South Damerham is striking because there was such a concerted effort to suppress the poor here, which continued for years perhaps because it was so 'close' in terms of power. Here the magistrates were absent, failed to check up on the parish relief system, or to be present and therefore accessible when the poor needed redress. Many of the legal processes within the welfare process were not working as well as we might often assume. Henvill and Rutter were the critical voices of the system when the voices of the poor were stifled or shut away. By exploring more pamphlets of this type, we can understand more about those moments when the poor could not negotiate poor relief or seek redress within the welfare process alone.

---

[147] *Report from His Majesty's Commissioners for Inquiring into the Administration and Practical Operation of the Poor Laws*, (Parl. Papers 1834), [C. 44] appendix A, *Reports from Assistant Commissioners*, part 1, report 3, D.O.P. Okeden, p. 12.

[148] DHC, BG/SY A1/1, Shaftesbury union minute book, 2 Nov. 1835.

[149] Review of Henvill, *A Brief Statement*, in 'Monthly Catalogue', *The Critical Review; or, Annals of Literature; extended and improved by a society of Gentlemen*, xxx (1800), 235.

[150] Title pages of Rutter, *A Brief Sketch*, and Henvill, *A Brief Statement*.

Interlude 6
Abel Rooker (1787–1867), surgeon
Janet Kisz

Abel Rooker was a surgeon in Darlaston, Staffordshire. Like the majority of bills submitted by doctors and surgeons to parish overseers, those submitted by Rooker to the parish of St Lawrence were very detailed, setting out precisely what he had done for his patients. Giving an insight into the level of care that the Old Poor Law system could encompass, a bill from 1816 shows that he passed a seton (to assist in the drainage of fluid) into the neck of John Adams; amputated the thumb of the widow Hubbard's son; opened a large tumour on the side of Richard Nightingale; and reduced the arm of Ann Cotterill's child.[1] The range of treatments Rooker provided for Darlaston's poor can be compared to the care given to Thomas Woolgar in East Hoathly and contrasted with the neglect of the poor discussed in Chapter 6.[2]

The payment of bills from physicians constituted significant outlays for parish overseers. As they tended to be submitted sometime after treatment had been given, their detailed nature suggests that Abel was in the habit of accounting clearly for any expenditure. It was only later (and certainly by 1822) that Rooker was paid by Darlaston under the terms of a half-yearly contract amounting to £7 10s (Figure 6.2).[3]

Rooker came from a distinguished background. His parents were active in a Dissenting congregation and his family participated in the Walsall riots of 1751.[4] His great-grandfather Samuel Rooker (c.1694–1768) was a cooper from West Bromwich and a member of the Dissenting congregation that met at Bank Court in Walsall.

---

[1] SRO, D1149/6/2/1/3/38, 11 Sept. 1816.

[2] See Interlude 1 (J. Irvin, 'Thomas Woolgar, the mystery man') in this volume.

[3] SRO, D1149/6/2/7/5/12, 29 Sept. 1822.

[4] A. P. F. Sell, 'The Walsall riots, the Rooker family and eighteenth century dissent', *Transactions of the Lichfield and South Staffordshire Archaeological Society*, xxv (1985), 50–71.

Abel Rooker (1787–1867), surgeon

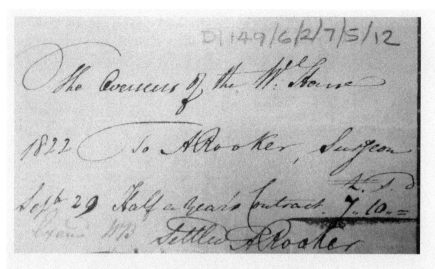

Figure 6.2 Payment to Abel Rooker for half a year's contract, for Darlaston Workhouse, Staffordshire, 1822. Reproduced courtesy of Staffordshire Record Office.

Rooker was born in 1787, the son of James and Mary Rooker, and baptized in the independent chapel in Walsall.[5] He was apprenticed to the surgeon Francis Watkin Weaver, a member of the same Dissenting congregation. Weaver paid apprentice tax for Abel in 1803.[6] Such an apprenticeship would not have been cheap, but it would have opened up opportunities for a professional career that did not require a university degree. Provincial medical schools like Birmingham's did not emerge until the 1820s.

Rooker was married twice, first to Susanna Brevitt and then to Frances Fletcher. He fathered eleven children, retired as a surgeon in 1854 and then moved to Lower Gornal, where his eldest son was the vicar. He died in 1867. Three of Abel's sons became Anglican clergymen during a period when the evangelicalism underpinning Nonconformist communities helped to reshape the Anglican Church.

Rooker was one of several Nonconformists involved in parish relief in the Midlands. The role they played is also evident in Uttoxeter's

[5] TNA, RG/4/2702, Walsall, Bridge Street Chapel (Independent), Births and baptisms, born 18 Oct. 1787, baptised 20 Feb. 1788.

[6] TNA, IR1/71, Country apprentices, 1710–1808, 26 Jan. 1803.

overseers' vouchers relating to Thomas Norris and to the Summerland family, and in the diaries of Congregational missionaries working in Birmingham's back streets used by Chris Upton in his research on the Birmingham parish workhouse.[7]

---

[7] For further details see jmkrolik, 'Abel Rooker, surgeon in Darlaston (1787–1867)' parts 1 and 2 (2021), The Poor Law <https://thepoorlaw.org/abel-rooker-surgeon-in-darlaston-1787-1867-part-1> <https://thepoorlaw.org/abel-rooker-surgeon-in-darlaston-1787-1867-part-2-nonconformist-antecedents>; P. Collinge, 'William Summerland (1765–1834), butcher, Uttoxeter' (2018), The Poor Law <https://thepoorlaw.org/william-summerland-1765-1834-butcher-uttoxeter> [accessed 20 June 2021]. The blog posts are made available under a Creative Commons Attribution-Non Commercial 4.0 International License (CC BY-NC 4.0); C. Upton, *The Birmingham Parish Workhouse, 1730–1840* (Hatfield, 2020).

III. Public histories

7. Public histories and collaborative working

Louise Falcini and Peter Collinge

Engagement with the past can never be the sole preserve of the academic historian. In the twenty-first century the issue of how, and more importantly who and what, we publicly commemorate is a pressing concern.[1] Yet rather less noise has been generated over the histories of marginalized people, those who have hitherto been missing from the public record. Moreover, the question of who should research and write these alternative 'small' lives and flesh out the life stories of paupers, shopkeepers and petty officials, the men and women who were the very essence of our communities, is rarely asked. The 'Small Bills' project was conceived, in part, to rectify this by collaborating with archival volunteers and repositories to research and write biographies of marginal figures, producing short histories of men and women from across the long eighteenth century. The broader starting point for the 'Small Bills' project was cataloguing, transcribing and categorizing the rich detail contained in thousands of overseers' vouchers, held by three partnered county archive services. These ephemeral documents encompass the bills, receipts and accounts passed between local tradesmen and women to the overseers in the process of providing for the poor under the Old Poor Law. The vouchers contain a plethora of information mapping the quotidian lives of the poor, from names and circumstances of the sick and frail to detailed lists of textiles, haberdashery and clothing supplied to the impoverished. By working collaboratively with three county record offices, numerous researcher volunteers and academic historians from two universities, this project has created a dataset containing almost 41,500 items relating to the goods and services provided to the poor, a series of new archival catalogue entries and over 200 short articles and biographies.[2]

---

[1] D. Olusoga, 'As Colston's statue lies forlorn in a lock-up, Bristol is working out what its toppling means', *The Guardian*, 12 July 2020 <http://www.theguardian.com/commentisfree/2020/jul/12/as-colstons-statue-lies-forlorn-in-a-lock-up-bristol-is-working-out-what-its-toppling-means> [accessed 30 Mar. 2021].

[2] The partners in the Arts and Humanities Research Council-funded project are Keele University, the University of Sussex, Cumbria Archive Service, Staffordshire and Stoke on

L. Falcini and P. Collinge, 'Public histories and collaborative working' in *Providing for the Poor: The Old Poor Law, 1750–1834*, ed. P. Collinge and L. Falcini (London, 2022), pp. 199–218. License: CC BY-NC-ND 4.0.

The central focus of this volume is the economics of the parish, much of which can be viewed through the presence or absence overseers' vouchers. But, just as importantly, the 'Small Bills' project has also sought to create a new model of collaborative working across institutional and community boundaries towards a common purpose. This chapter considers those institutions and the research volunteers that have worked as partners, contributing their knowledge, labour and expertise to the project. It examines the landscape of volunteering and the technical infrastructure that made data collection possible. It seeks to demonstrate and reflect on one model of how history can escape the academy and work constructively with new partners.

Historiography

The creation of histories for and by different publics in the 1960s and 1970s marked the beginning of new forms of collaborative history-making. Allied to the growth in local and family history societies, these 'new' methods of creating and writing histories were captured in Raphael Samuel's observation that 'history is not the prerogative of the historian … It is, rather, a social form of knowledge; the work in a given instance, of a thousand different hands'.[3] For very many, Samuel and the History Workshop Movement provided the impetus for this new form of history. As one of the early founders of the History Workshop project, Samuel advocated a model of writing history that is participatory and in which the role of the academic historian is sublimated, giving way to other voices and respecting the sharing of knowledge and expertise.[4] In the decades since Samuel's 'collaborative enterprise', much of 'public history' has incorporated both the methodologies encouraged by the History Workshop Movement and its ethos of 'history from below', as advocated by Samuel and his fellow traveller E. P. Thompson.[5] Over those same decades, however, collaborative public history has also been shaped and reshaped to suit the perspective of very different practitioners with different intellectual agendas.[6] Even now

---

Trent Archive Service and East Sussex Record Office.

[3] Quoted by P. Ashton and H. Kean, 'Introduction: People and their pasts and public history today', in *People and Their Pasts: Public History Today*, ed. P. Ashton and H. Kean (Basingstoke, 2009), pp. 1–20, at p. 1.

[4] J. Kalela, *Making History: Historians and the Uses of the Past* (Basingstoke, 2012), p. 162.

[5] 'About HWO', *History Workshop* (21 June 2010) <https://www.historyworkshop.org.uk/about-us> [accessed 30 Mar. 2021]; E. P. Thompson. 'History from below', *The Times Literary Supplement* (7 April 1966), 279–80.

[6] See B. E. Jensen, 'Usable pasts: comparing approaches to popular and public history', in *People and their Pasts*, ed. Ashton and Kean, pp. 42–56.

there remains a divide among public history practitioners between those who see it as a branch of academic history writing for the general public (building in a central role for the 'professional historian') and those, like Samuel, who saw public history as a collaborative work in progress ideally led 'from below' and from outside the academy.[7] Between these poles, the public historian comes in a wide range of forms and can be found in many quasi-academic roles, including practitioners who interpret collections in museums and galleries, who curate oral histories and who manage local history collections, heritage buildings or monuments. Many draw on their audiences to assist in this task but are 'public history' practitioners by dint of their direct engagement with the public rather than collaboration. Equally important are the many thousands of community, local and family historians and a wider constituency of enthusiastic 'citizen historians'.

The 'Small Bills' project takes the widest possible view of public history, particularly in the processes and methods used in creating collaborative histories. Since the turn of the twenty-first century, participatory projects, shared resources and the ability to reach wider audiences have been transformed by the internet. The advent of Web 2.0, and the participatory or social web, created new spaces for dialogue between the engaged public and heritage institutions. Initially used for creating communities of enthusiasts, this was very quickly turned to practical use, producing collaborative projects of extraordinary breadth. In 2006 Jeff Howe coined the term 'crowdsourcing'. The expression, which had grown out of technical and commercial requirements, was very quickly adopted by numerous projects.[8] Many of those early projects have matured with the likes of Wikipedia and the 'citizen science' project Zooniverse.[9] These online projects typically engaged hundreds of participants in mutual tasks, including transcribing, describing, tagging and geolocating resources. There have been several attempts at creating broadly defined typologies for these projects, ranging from identifying the types of tasks carried out to areas of application and outcomes.[10] Jason Heppler and

---

[7] D. Dymond, 'Does local history have a split personality?', in *New Directions in Local History since Hoskins*, ed. C. Dyer, A. Hopper, E. Lord and N. Tringham (Hatfield, 2011), pp. 13–28.

[8] J. Howe, 'The rise of crowdsourcing', *Wired Magazine*, June 2006 <http://www.wired.com/wired/archive/14.06/crowds_pr.html> [accessed 20 Mar. 2006].

[9] H. Riesch and C. Potter, 'Citizen science as seen by scientists: methodological, epistemological and ethical dimensions', *Public Understanding of Science*, xxiii (2014), 107–20, doi: 10.1177/0963662513497324.

[10] E. Estellés-Arolas and F. González-Ladrón-de-Guevara, 'Towards an integrated crowdsourcing definition', *Journal of Information Science*, xxxviii (2012), 189–200, doi: 10.1177/0165551512437638.

Gabriel Wolfenstein note how crowdsourcing 'fosters engagement with new publics, and … opens up data sets and skills that were formerly difficult, if not impossible, to access'.[11] This was very much the philosophy behind the 'Small Bills' project, though the model of crowdsourcing adopted was, by choice, smaller and more directly engaging. It is sometimes referred to as socially engaged crowdsourcing or 'community sourcing'.[12] This version uses the affordances of the internet to collect data, but small groups also meet and work together, directly sharing knowledge and expertise rather than working remotely, where the shared experience is diminished. This work can also be referred to as 'participatory transcription' or transcription plus.[13] In the case of the 'Small Bills' project, participants both engaged in transcription and were required to seek out selective elements of data, to categorize items in some fields and to add geolocations if they were able. The 'Small Bills' project has chosen to refer to this element of the project as crowdsourcing, since it reflects a wider range of tasks undertaken by the archival research volunteers. It is with those same research volunteers that we begin this examination of the volunteering landscape.

Research volunteers

Collaborative heritage projects are not new. Family and local historians have a long track record of working with their local archive or museum on projects of mutual interest.[14] The digital shift, however, has increased the involvement of academic historians in large-scale projects. Working together with archive professionals and volunteer researchers, this recent phenomenon is beginning to identify new modes of working and blended methodologies in the production of collaborative public histories. For some repositories these technologies represent a continuation of manual projects begun in an age of card indexes, hand sorting and the calendaring of documents. The affordances of new technologies, however, have changed many of these collaborations, moving from automated indexing to digital surrogates and online participation within a handful of years. In parallel,

[11] J. A. Heppler and G. K. Wolfenstein, 'Crowdsourcing digital public history', *The American Historian* <https://tah.oah.org/content/crowdsourcing-digital-public-history> [accessed 26 Aug. 2020].

[12] Heppler and Wolfenstein, 'Crowdsourcing digital public history'.

[13] S. Ahmed, 'Engaging curation: a look at the literature on participatory archival transcription', in *Participatory Archives: Theory and Practice*, ed. E. Benoit III and A. Eveleigh (London, 2019), pp. 73–83.

[14] M. Ridge, 'The contributions of family and local historians to British History Online', in *Participatory Heritage*, ed. H. Roued-Cunliffe and A. Copeland (London, 2017), pp. 57–66.

there has been a shift in cultures of volunteering; the rise in popularity of family history has brought new audiences to the archive. In addition, an increase in leisure time, particularly among the newly retired, has provided a rich source of enthusiastic participants. Archival institutions were encouraged to participate actively in these changes by establishing or rejuvenating volunteering groups, often supported by the availability of small community project grants. This engagement was boosted from 1994 by the appearance of the Big Lottery Fund (now the National Lottery Community Fund), with significant funds made available for collaborative projects. In response, the archival profession began to acknowledge the significant shift in their relationship with the wider community. Stakeholders' views were actively sought through volunteer and user bodies, and systems to capture this information were required by the new national accreditation system. The role played by archival volunteers and policies in supporting and directing this work is now recognized as a means of enhancing 'competent professional performance'.[15] While archive professionals built relationships with volunteer groups over many years, it is only recently that universities have actively pursued partnerships with volunteer researchers. Much of this has been driven by the research agendas set by the Research Excellence Framework (REF) mandating impact and engagement as a metric for measuring research performance.[16] By building on initial contacts with archives and forging new partnerships, academic historians and archival repositories have found common ground on which to develop project-based relationships.[17] The AHRC project 'Small Bills and Petty Finance: Co-creating the History of the Old Poor Law' was built on one such relationship and developed over the following two years.

In 2015 Alannah Tomkins of Keele University approached Staffordshire Record Office about a small-scale project, using volunteer researchers to calendar and catalogue overseers' vouchers held in their parish collections.

---

[15] The National Archives, *Archive Service Accreditation Standard* (London, June 2018), p. 6. <https://www.nationalarchives.gov.uk/documents/archives/archive-service-accreditation-standard-june-2018.pdf> [accessed 6 Jan. 2021].

[16] L. King and G. Rivett. 'Engaging people in making history: impact, public engagement and the world beyond the campus', *History Workshop Journal*, lxxx (2015), 218–33, doi: 10.1093/hwj/dbv015; B. R. Martin, 'The Research Excellence Framework and the "impact agenda": are we creating a Frankenstein monster?', *Research Evaluation*, xx (2011), 247–54, doi: 10.3152/095820211X13118583635693.

[17] One of these early projects was coordinated by Nigel Goose at the University of Hertfordshire in the 1990s. Goose collaborated with local family history societies to transcribe and index the 1851 Hertfordshire census returns: N. Goose, *Population, Economy and Family Structure in Hertfordshire in 1851*, i, *Berkhamsted Region* (Hatfield, 1996).

Staffordshire Record Office had a strong track record of volunteer projects and previous academic partnerships, which made it an ideal archival partner. Matthew Blake, Staffordshire's participation and engagement officer, proved invaluable, hosting a pilot project and embedding it in their regular calendar of volunteer work. This allowed academic partners to gauge the viability of a larger, more focused project, and the archive to identify some of the potential benefits of a larger-scale undertaking. By carefully positioning itself at the intersection of family and academic histories, the 'Small Bills' project sought to encourage its research partners to share their knowledge and expertise in forms of co-creation and the collective production of resources. The project was formed of two collaborative elements. The first catalogued, categorized and collected data from the overseers' vouchers. These often flimsy slips of paper were the bills, receipts and accounts generated in the process of providing for the sick and the impoverished under the Old Poor Law. Then, using the vouchers as a starting point, volunteers were invited to research and write biographies of those mentioned in these ephemeral sources. The research methodologies selected by the 'Small Bills' team reflected their preference for close engagement in their participatory practice, while their use of digital technologies allowed for some flexibility around this method of working. But the notion of a large-scale crowdsourced project, with multiple passes over data, mediated by an algorithm or dedicated editors was precluded in favour of a project committed to small-group research.[18] Research volunteers were encouraged to join weekly sessions, in the hope that they would create new communities of researchers who were invested in their collective contributions. Trevor Owens noted that the 'true value of crowdsourcing lies not in the work product per se ... but in the process of engaging audiences in the mission of the museum, library archive or research initiative'.[19] This process has created the high-quality transcriptions that the project sought, together with a uniform categorization of the data. These have been achieved largely through group interactions and discussions involving the contextualization of material. The research volunteers were very much embedded in those discussions of locality, meaning and significance, and, as Sarah Lloyd and Julie Moore suggested, they have been 'closing the distance between popular stories and formal knowledge', using 'new distinctions, language and hierarchies'.[20] Research volunteers often

---

[18] Various formats for crowdsourcing are discussed by Heppler and Wolfenstein, 'Crowdsourcing digital public history'.

[19] N. Proctor, 'Crowdsourcing – an introduction: from public goods to public good', *Curator: The Museum Journal*, lvi (2013), 105–6, doi: 10.1111/cura.12010.

[20] S. Lloyd and J. Moore. 'Sedimented histories: connections, collaborations and co-

bring these nuances to life, which might be as simple as asking 'Was benefit fraud the same as pauper agency?' In the process of this mutual work, the project created opportunities for the research volunteers to learn about the historic contexts of the vouchers, to share local knowledge and, if they chose, to develop new competencies in archival research and life writing. These small, intimate research groups are far from the largely anonymous crowds that participate in some of the enormous science-based projects. They are, however, more typical of a heritage-sector crowdsourced project.[21]

At the start of the 'Small Bills' project, initial objectives included consolidating the archival research group at Staffordshire Record Office and establishing a dedicated group of volunteers at each of its other two partner archives. This was facilitated by developing a project pack, beginning with a description of the volunteering role. The advertising was targeted at those with an interest in family, local or social history by promoting the project on council and archive websites, in history society newsletters and in the local press. In retrospect, more specific advertising, better targeted taster sessions and reaching out to other community groups might have increased the diversity of the research volunteers. Further collaborative work with a member of staff responsible for archive outreach or other partner organization is essential in identifying new and more inclusive strategies to offer research volunteering to wider audiences. The three research groups turned out to be quite distinctive and developed slightly different methods of working, largely based on their previous experience. Most were drawn from local or family history societies, although much less so for the East Sussex cohort; all identified an interest in social or local history.

After an initial repository induction, management of the volunteer groups was devolved to the 'Small Bills' project staff. This was done, in part, by earning the trust of each repository, with regular visits and ongoing support for volunteers. Staffordshire Record Office identified the importance of this element when they observed that 'What this [project] does better than others is the commitment from [the Keele University academics] in terms of the time they spend with the volunteers; more or less every week one of them will be there. It is not just a means to get funding but a genuine commitment.'[22] The crowdsourcing elements of the project

---

production in regional history', *History Workshop Journal*, lxxx (2015), 234–48, at 235, doi: 10.1093/hwj/dbv017.

[21] T. Owens. 'The crowd and the library', Trevor Owens: User Centred Digital Memory (blog), 20 May 2012 <http://www.trevorowens.org/2012/05/the-crowd-and-the-library> [accessed 21 Jan. 2021].

[22] *The Small Bills Project: Qualitative Evaluation Report* (Coventry, 2020), p. 13.

enabled the groups to bond in a common purpose. Volunteers noted the 'camaraderie' and mutual assistance in the research groups, and particularly the input from academic staff. A sense of community curiosity began to form as bills for burials and medical treatment for familiar individuals emerged, matched by a sense of foreboding when a pauper inventory was spotted or hilarity when another receipt for drinks at the vestry appeared. These relationships were cemented by self-organized trips by the research volunteers. For instance, the East Sussex volunteers planned a field trip to a specific parish, negotiating a visit to a private home that had formerly been the location of the village shop and home of the overseer of the poor. The project responded to this growing intellectual curiosity by providing specialized workshops and other training to give this new information a broad historical context. Volunteers were able to share their own specialist knowledge in these sessions and independent research was encouraged by academic staff. Many of the volunteers reported that intellectual stimulation was a key part of their motivation for joining the project; keeping the mind active in retirement or during periods of unemployment was a valuable and even enjoyable element of volunteering. In Cumbria academic and volunteer input combined to take the 'Small Bills' project into a primary school to run workshops on poverty and the Old Poor Law.

The move by volunteers from data capture to researching and writing biographies marked a subtle but important change in their role. Volunteers now became users of the data rather than contributors. Their biographies took hitherto separate pieces of data and wove them into cohesive narratives, bringing together their local knowledge and research expertise in a single life story. This was a new and different form of knowledge production. Each volunteer chose and wrote on subjects and people that they found personally appealing or that reflected their own research and interests. The only proviso was that they use the vouchers as a starting point. Volunteers were encouraged to share these short pieces of research with the group and later, more widely as a blog post, several of which appear as interludes in this volume. Through these processes, volunteers were able to upskill, improving their research and writing. New skill sets and information on the historic background to the Poor Law accrued during the data-gathering phase that enabled the volunteers to think more critically about how and what they wrote. Making connections and finding new perspectives was a satisfying element of these new research skills, such as when one volunteer noted that the 'material represents a national system of which there is a "textbook" version and then the concrete reality – we're looking at the latter.

It's about people's lives.'[23] Dialogue with academic and archival practitioners provided a sounding board for these nascent skills, supporting a variety of new writing on those 'small' lives of our rural villages and growing towns.

Like most volunteer projects in 2020–1, work was curtailed by the COVID-19 virus. Although some online transcription was possible, the collegiate aspects of the project were severely hampered. As one volunteer commented, physically holding the vouchers, feeling the texture of the paper and seeing the names, handwriting and watermarks made the people seem more real. A series of proposed events in each of the counties had to be postponed. Nonetheless, support for volunteer groups has continued online. Legacy planning has allowed elements of the project to continue, while the emphasis of some volunteering will shift to more self-sustaining projects. The practical journey towards forming effective partnerships is not necessarily an easy one, and valuing and including the research volunteers' voices in that process is an important element of new collaborative arrangements.

Technical infrastructure and data collection

The broad parameters of the 'Small Bills' project were set well before there was any detailed consideration of the data collection and management. Those parameters determined much of the subsequent landscape for developing a bespoke system for data entry and largely precluded integrating a well-established platform.[24] Capturing and managing the data generated by our volunteer collaboration was fundamental to the success of the project, and dominated the early stages of its development. The initial pilot project at Staffordshire Record Office established the feasibility of research volunteers collecting small-scale data from the overseers' vouchers. This worked well for the small group concerned, providing significant numbers of archival catalogue entries. The data collection, however, was initially limited. Data were entered in separate spreadsheets with between eight and ten columns, using a proprietary spreadsheet package. However, data entry standards varied over time and between volunteers. As the project expanded following the award of AHRC funding, a set of clearly articulated outcomes called for a reassessment of data collection methodologies. It soon became clear that research volunteers would struggle to record data in a consistent way, reflecting the full content of the vouchers. In addition, the difficulties of record transfer and management across disparate systems,

---

[23] Cumbria volunteer in *Small Bills Project: Report*, p. 10.

[24] S. Dunn and M. Hedges, 'Crowd-sourcing as a component of humanities research infrastructures', *International Journal of Humanities and Arts Computing*, vii (2013), 147–69, doi: 10.3366/ijhac.2013.0086.

together with a secure method of aggregating the data and regular back-up, proved challenging. In response, a data entry portal was created to ensure consistency in data collection, and to facilitate data management. The new data model included a number of different formats from transcription to data classification and the addition of geolocations. Direct data capture through this online portal solved many of the initial issues, particularly those of data transfer and management; it also removed the responsibility of data back-up from the researcher. Issues of scale and consistency were mitigated by the development of a framework for the collection of structured data. The nature and configuration of these data, however, generated particular complexities of its own. As a group, overseers' vouchers were the product of multiple hands; the individual bills and receipts varied in structure and format from a single entry to 200–300 entries on a single item. Physical formats also varied. Bills were presented occasionally on a pre-printed form with an elaborate heading, and at other times on a small scrap of paper written in an unsure hand. To capture as much of the rich texture of these documents as possible, the project opted to include both direct transcriptions of all text, in combination with pull-down menus allowing volunteers to categorize goods and services using a controlled vocabulary. This allowed details, including names of providers, payees and beneficiaries; dates; sums of money; and, where known, occupations and geolocations to be entered consistently, and for each line of the bill to be translated into a line of data. The classifications of occupations used the well-established Booth-Armstrong categories. Although this occasionally proved difficult to interpret, given the fluidity of work and occupations in the long eighteenth century, it nevertheless provided a strong basis for statistical analysis. The categorization of goods and services were project-specific, and a taxonomy based on pilot data was created prior to large-scale data collection. This taxonomy used twelve major and seventy minor fields for sub-classification. Frequent and ongoing discussions between volunteers and project staff ensured continuity in the correct allocation of goods or services to the categories identified in pull-down menus. Designing a project-specific data collection tool and adopting a simple intuitive interface for multi-user data capture proved invaluable. Help texts were embedded in the input screen to assist users, together with a contact button to alert project staff during remote working sessions. Over the course of the project, iterations of the tool were rolled out, incorporating suggestions made through the volunteer research groups. For example, the system for locating and editing entries proved difficult to negotiate initially, particularly if the reference number contained a small error. This was later replaced by a tab that generated a full list of all entries created by a single volunteer; allowing them to scroll though and click directly on previous work. It also acted as a place marker, identifying the last entry made by that volunteer. A search function was also added, allowing volunteers to search across any field on the input screen. The results were then downloadable in several formats including as a CSV file for analysis in a standard spreadsheet package. This enhanced search facility supported research across bills for names, welfare processes or broad categories of goods, for example clothing and footwear, food and drink, or fuel. The Staffordshire research group, who had been part of the pilot project, found the transition to this new system more problematic than other groups did. They had enjoyed a large degree of autonomy during the pilot project and now found it frustrating to work in a more formal data-entry environment. They reported how research became 'more difficult as the [online] database was not as easily searchable as the original spreadsheets'.[25] The transition ensured that the new data would be entered in a more consistent and usable form, but it was nevertheless a missed opportunity for the 'Small Bills' project to develop additional resources to support the transition. The later addition of an easier method for downloading the whole dataset as a spreadsheet for personal research provided a simple resolution to this issue. In addition, clearer information on subsequent plans for making the data freely available and using them to provide enhanced archival catalogue entries should have been made available.

The data collection tool was designed with the capacity to support images associated with the relevant item. This allowed participants to work remotely and also facilitated image manipulation, allowing the user to magnify the document or as part of a process to enhance the text. These images were created in accordance with repository guidelines, using mobile phones. But the labour of taking pictures and laboriously relabelling and uploading them to the data capture tool, one image at a time, was significant. As a result, the project developed a phone app allowing the document reference number and repository identifier to be embedded in the image metadata. Bulk upload of these images to the data capture tool allowed data and image to be associated. Where no data had been entered, a new record was created. The final element of this tool was the ability to auto-create an item-level entry for each voucher for the archival catalogue of the three partner repositories. The differing needs of each repository and their specific use of the CALM platform required further collaboration to come up with a format that requires the minimum of additional editing on behalf of the repository. These data entry tools were originally designed to support collective activity, although, fortuitously, they also made remote working possible. When

[25] *Small Bills Project: Report*, p. 9.

COVID-19 closed repositories, a transition to online working was effected with minimum effort. The volunteers, however, found working in isolation difficult and many preferred not to make the transition. Several switched their volunteering efforts to more pressing COVID-19-related projects.

While electronic methods of data capture can increase inclusion through remote working and adaptation of working practice, it can also create its own barriers. Not everyone owns or has access to a laptop computer, and the provision of appropriate technology wherever possible is key to increasing digital inclusion. The difficulties of access, however small, can easily discourage new and more diverse participants. The 'Small Bills' project was able to tackle this issue, in part by repurposing some superseded laptops, thereby enabling all volunteers to work online. In the wider landscape of digital connectivity, 2020 and 2021 highlighted issues of data poverty and the fragility of the country's digital infrastructure. We are now very aware that data services can prove both expensive and unreliable. Therefore, the provision of a free, reliable data connection at each repository was fundamental to the digital data collection plan, but with two of the three institutions providing intermittent public access, this proved challenging. In East Sussex data connection was improved by using a portable Wi-Fi hotspot, with sufficient slots to accommodate those unable to use the public Wi-Fi. The data capture tool was subsequently improved, at the request of the research volunteers, to acknowledge the successful submission of an entry, thereby reassuring them that their data upload had been completed. In this wider consideration of digital infrastructure, the implications of the General Data Protection Regulation (GDPR) which was implemented under the Data Protection Act 2018, was of particular concern to the 'Small Bills' project. Personal data that might be accrued in the process of data collection was subject to these regulations. Therefore, all metadata identifying the inputter was automatically anonymized at the point of entry, including metadata attached to images; unique identifiers were allocated so that data input by a single participant could nevertheless be linked.

The approximately 41,500 lines of data created during this project are the product of significant labour and consideration of intellectual property rights (IP), and copyright proved difficult to resolve. The project staff's first thoughts were to vest IP rights in the 'Small Bills' project but, as the project is not a legally constituted body, this was not possible and the assignment of any rights to a specific member of academic staff seemed inappropriate. After some discussion, it was agreed that contributors should retain copyright in material they had added to the dataset and agree to license that data to the 'Small Bills' project for distribution under a Creative Commons Attribution-NonCommercial 4.0 International License (CC BY-NC 4.0).

Several of the volunteers were concerned that their work might be sold or made available behind a paywall, and this licensing process allowed all parties to find an agreed way forward and for the material to remain in the public domain. The copyright in the images of the overseers' vouchers remain the property of the relevant repository, and treatment of these varied between them. East Sussex would not permit the resulting images to be used outside of the project, while Cumbria Archive Service expressed an interest in using the images in their public-facing catalogue.

At the end of a large data collection project, particularly where multiple participants have contributed material, there is inevitably some form of data 'cleaning' or 'scrubbing'. These processes ensure an improved quality of data, providing internal consistency across what could be hundreds of thousands of entries with multiple fields. To minimize this job, and as an integral part of the 'Small Bills' data collection methodology, research volunteers were encouraged to self-edit. However, it took several weeks for them to become familiar with the vouchers, their palaeography and the system of input, and only then did they become confident enough to edit previous entries. This turning point encouraged additional feedback, which was particularly helpful in finding collaborative solutions to problems of data editing. For instance, the most intractable problem was identifying previous entries for editing; many were hidden from the search function by small errors in the reference code. The project team were able to minimize these errors by delimiting fields, for example, by ensuring that no blank spaces could be entered in the reference field, by capping other fields with maximum and minimum ranges, or by prohibiting invalid characters. While this did not prevent errors, it did help reduce a number of common problems. Editing was assisted by saving every iteration of the record, which allowed research volunteers to reinstate previous entries as necessary. There was no significant checking of transcriptions, although volunteers in all groups expressed concerns over the accuracy of their early efforts at transcribing documents. Sample checking, however, showed a high quality of transcription. A more collaborative approach to editing, where the volunteers formed temporary pairs, or used group sessions for checking previous entries, may have given them greater reassurance. The end of project data cleaning was undertaken by project staff to ensure consistency in the categorization of data from three counties. The data are freely available from the project and in other data repositories.

Archival relationships

The digital turn in archives has created profound change. Archival staff have been required to engage with innovative digital practices in both cataloguing and processing born-digital collections.[26] From digital tools and the wide-scale digitization of material, a new archival landscape emerged. Renewed expectations over how and what repositories should deliver as part of their core services began to shape the ways in which archives were conceived and developed. In parallel, broad conversations around 'democratising knowledge production' in the archive began to gain traction among communities of users, academic researchers and archivists.[27] This dialogue encouraged many repositories to engage with community archives and local groups to identify mutually supportive ways of filling archival silences.[28] This intellectually urgent work has come, however, during years of financial strictures, leaving many repositories unable to respond to these new initiatives. Some of these difficulties have been bridged by grant-funding streams, which have enabled repositories to work in partnership with other institutions, and have driven innovative practice and further collaborative projects.[29] Schemes like the Revisiting Archives initiative, developed by the Museums, Libraries and Archives Council (MLA) advocated for community engagement with archival collections. The MLA has encouraged archives to identify the 'wealth of new understanding and expertise' that local communities could bring to the interpretation of their collections.[30] In concert with academic engagement and a new willingness for volunteers to participate in heritage research projects, this mutual labour has engendered the 'participatory

[26] F. X. Blouin Jr and W. G. Rosenberg, *Processing the Past: Contesting Authority in History and the Archives* (Oxford, 2011), p. 207.

[27] A. Flinn, 'An attack on professionalism and scholarship? Democratising archives and the production of knowledge', *Ariadne*, lxii (2010) <http://www.ariadne.ac.uk/issue/62/flinn> [accessed 20 Mar. 2021].

[28] For a longer discussion on these processes see M. Stevens, A. Flinn and E. Shepherd, 'New frameworks for community engagement in the archive sector: from handing over to handing on', *International Journal of Heritage Studies*, xvi (2010), 59–76, doi: 10.1080/13527250903441770; A. Flinn, 'Community histories, community archives: some opportunities and challenges', *Journal of the Society of Archivists*, xxviii (2007), 151–76, doi: 10.1080/00379810701611936.

[29] These funding programmes include those administered by The National Archives to provide opportunities for innovative practice <https://www.nationalarchives.gov.uk/archives-sector/finding-funding/collaborate-and-innovate/about-collaborate-and-innovate> [accessed 9 Feb. 2021], and the Connected Communities programme administered by the AHRC to encourage collaborate working between academic institutions and other bodies <https://connected-communities.org> [accessed 9 Feb. 2021]. Other schemes involve those administered by the Heritage Lottery Fund and the Wellcome Trust.

[30] Collections Trust, *Revisiting Archive Collections: A Toolkit for Capturing and Sharing Multiple Perspectives on Archive Collections*, 3rd edn (London, 2009), p. 3 <https://collectionstrust.org.uk/wp-content/uploads/2017/02/Collections-Trust-Revisiting-Archive-Collections-toolkit-2009.pdf> [accessed 11 Mar. 2021].

archive'.[31] Some of these new relationships have not been easy. There is still institutional resistance to using volunteer labour for hitherto archival tasks. However, archive professionals can no longer catalogue every collection down to item level. This leaves inherent tensions in participatory archival practice. As Alexandra Eveleigh identified, the benefits in the democratization of professional archival practice through the 'co-creation of historical meaning' have to be balanced against their role in 'subverting' the 'power relationships between records, researchers and archivists'.[32] These considerations create a profound underlying anxiety among some archive professionals that a 'contributor might be wrong, or that descriptive data might be pulled out of archival context'.[33] Academic historians can assist in breaking down some of these misconceptions by using co-created resources in their research, thereby giving authority to this new form of history-making. The visibility of such work normalizes its use and assists in forming a trusted relationship between archive, academic and volunteer researcher.

Taking preliminary steps in the seemingly complex world of collaborative academic partnerships, grant funding and public engagement is a daunting prospect for any archive, particularly when there are few formal opportunities to develop these relationships. Repositories, however, are able to drive some initiatives from their own resources, with directed showcases, social media posts and approaches tailored to specific academic interests. This initial work, however it is done, is an essential prerequisite to breaking down barriers and making new academic relationships, since the benefits accrued from such collaborative projects can be substantial. Research on behalf of the National Archives has identified significant areas of benefit for the archive, including enhanced impact and profile raising, knowledge exchange, user/audience development, new interpretation of archives, access to specialist expertise and new research, and access to grant funding streams.[34] For collaborative projects involving community and academic partners, the existence of a well-developed culture of volunteering makes these approaches both easier and more likely. In these initial stages, particularly when discussing the possibility of a grant funding application, it is important that all partners are able to articulate their expectations. The balance of responsibility between

---

[31] E. Benoit III and A. Eveleigh, 'Defining and framing participatory archives in archival science', in *Participatory Archives*, ed. Benoit and Eveleigh, pp. 1–12, at pp. 1–4.

[32] Alexandra Eveleigh, quoted in Benoit and Eveleigh, 'Defining and framing participatory archives', p. 7.

[33] Alexandra Eveleigh, quoted in Benoit and Eveleigh, 'Defining and framing participatory archives', p. 7.

[34] P. McNulty and M. O'Rourke, *A Guide to Collaboration for Archives and Higher Education*, 2nd edn (London, 2018), pp. 11–12.

partners is largely determined by these preliminary discussions; repositories should ensure that they advocate for their own needs during this initial design process.[35] The 'Small Bills' project was specifically developed to fit with repositories where there was a firm commitment to volunteering. The parameters of data collection and associated research questions were set by academic partners and agreed. The research model used limited crowdsourcing, where there was significant contact with research volunteers, enabling them to upskill and to move to the writing element of the project if they chose. The consequent research and writing of connected biographies used a co-creation model, with research volunteers choosing and setting their own subjects, using the overseers' vouchers as their starting point. This blended model required significant input from academic partners through supporting research volunteers, providing training and offering a platform for volunteer blog posts. In return, one of their partners, Staffordshire Record Office, was able to offer a 'good volunteering model', since they knew 'how to recruit, organize, and look after volunteers'.[36] Jason Heppler and Gabriel Wolfenstein emphasize that for a crowdsourced project to function effectively it cannot be 'left to its own devices nor … used only as a provider of information or mechanical work'.[37] Those involved need to feel that their contributions are valued and appreciate being informed about how their work is reflected in the various outputs of the project including academic articles, conference presentations, public workshops, talks to local history groups and blog posts. In each instance recognizing the contributions made by participants helped give them a sense that their work was valued; in effect, they become partners in the process. This is just as true for the partner archive as for the research volunteer. The sharing of knowledge and engagement with the research volunteers becomes central to the project. The close involvement of academic project staff, and a degree of trust built up between partners, allowed responsibility and support for the volunteer groups to be passed to the 'Small Bills' project very quickly. This ensured that research groups were able to run independently while freeing up archival capacity for other projects. As the 'Small Bills' project rolled out to two additional partner archive services, in Cumbria and East Sussex, the expansion of the project led to additional material benefits

[35] E. Benoit III and A. Eveleigh, 'Challenges, opportunities and future directions of participatory archives', in *Participatory Archives*, ed. Benoit and Eveleigh, pp. 211–18, at p. 215.

[36] Participation and engagement officer, Staffordshire Record Office, in *Small Bills Project: Report*, p. 13.

[37] Heppler and Wolfenstein, 'Crowdsourcing digital public history'.

accruing to the participating archives: the creation of item-level entries for their catalogues and, for the repositories that so wished, an associated image of the document for reuse. The participating archives found these new relationships to be very positive, and they provided a blueprint for other collaborative partnerships. In Cumbria the relationship paved the way for establishing a collaborative doctoral award, based on material held by the archive service. An additional benefit of the project for the archives was that it provided evidence of cross-sector collaborations during the archive reaccreditation process. All the partner repositories found the collaboration a positive experience, particularly the academic partners' engagement with the volunteer groups. Moreover, they valued a strengthened relationship between themselves and academic institutions that would provide firm foundations for future collaborations.

Academic relationships

Academic need is often the powerful motivator behind crowdsourcing projects connected to universities. Inaccessible primary sources or those at a scale requiring many hundreds of hours of transcription, analysis or categorization demand innovative approaches. As Louise Seaward identified for the Transcribe Bentham project, crowdsourcing simultaneously contributes to academic research, helps to preserve documents and promotes access to them.[38] In normal circumstances, creating 41,500 lines of data of the sort generated by the 'Small Bills' project would be well beyond the capability of one or two dedicated researchers.[39] But, by collaborating with research volunteers and archive professionals, significant projects can be realized, with valuable results for all parties and creating new audiences for historic resources. The attraction of this wide-scale public participation goes well beyond the cursory 'engagement' metric of attendance at a conference or exhibition, and provides more lasting benefits to research volunteers, archives and other academics. As Mia Ridge argues, 'participation in crowdsourcing should also be recognized as a valuable form of public engagement with cultural heritage'.[40] Indeed, among several motivations

---

[38] L. Seward, 'Crowdsourcing the past', The Social History Society (blog), 12 Sept. 2018 <https://socialhistory.org.uk/shs_exchange/crowdsourcing-the-past> [accessed 26 Aug. 2020].

[39] S. Dunn and M. Hedges, 'Crowd-sourcing as a component of humanities research infrastructures', *International Journal of Humanities and Arts Computing*, vii (2013), 147–69, doi: 10.3366/ijhac.2013.0086.

[40] M. Ridge, 'From tagging to theorizing: deepening engagement with cultural heritage through crowdsourcing', *Curator: The Museum Journal*, lvi (2013), 435–50, doi: 10.1111/cura.12046.

for getting involved with the project, one volunteer from Cumbria noted their own lack of knowledge of the history of the city in which they were born. Projects that partner with family and local historians form particularly fruitful relationships and benefit from highly engaged participants, many of whom are very willing to share their local expertise. For the academic historian, crowdsourcing also generates opportunities for student engagement, giving rise to a richer student experience as well as enhancing practical research skills. The socially engaged crowdsourcing provided by the 'Small Bills' project encouraged volunteers, including student volunteers, to participate in work beyond data collection, with opportunities to research and write related blog posts. This collaborative process often drew on the collective knowledge of more experienced volunteers and archival staff, and on occasion provided challenges in a joint endeavour to discover the outcome of specific events. In the process, this work has contributed to our communal knowledge of smaller communities and the Poor Law.

Undoubtedly, collaborative partnerships support higher education institutions in their REF, TEF and KEF submissions, while there are wider societal benefits for repositories and research volunteers.[41] Some of this is captured by academic metrics, but much of the real camaraderie, the mutual support, the feeling of being valued and the improved sense of well-being experienced by volunteers and partners alike is difficult to quantify. As Laura King and Gary Rivett have noted, the 'constraining model of engagement' in the academy does not sufficiently value the two-way knowledge exchange that is fundamental in co-created projects.[42] Continuing work by the National Co-ordinating Centre for Public Engagement to embed public engagement in the wider academic framework has made some progress in these areas, providing opportunities for stakeholders to shape future policy development.[43]

The legacy of these relatively new collaborative partnerships forms an important element in the development of co-created resources and provides a renewed focus for public history. The days of small datasets stored on individual hard drives are numbered. Yet the intellectual labour of reimagining a project as a digital resource and of creating a platform to support this work, and the resulting dataset, are insufficiently valued. Tangible assets such as articles and books, although part and parcel of the historian's craft, still form the primary currency of intellectual esteem, with

---

[41] Research Excellence Framework (REF), Teaching Excellence and Student Outcomes Framework (TEF) and Knowledge Exchange Framework (KEF).

[42] King and Rivett, 'Engaging people in making history', p. 220.

[43] See <https://www.publicengagement.ac.uk/about-engagement/current-policy-landscape> [accessed 20 Feb. 2021].

little room for any other format. Digital artefacts are a valuable contribution to the intellectual project of the historian and the communities they serve. This is particularly important to those working in public history who need to represent not only their own contribution but also the labour of others and the 'value' of publicly funded projects. The digital platform created by the 'Small Bills' project for the collection of data and as a resource for creating catalogue entries is an important contribution to the project of 'public history'. The methodological innovation that it represents, combining digital methods and close collaborative working, is a new way forward in the creation of knowledge and the writing of the history of the Old Poor Law. The conclusion that the practice of history is confined to a few in academic positions is now old hat, and, just as they took place in archival circles, the conversations about the democratization of knowledge production have to continue and develop in the academy.[44] Understandably, this work is hard for the academic historian who has hitherto worked in an environment predicated on personal achievement. Those who have created and maintained collaborative networks understand the commitment and personal investment necessary for such work, which should not be underestimated. However, it is important to remind the academic historian that, on many occasions, they should step back from their role as the perceived principal source of historic knowledge to facilitate the work of those who know more.[45]

Conclusion

By any empirical measure the 'Small Bills' project has succeeded. It has created a large dataset, produced a host of published outputs and generated numerous blog posts written by volunteers. The flexible format of the data created will provide the basis for further detailed analysis of topics ranging from the economics of the parish and seasonal patterns of expenditure to the material culture of the poor. Each of the partner institutions, universities and repositories has made quantifiable gains from the collective work of the project. It is believed that the volunteer researchers – those at the very centre of the project – have gained what they anticipated from the project; indeed, it is hoped that the project has exceeded their expectations. While some go away with very tangible achievements – chiefly, a blog post, hundreds of entries on a public dataset or new skills in researching or writing – others leave with much more: a sense of working for a common

---

[44] Flinn, 'An attack on professionalism and scholarship?'

[45] L. Westberg and T. Jensen, 'Who is the expert in participatory culture?', in *Participatory Heritage*, ed. Roued-Cunliffe and Copeland, pp. 87–96.

purpose, camaraderie and knowing that their contributions are valued by others, particularly the academic staff with whom they worked. Along the way the project has facilitated so much more than data gathering. It has created what Raphael Samuel called a 'social form of knowledge', not quite by a thousand hands but certainly by hundreds. All of the 'small' lives written by the volunteers are part of a much bigger history, and it is only when these are considered collectively that it can truly be said that we have begun to write a co-created history of the Old Poor Law. By using these shared experiences as a foundation for further initiatives, both the original methodologies and the platforms for further research in public and community histories will be enhanced.

Conclusion

Alannah Tomkins

The 'Small Bills and Petty Finance' project was born out of frustration at the limitations of overseers' accounts for investigating the economic detail of poor relief and apprehension of the massed data folded within overseers' vouchers. Research over three counties and five years has pointed up the documentary interplay between accounts and their ephemera, where focus on one archival genre within the ephemera clearly brings some questions to the fore and leaves others in the background. This volume has therefore followed work by Keith Snell on settlement examinations, and Steven King on pauper letters, by bringing vouchers into prominence for framing questions about welfare processes under the Old Poor Law.[1]

Part I of this volume interrogated the vouchers for their capacity to illuminate the lives of the poor, specifically in relation to agency and visibility. Parish paupers have been the beneficiaries, in historiographical terms, of the drive for history from below, which has characterized English social history for the last fifty years. Multiple local studies, particularly those that examine accounts of poor relief in parishes either possessing censuses or reconstructed by the Cambridge Group for the History of Population and Social Structure, have addressed quantitative aspects of parish welfare for paupers in cohorts.[2] The elderly, widows and children have been made prominent as types among the poor. Letters between parishes have demonstrated the involvement of the settled-but-not-resident poor in negotiations for relief. Vestries may have held the upper hand and yet still found it necessary to acknowledge or pacify those paupers who knew or worked out how best to influence the process.

The vouchers studied in the project counties have revealed the poor obliquely, given relief claimants' coincidental participation in the economic

---

[1] K. Snell, *Annals of the Labouring Poor* (Cambridge, 1985); S. King, *Writing the Lives of the English Poor, 1750s–1830s* (Montreal, 2019).

[2] S. Williams, *Poverty, Gender and Life-Cycle under the English Poor Law, 1760–1834* (London, 2011).

A. Tomkins, 'Conclusion' in *Providing for the Poor: The Old Poor Law, 1750–1834*, ed. P. Collinge and L. Falcini (London, 2022), pp. 219–226. License: CC BY-NC-ND 4.0.

transactions being recorded. From the point of view of a Sussex overseer and the shoemaker he commissioned, for example, it mattered little whether a pair of shoes was being purchased for Ann Vinal or Elizabeth Sinden. The significance of the paupers named in vouchers, therefore, is amplified by teaming subsets of voucher data with additional sources, as in the chapters by Louise Falcini (Chapter 1) and Tim Hitchcock (Chapter 3). Enforced or 'knobstick' marriages are assumed to have been foisted on pauper spouses, on the basis of anecdotes of husbands absconding; in contrast the material for East Hoathly, which uniquely permits the conflation of overseers' accounts with an overseer's diary, shows that the terms of such marriages could be shaped by the couple to their own (as well as the parish's) long-term advantage. The parochial relief system was designed to work in tandem with the vagrancy laws, so it might be expected that the vouchers have little to say about the mobile poor. Glimpsed in the vouchers are public meetings regarding vagrancy and the devolving of parish responsibility for it, payments to and for vagrants and contributions to mendicity societies.[3] The 'vanishingly small' proportion of data on this topic in the three counties, however, indicates the '"dark figure" of unrelieved poverty'.[4] The paucity of overlap between the vouchers, the 'Vagrant lives' dataset, and the national Parliamentary Returns on vagrants indicates a solidity to the administrative boundary between settled and migrant poor, though their material circumstances may have been identical.[5]

The appearance of paupers in vouchers is serendipitous: the presence of things, in contrast, is central to the existence of vouchers. Vouchers convey information on what appear at this remove to be mundane transactions and interactions, but the goods and services they record provide the material evidence of processes that impacted on often fragile lives and on local economies. Objects are described with often acute specificity, if only because they carry a price, but food, drink, cloth, fuel and other commodities were given additional indicators of weight, length, texture, colour, quality and intended usage. This level of detail arose from the needs of tradespeople to account for goods and services supplied when there could be significant time lags between delivery and the settling of accounts, and from overseers' need to track the precise reasons for debts

---

[3] CAS, PR36/V/7/33, Wigton, 1777; SPC21/8/11/80, Threlkeld, June 1802–Oct. 1803; SPC44/2/38/37, Dalston, 4 July 1818; PR60/21/13/6/9, Brampton, 3 Apr. 1828; SRO, D925/5/2/12, Rocester, 9 Apr. 1800; ESRO, PAR378/31/3/12/13, East Hoathly, 1773.

[4] See Chapter 3.

[5] For example, see *Returns of Persons Committed under the Vagrant Laws to the respective prisons and houses of correction in England and Wales from 1 January 1820 to 1 January 1824* (Parl. Papers 1824).

incurred (given the annual nature of most parish officers' appointments). The historical yield of these minutiae is significant, since the chapter on textiles shows how the mundane items recorded in vouchers can be used to help to define the parish as a site for everyday life and consumption. Elizabeth Spencer's analysis of vouchers on the specifics of yardage, price per yard and durability in Chapter 2 mapped diversity in parish purchasing, local preferences (for example, for blue duffel cloth in Cumberland) and individual intimacies (where traditional linen for shifts and shirts worn next to the skin gave ground to cotton).

Part II considered the people who are merely surnames in most volumes of accounts but whose investment in the Poor Law, both personal and commercial, was more substantive than these fleeting name checks imply. The suppliers and administrative enablers of the Poor Law are present in vouchers as accountants, signatories, retailers and commissioners of bill-head art. They might even use vouchers sporadically as a vector for correspondence, communicating in the same business language conventions adopted by international traders.[6] Their levels of literacy and orthography, the quality of their communications on paper, and the paper itself, varying from printed bills to torn scraps and reused handbills, all indicate their immersion in parish business. Furthermore, the array of trades and services represented on paper speak to fluctuations or cycles in parish policies of provision; the choice of goods, the preferences in favour of some businesses but not others, the patterning of interactions in daily, weekly, monthly or annual points of contact and the readiness to pay, are inscribed in vouchers but not typically transferred to accounts.

Flows of both goods and paper, in a triangulation of parish officers, service or commodity providers, and the poor, draw people forward who are easy to overlook when using other documents. In Chapter 4 Peter Collinge spoke to both Poor Law economics and the world of retailing more widely when tracing female suppliers of workhouse foodstuffs and other parish goods. Shifting the focus from women as recipients of relief to women who were often missing from trade directories and newspapers: the latter were nonetheless prominent in transmitting goods, working as business owners or assisting in the trades of others. As such, the vouchers provide a new pathway for research into the role of women (and men) in the commercial arena and the mechanics of business. Similarly, where assistant overseers have previously been regarded as generic, the vouchers enable the research by Tomkins in Chapter 5 to be specific.

---

[6] P. Hudson, 'Correspondence and commitment: British traders' letters in the long-eighteenth century', *Cultural and Social History*, 11 (2014), 527–53.

Both of the chapters in Part II narrow the social distance between the paupers and their providers and thereby allow researchers to problematize their understanding of regional trends under the Old Poor Law. From his analysis of poor law accounts in the south and east, King suggested that parish authorities there may have intervened earlier than in the north in 'the descent of individuals and families into poverty', but it is evident in East Sussex, Staffordshire and Cumbria that, by appointing individuals to parish posts or by permitting businesses to charge slightly higher prices, parishes acted even earlier in the process in some instances.[7] Parishes supported individuals, businesses and the local economy to respond to financial jeopardy, or the risk of fragility, in a proactive way. The ratepayers identified by Williams in Campton and Shefford, Bedfordshire, found that there could be a fine line between independence and dependence.[8] Chapters 4 and 5 by Collinge and Tomkins, respectively, indicate a more dynamic possibility: people did not simply experience declining circumstances with no recourse beyond their own efforts, but could be shored up by Poor Law contracts and salaries. Grocery and material supplies in parishes of the Midlands and north, for example, demonstrate common provision practices – multiple suppliers, similar pricing and frequent purchases – that muddy the waters in analyses of regional and local diversity and any attempts to define businesses based on their customers who were middle class and above.

The final chapter of the second section, Chapter 6, goes to the heart of national welfare provision and asks who historians should include in the complexities of unpicking the Old Poor Law. The volume opened with Jane Sewell's appeal to the magistrates challenging parish decisions regarding welfare relief, drawing attention to the range of individuals and mechanisms involved in allocating poor relief. Shave's chapter builds on this to extend the 'gene pool' of those who should be considered when discussing Poor Law provision. Whenever problems arose, where parishes denied relief, tried to coerce the poor, were inadequately informed of their duties or responsibilities, or where they failed to perform their legal responsibility to a satisfactory standard, enquiries and proposals for reform came from those beyond the custom and practice boundaries of the Poor Law system.

Throughout all of these chapters, the focus on individuals and their preoccupations drawn from massed data enables purposeful genealogy within an academic remit. Too often the study of family history is characterized as merely popular or marginalized as inaccurate, typically by

---

[7] S. King, *Poverty and Welfare in England, 1700–1850: A Regional Perspective* (Manchester, 2000), p. 257.

[8] Williams, *Poverty, Gender and Life-Cycle*, pp. 162–3.

people who forget that historical research is frequently concerned with the descent of other people's families. The 'Small Bills' project has knitted the skills of volunteers together with questions beyond the remit of a single surname or lineage, ensuring that there is a direct connection between the life stories of professional and quasi-professional men such as Abel Rooker and James Finlinson, for example, and the unpacking of modest or tenuous careers in parish service.

Steven King noted that 'we are still a long way from having the databases to map intra- and inter-county variations on any definitive basis, let alone explaining them'.[9] The 'Small Bills' project has provided a methodology for doing so. In particular, the chapters in this volume and the articles that continue to be written by project staff forecast the value of Poor Law vouchers in enabling research into provision and consumption practices. The close description of mundane objects and substances purchased for the poor contained in receipts offers something new to material history: an article about the voucher data for the patterns of acquisitions and uses across the three counties is in progress. Similarly, a study of the personnel involved in apportioning ratepayers' money to local trades is in draft, raising the question of whether the use of parish officers as suppliers was actively corrupt or an efficient use of social capital. Ultimately, this methodology can be expanded to include other voluminous collections of bills and receipts, such as those retained by estates, councils and corporations, to produce a new sort of economic history.

The research agenda emerging from the study of vouchers is important because it intersects with concomitant shifts in the macro-economic historiography of the Old Poor Law. Peter Solar argued a generation ago that the Old Poor Law 'functioned in ways that promoted economic development', supporting local economies by stimulating the churn of money.[10] At the time of writing, the national economic significance of rising poor-relief expenditure is being re-examined as a phenomenon beyond the explanatory capacity of either population growth or wage/price inflation.[11] Waddell speculates that this expansion was driven by demand from the poor rather than by generosity among rate-payers; from this book onwards, the influence on expansion emanating from parish suppliers must be accommodated as well.

---

[9] King, *Poverty and Welfare*, p. 260.

[10] P. M. Solar, 'Poor relief and English economic development before the Industrial Revolution', *The Economic History Review*, 48 (1995), 1–22, at 6–8.

[11] B. Waddell, 'The rise of the parish welfare state in England, c.1600–1800', *Past & Present*, ccliii (2021), 151–94.

In addition to the historical questions that can be asked of vouchers, research should also stress the physical experience of encountering them in the archive as contradictory but instructive. Murphy and O'Driscoll noted in relation to *printed* ephemera that it 'mattered very much' at the time it was distributed, despite the apparent ease of its loss or destruction.[12] The same could be said of the thousands of handwritten bills that make up the majority of overseers' vouchers. The historical neglect and patchy survival of overseers' vouchers until now does not override this conclusion: for once in historical research, the near-ubiquitous production of these documents can be assumed, rendering the specifics of retention and survival less central than is usual. Indeed, fingertip engagement with surviving vouchers – months and years of handling dirty, scrunched or fragile objects – compounds the sense of their one-time significance. Simultaneously, their consistent inconsistencies speak to reliable patterns amid the diverse details. Indeed, the three counties studied by the 'Small Bills' project exhibit a complex and often personal mix of localized systems of supply and recording. The vouchers demonstrate that, across counties and above the level of regional difference, parishes were not spendthrift but checked and rechecked expenditure, a practice that in Lichfield generated inked confirmations. These scraps were vital for accounting and accountability everywhere and their importance did not leach away immediately when magistrates endorsed overseers' ledgers. By the time they were recognized as irrelevant to a parish's rigorous financial management, they had already become fragments of parochial history.

The composition and content of vouchers was aligned to the immediate requirements of their uses and users: 'the transient documents of everyday life ... [were] ... essentially produced to meet the needs of the day, such items reflect the moods and mores of past times in a way that more formal records cannot'.[13] If the overseers' account book is the Poor Law historian's canonical text, then the voucher is its apparently disposable context and, like researchers in parallel fields, those involved in the 'Small Bills' project are in the business of ephemeralizing the canon.[14]

Placing vouchers at the centre of research, these chapters have provided content and context for the raw information they contain. Meeting at the

---

[12] K. D. Murphy and S. O'Driscoll, 'Introduction', in *Studies in Ephemera: Text and Image in Eighteenth-Century Print*, ed. K. D. Murphy and S. O'Driscoll (Lewisburg, Penn., 2013), pp. 1–28.

[13] M. Rickards, 'History's other half: world search and rescue', *Private Library*, 3 (1980), 8–15.

[14] Murphy and O'Driscoll, 'Introduction'.

points where the poor, the parish and the providers intersect or overlap, the vouchers have generated questions regarding the relationships and degree of agency between those who came into contact with the Old Poor Law. They have been used to reconstruct and reveal networks, negotiations, exchanges and interactions between groups of people who are often treated in isolation. Ephemeral as they are, vouchers nevertheless constitute the managing of information and data and the 'enduring materiality of economic transactions'.[15]

Furthermore, the project team is inclined to reflect on a voucher's 'sociability – that is, its embedding in numerous networks and its reliance on multiple mediators'.[16] As with books in the long eighteenth century, how overseers' vouchers were used could be as significant as the information they contained.[17] As an item of communication, a typical voucher was generated by a tradesperson or service supplier, handed to one or more parish officers, read, checked and authorized, returned to its author or an assistant for signature in recognition of payment, carried to meetings of vestrymen at local inns, potentially parsed by magistrates and finally bundled with other vouchers pending queries. Indeed, once accounts were settled, the vouchers were often 'folded in thirds, labelled, stacked, bundled … tied into bricks', stored on spikes or pasted into ledgers to be stored.[18] In the modern archive the same bundle is unwrapped, unfolded, flattened, interpreted and calendared. Under the auspices of the 'Small Bills' project, as many or more hands transmit the vouchers as in their initial circulation, particularly whenever legibility is queried, or a single scrap is passed from hand to hand to construe the meaning of arcane wording.

The sociability of vouchers has related directly to the activity of volunteers. In their article on 'sedimented histories', Sarah Lloyd and Julie Moore, have commented that co-production is about 'dispelling the idea that research is only for the institutionally-trained historian and introducing the beauty of collaborative history as a process of taking everyone's contribution to build a bigger picture'.[19] When people are encouraged to explore 'stories from

---

[15] S. Rockman, 'The paper technologies of capitalism', *Technology and Culture*, 58 (2017), 487–505, at 489–90.

[16] R. Felski, 'Context stinks!', *New Literary History*, 42 (2011), 573–91. For the implications of receipts for reciprocity and record-keeping practices, see also F. Maguire, 'Bonds of print and chains of paper: rethinking print culture and social formation in early-modern England *c.*1550–*c.*1700' (unpublished University of York PhD thesis, 2017), ch. 4.

[17] A. Williams, *The Social Life of Books: Reading Together in the Eighteenth-Century Home* (New Haven, 2017), p. 6.

[18] Rockman, 'The paper technologies of capitalism', 488.

[19] S. Lloyd and J. Moore, 'Sedimented histories: connections, collaborations and co-production in regional history', *History Workshop Journal*, lxxx (2015), 234–48, at 239.

their own locality', knowledge and experiences are generated in ways that are 'unlikely to emerge through more orthodox academic processes'.[20] This volume unites these same stories with academic publishing by means of an extended sociability that, it must be hoped, will soon become orthodox across both academic and archival sectors.

The context of this sociability has been the archive. Chapter 7, on public histories, evaluates the pursuit of knowledge in collaboration with the project's partners, establishing parity of purpose between the academic goals of the project and its social process. In an era of public sector austerity, which looks set to become more acute, triangulation of effort has generated added value for hard-pressed archives.

Finally, the digital distribution and global availability of the vouchers' contents extends the metaphor of sociability beyond the limits of a paper artefact. At the time of writing, friends of the project are making use of voucher data, either in clumps or in snippets, to resource histories of men's body hair, women's clothes and the furnishings of poor households.[21] The very granularity that has hitherto withheld serious attention from the vouchers is nonetheless finding an enthusiastic audience.

---

[20] Lloyd and Moore, 'Sedimented histories', 237, 241.

[21] A. Withey, *Concerning Beards: Facial Hair, Health and Hygiene in England, 1650–1900* (London, 2021); J. Harley, *At Home with the Poor: Consumer Behaviour and Material Culture of the Poor in England, 1650–1850* (Manchester, forthcoming).

Index

Page references in italic refer to the illustrations.

Abbots Bromley, Staffs., 6, 14, 18, 101
   clothes and clothing, 62, 65, 66, 75
   population, 6
Abell, Thomas, Brede, Sussex, 148, 155, 159–60
able-bodied poor, 1, 4, 10
Acts of parliament, *see* statutes
Adams, Henry, vagrancy contractor, 84, 92, 94
Adams, Peter, 30–1, 44
advertising and advertisements
   advertisement for an assistant overseer of Greystoke, 1835, *149*
   advertisement for a master and mistress of St Mary's Workhouse, Carlisle, 1785, *149*
   for assistant overseers, 139, 150, 151
   for groceries, 113
   for London Genuine Tea Company, 120–1
accommodation, alternatives to workhouse, 177–82, 193
agency, pauper, 26, 35
Aldridge, Staffs., 155, 156, 158–9
Allen, Thomas, contractor of the poor, 13
allowances, 13, 173
Annals of Agriculture, 172
apprenticeship (pauper), 54, 75, 90
archival absences, 17, 26, 198, 210
archival practice, 16–17, 211
Arnett, Charles, 146, 147, 155, 161
Ashdowne, John, 146
assistant overseers, 137–63
   advertisements for, 139, 150, 151

Advertisement for an assistant overseer of Greystoke, 1835, *149*
   applications for position of, 139, 144, 150, 151
   character references and testimonials, 152, 153, 154
   duties, 144, 146
   misconduct, 148, 159
   other occupations, 17, 18, 145
   parishes making use of, 142,
   salaries, 142, 145, 156
   status of applicants, 143,
   targets of violence, 147, 148, 150

badging the poor, 55
bankrupts, 118, 120, 142
bastardy bond, 28, 34
Beard, John, assistant overseer, Whittington, Staffs., 155
Becher, Rev., J. T., 177
Bedfordshire, 46
Bethlem Hospital, London, 78, 80–1
Bevill, Soloman, assistant overseer, Hastings St Clements, Sussex, 155
biographies, 197
   research and writing, 202, 204
Birch, Thomas, 97
Bird, Isaac, grocer, Brampton, 118, 122, 123, 130
Bird, James, 146
Bird, Major Nicholas, assistant overseer applicant, 153
Blake, Matthew, Staffordshire Record Office, 202
Blakemore, James, vagrant, 101
blog posts, 204, 212, 214–15

227

Bolton, Lancs., 7–8
Brampton, Cumb.,
    businessmen, 111, 112, 118, 122–3
    businesswomen, 111, 112, 114, 117–22, 130
    economy, 110
    farming the poor, 13, 14
    foodstuffs, 122
    legal expenses, 91
    occupations, 112
    overseers' vouchers, 112, 113, 123
    pensions, 13
    pauper clothing, 76
    poor rate, 111
    poor relief, 76
    poor relief costs, 91, 111
    population, 13, 110
    provision of textiles, 61, 62, 67
    size of parish, 13
    workhouse, 13
    workhouse diet, 122
    workhouse inmates, 14, 111
Brazier, Thomas, 32
Bromwich, Thomas, vagrant, 101
Brown, George (b.1812), butcher, Lichfield, Staffs., 126–7
Brown, Grace (1780–1876), butcher, Lichfield, Staffs., 123, 126, 129
Brown, John Samuel (b.1815), butcher, Lichfield, Staffs., 126–7
Brown, John (1790–1833), butcher, Lichfield, Staffs., 126
Brown, John, Sedgefield, assistant overseer applicant, 154
Brown, Richard, assistant overseer, Hayton near Brampton, Cumb., 155
Buckley, Mary, 97
Burgess, Joseph, 40
Burn, Richard, 141
Burn, Thomas, assistant overseer, Greystoke, Cumb., 155
businesswomen, 107–32

butchers, 112, 116, 118, 126, 127, 156. *See also* Grace Brown, Ann Hill
Butterton, Staffs., 104
Butterton-in-the-Moors, Staffs., 92, 103–4
Buttery, William, assistant overseer, Wigton, Cumb., 155, 162

Cain, Ann, 30–1, 44, 47
Cairns, John or George, pauper, 165
Campton and Shefford, Bedfordshire, 46
candles, 51, 122, 123
Captain Swing, 148, 150
Carlisle Patriot, 121, 134
Carlisle, Cumb.
    advertisement for a Master and Mistress of St Mary's Workhouse, 1785, *149*
    grocers and tea dealers, 120, 121
    parish of St Mary, 143
    population, 12
cash, circulation, 2, 5, 48–9, 53
charity, as part of poor relief, 8, 37, 57, 80, 178, 191
Chetwyn, M.P., George, 88, 96
children
    apprenticeship, 75
    boarding out, 13
    clothing, 65, 72, 73, 74, 75, 77
    illegitimate, 2, 27, 31, 33, 43, 44, 45, 46, 48, 49
    in receipt of relief, 12, 14, 18, 39, 111
    widows and, 87, 88, 103, 104, 120, 131
    work, 172
Churchwardens' and Overseers' Guide and Director (1824), 146
clergy, 169, 176–7
Clerkenwell, Middlesex, 94
Clinch, Stephen, 35
clothing
    aprons, 60, 62, 65, 69, 73, 81, 87

Index

children's, 65, 70, 72, 73, 74, 75, 77
cloaks, 61, 62, 68, 73
cloth, 55, 59, 60, 61, 62, 63, 64, 65, 66, 67, 69, 71, 72, 218, 219,
detail of a bill for material supplied by Joshua Harrison, 1776, *63*
gowns, 61, 62, 66, 67, 73
haberdashery, 68
hats, 59, 69, 72, 75, 112
making, 66, 70, 72, 73, 75, 79
Margaret Fenton's bill for making gowns, frocks and stays, 26 April [1823], *71*
men's, 72, 75
pawning, 71, 76
shirts, 60, 65, 66, 70, 71, 72, 219
shifts, 60, 66, 70, 72, 219
stays, 73
stockings, 69, 70, 72, 73, 81
supply, 42, 197
women's, 60, 61, 62, 65, 66, 67, 68, 69, 70, 72, 73, 81, 87, 219
Cobbett, William, 148
Cockermouth, Cumb., population, 12
co-creation, 202, 211–12, 214
Coles, John, stationer, 21
Collinson, Rev., John, 151–3
contractors of the poor, 14, 18, 141
See also farming the poor
Cooke, Jonathan, assistant overseer applicant, 153
Cooper, Elizabeth, 97
Corporations of the Poor, 3
Cormick, Patrick, assistant overseer, Aldridge, Staffs., 155, 158–9
correspondence, 144, 150, 151–4, 217, 219
See also pauper letters
Courthope, George, J.P., 25, 32, 37
COVID-19 virus, 205, 208
Cowfold, Sussex, 150
credit, 20, 120, 125, 128
creditors, 120, 155, 158

crowdsourcing, 199–200, 202–3, 212–14
Crozier, Timothy, Dalston, Cumb., 70
Cumberland Pacquet and Ware's Whitehaven Advertiser, 121
Cumberland,
agriculture, 3, 12
contracting of the poor, 18, 141
economy, 12
income from charitable bequests, 9
industry, 12
legal fees, 91
percentage of assistant overseers, 141
pensions, 19
poor rate, 7, 8. *See also individual parishes*
poor relief, 5, 91
population, 85
removal expenditure, 91
vagrants, 92, 94, 96
See also individual parishes
Cumbria Archive Service, 209, 212
Cumwhitton, Cumb., 85

Dalston, Cumb.,
assistant overseers, 137, 156, 160, 164–5
provision of textiles, 65, 70, 71, 73
Dann, Elizabeth, 45
Dann, John, 45
Darlaston, Staffs.,
economy, 14, 84
Fletcher, Elizabeth, pauper, 94
numbers in receipt of outdoor relief, 14
non-resident relief, 85
overseer, 101
payment to Abel Rooker for half a year's contract for Darlaston Workhouse, Staffordshire, 1822, *193*
population, 14, 85
Rooker, Abel, surgeon, 192–4

vagrants, 94
workhouse, 14
Darling, John, 46
data
   capture, 204–8, 212–17
   capture tool, 207, 210, 215
   consistency, 205
   dataset, 197
   download, 207
   editing, 206
   format, 215
   GDPR, 208
   poverty, 208
   structured, 205
Davidson, Jane (1748–1827), grocer, Brampton, Cumb., 121–3
Dawes, Elizabeth (1768–1852) grocer and tea dealer, Lichfield, Staffs., 107
Day, Ann, 36
Day, Elizabeth, 36–38, 41–2, 45, 47
Day, Sarah Durrant, 37, 45
Day, Thomas, 36
debt, 31, 44 118, 158,
deserving poor, 9, 91, 143, 148
Devon, 98
Dickinson, Daniel, grocer, Workington, Cumb., 113
digital,
   inclusion, 208
   infrastructure, 198, 208
   technologies, 202
   turn, 209
disability
   use of arm, 33
   blind and maimed musicians, 87
   soldiers, 86
disorder, 92, 96–7, 148, 185
drink
   ale, 104, 124
   coffee, 121, 122, 123, 126
   gin, 124
   milk, 122, 177
   tea, 113, 121, 122, 123, 125, 128
   wine, 50
Dunglinson, Daniel, workhouse master, Kendal, Westm., 78
Durrant, Ann, East Hoathly, Sussex, 25–6, 31–4, 36, 39, 42
Durrant, John, East Hoathly, Sussex, 25, 32
Durrant, Joseph, East Hoathly, Sussex, 43
Durrant, Robert, East Hoathly, Sussex, 36–7, 42
Durrant, Robert Argles, assistant overseer, Ringmer, Sussex, 155, 157–8

East Hoathly
   assistant overseer, 156
   charity, 9, 12, 38
   children in receipt of relief, 12, 37–9
   economy, 11
   expenditure on poor relief, 6, 39, 41, 51
   illegitimacy, 25–49
   management of unmarried motherhood, 49
   maintenance payments, 37–8, 42, 45
   marriage in, 40–1, 218
   medical attendance, 50
   numbers in receipt of relief, 12
   number of houses, 11
   overseer of the poor, 32,
   overseers' vouchers, 30, 50–1, 78, 81
   poor rate, 12, 40, 42–3
   poor relief, 12
   population, 11, 85
   rector, 35
   settlement in, 32, 36–7, 42, 44, 80
   sick poor, 192
   travellers, 83
   vestrymen, 30, 34, 38, 43
economic crises, 5, 6, 171
   impact on poor, 171–2

Index

economy
   local, 43, 48–9
   of makeshifts, 8, 57
   management, 46
Eden, Frederick Morton, 12, 18
Edge, John, 46
Edwards, Richard, Winchelsea, Sussex, 147
elderly, 1, 4, 10, 12, 217
Elliott, John, assistant overseer applicant, 152, 153
Eldridge, Susannah, 45
enabling legislation, 4, 9, 16
Essex, 97
Evenden, Mary, 44

family history, 198–9, 200–3, 214, 220
farming the poor, 3, 12, 15, 18. *See also* contractors of the poor
fathers of illegitimate children, 25, 27–8, 30–3, 36–9, 44–9, 90
Finch, John, assistant overseer, Ringmer, Sussex, 156
Finlinson, James (1783–1847), assistant overseer, Dalston, Cumb., 137, 145, 156, 164–5
Fletcher, Elizabeth, 93–4
food
   barley, 12, 122, 123, 129
   barm, 124
   beef, 34, 35, 127, 177
   bread, 12, 126
   butcher's meat, 129
   cardamom, 125
   flour, 42, 113, 122, 123, 125, 129
   ginger, 125, 126
   hasty pudding, 122
   mustard, 126
   mutton, 127
   oatmeal, 122, 125, 129
   pepper, 113, 122, 125, 129
   porridge, 122
   salt, 125

   sugar, 122, 123, 125, 129
   treacle, 122, 126, 129
   veal, 127
Forster, Joseph, grocer, Brampton, Cumb., 118, 119, 123, 130
Fothergill, Anthony, physician, 114
Fox, Ann, 46
Francis, Mary, coal dealer, Lichfield, Staffs., 116
French, Jeremiah, farmer, 34–5, 37, 43
friendship, 44, 143. 175–6
friendly societies, 8
Fuller, Joseph, 35, 43
Fuller, Thomas, 35, 40
Funnel, Will, brickmaker, 38

Garnett, Stephen, assistant overseer, Kirkby Lonsdale, Westm., 139, 156
General Data Protection Regulation (GDPR), 208
Gibbs, Sarah, pauper, 182, 188
Gilbert Unions, 4, 47
Gisborne, Rev., Thomas, 177
Gnosall, Staffordshire, 46
Goad, William, 33, 35
Godwin, Jane (1770–1852), innkeeper, Turk's Head, Lichfield, Staffs., 123–5, 128, 131–2
Goodwin, John, assistant overseer, Dymchurch, Kent, 150
Graham, Mary, grocer, Brampton, Cumb., 118, 123
grant funding, 210
Greystoke, Cumb.
   administration of poor relief, 13
   Advertisement for an Assistant Overseer, Greystoke, 1835, *149*
   Burn, Thomas, assistant overseer, 155
   farming the poor, 13
   applications for post of assistant overseer, 150
   poorhouse, 13
   poor relief, 9

231

size of parish, 12
textiles and clothing, 66, 73
townships and chapelries, 12–13
Wannup, John, assistant overseer, 156
Griffin Inn, Penrith, Cumb., 133–5
pre-printed bill for expenses at the Griffin Inn, Penrith, submitted to the overseers of Threlkeld, c.1800, *133*
grocers and tea dealers,
in Brampton, 112, 118, 119–23
in Carlisle, 120–1
in Lichfield, 112, 123
in Workington, 113
grocery prices, 130
Guy, Richard, brickmaker, 38
gypsies, 85–6, 88, 97

haberdashery, 68, 197
hairdressers, 112, 115
Hall, Jane, pauper, Dalston, Cumb., 165
Hall, Thomas, vagrant, 101
Halmarack, James, overseer, Madeley, Staffs., 142
Hannon, Mary, 101
Hart, Elizabeth, 46
harvest workers, 86–7
Haskol, Elizabeth, pauper, 180–1, 187, 191
Hayton near Brampton, Cumb.
Brown, Richard, assistant overseer, 155
contracting out of poor relief, 13
population, 6
provision of textiles, 67
Haywood, John, vagrant, 101
Hearnden, Isaac, 147
Hellingly, Sussex, 40–1
Henvill, Philip, curate, South Damerham, Wilts., 167–93
Hertfordshire, 46, 96

Hill, Anne (1748–1833), butcher and innkeeper, Lichfield, Staffs., 127–8
Hill, Reuben, Dursely, Glos., assistant overseer, 148
historians, 88–9, 102, 108, 130, 140, 167, 173, 175, 198, 215, 220
academic, 197–201, 211, 214–15, 223
family, 199–200, 214
local, 199–200, 214
history from below, 198
History Workshop Movement, 198
Holland, Sarah, Lichfield, Staffs., 115
Hook, Robert, shoe maker, Sussex, 32, 43
hop-pickers, 87–8
Hope, Richard, 44
Horton, Thomas, overseer, Darlaston, 101
houses of correction, 91, 93, 96
Hunter, John, pauper, Greystoke, Cumb., 13
Hutchinson, William, 13
Hyland, George, Laughton, Sussex, 31–4, 36, 39, 41–2

illegal trading, 113
impotent poor, 1
illegitimacy
children, 2, 12, 19, 27, 33, 35, 37–9, 41–6, 48, 89, 159
coerced marriage, 27, 33, 35, 41, 49
demographic change, 26
expenditure, 26, 41–2, 46, 49
maintenance payments, 19, 28, 31, 39, 42, 44–8
management, 26, 28–9, 35, 41–2, 46–7, 49
morality, 27
ratios, 25–7, 42, 45–6
regional variation, 27
settlement, 29–30, 32–3, 36–42, 44–5, 47, 49

Index

Instructions for Cutting Out Apparel for the Poor (1789), 67, 72
intellectual property rights, 208–9
Irthington, Cumb., number of surviving overseers' vouchers, 18
Isle of Ely, Cambridgeshire, 87
itinerant poor, 1, 2, 12

Jackson, Jeremiah, J.P., 86–7
Jobs, Joseph, 144
Jolliffe, Rev., Tovey, Skelton, Cumb., 177
Justice of the Peace, and Parish Officer (1755), 146

Keen, Anne (1771–1853), shoe dealer, Lichfield, Staffs., 117, 128
Kendal, Westm.
    Dunglinson, Daniel, workhouse governor, 78
    Sowerby, Sarah, workhouse inmate, 78
King's Bench, court of, 142
Kirkby Lonsdale, Westm.
    Garnett, Stephen, assistant overseer, 139, 156
    workhouse, 4
knowledge exchange, 211, 214
Knowledge Exchange Framework (KEF), 214

Lamesley, County Durham, 151–4
Lancashire, 4, 7, 88, 94, 98, 139
Lancaster, Joseph, assistant overseer, Wigton, Cumb., 156
Laughton, Sussex, 31–5
Laurence, David, assistant overseer, Winchelsea, Sussex, 156
Laws Respecting Parish Matters (1828), 146
Leek, William, assistant overseer, Lichfield, Staffs., 156, 161
Lewes, Sussex, 34, 38, 40, 48, 50
Lichfield, Staffs.,
    businessmen, 112, 125, 126
    businesswomen, 107, 108, 112, 115, 117, 123–8
    description, 14, 110
    Leek, William, assistant overseer, 156, 161
    occupations, 112
    relief given to travellers, 92
    population, 132
    Mendicity Society, 8
    parish of St Chad, 127
    parish of St Mary,
        Baker, Thomas, assistant overseer, 145
        cost of poor relief, 111
        numbers in receipt of relief, 111
        overseers' accounts, 18
        overseers' vouchers, 113, 115, 117
        provision of clothing, 73, 75
        provision of textiles, 62
        women supplying the parish, 108, 115–17, 123–8
    workhouse, 5
life writing, 203. *See also* biographies
Lincolnshire, 98
Ling (formerly Cain), Ann, 31, 45
Ling, Thomas, 31, 35
Littleton, Edward, 96
London, 59, 80, 84, 91–4, 98, 110, 134, 169
London Gazette, 120, 142
London Genuine Tea Company, 120–1
Longley, John, Hastings, Sussex, 144
Longtown, Cumb., 4
Lying-in, 34, 37, 47
Lyon, Samuel, assistant overseer, Alrewas, Staffs., 156, 159

magistrates, 3, 17, 28, 31, 37, 39, 87, 169, 101, 172, 177, 189, 191, 193, 220
    pauper appeals to, 220.

233

pauper examinations, 90, 93
Malbon, Elizabeth (c.1743–1801), pauper, Wednesbury, Staffs., 91–2, 103–4
Extract of an Overseers' Voucher for Darlaston, Staffordshire, showing ale for E. Malbourn's funeral, 1801, *104*
Manchester, proportion of women in business, 111
Marchant, James, tailor, East Hoathly, 51
Marlow, Edward, pauper, 181, 188, 191
Martin, Lydia, 97
Martin, Thomas, assistant overseer, Dalston, Cumb., 156, 160–1
Mayfield, Sussex, 48
Mayhew, Henry, 86
medicines, 42, 50
microeconomics, 43, 48
microhistories, 26
micro-politics of the parish, 29, 168, 171, 187–92
Middlesex, 92–3, 94, 97–8, 102
migration, 85, 98, 102
Millard, Mary, 101
Miller, Joseph, assistant overseer applicant, 152
milliners and dressmakers, 70, 112, 114, 121
Mills, Thomas, 101
morality and duty regarding the poor, 183–7
Museums, Libraries, and Archives Council (MLA), 210

National Co-ordinating Centre for Public Engagement, 214
Newcastle Courant, 151
Newell, Elizabeth, pauper, Yoxall, Staffs., 53
non-resident (out-parish) relief, 1, 21, 55, 56, 78, 85, 111
Norris, Thomas, assistant overseer, Uttoxeter, Staffs., 156, 162

Okeden, David, J.P., Dorset, 172, 192
Oliver, Sarah (1780–1832), grocer, Brampton, Cumb., 114, 120–1, 122, 123, 130
nursing, 42, 47
occupations, categorization, 206
Olney, Buckinghamshire, 88
outdoor relief, 2, 13, 14, 111, 182–3
overseers,
    appointment, 30
    accounts, 17–18, 19, 143, 188
    duties, 30–1, 37, 46, 83, 87, 101,143–4, 146
    misconduct, 17, 42, 48, 142, 158
    See also assistant overseers
overseers' vouchers, 15–16, 17–18, 20–2, 114–15
    absences, 26, 46, 198
    cataloguing, 197, 201–2, 205–6, 209
    contents, 18, 19, 20–1, 46, 53, 59–60,117, 120, 122, 124, 125, 127, 197
    copyright, 209
    extract showing ale for E. Malbourn's funeral, 1801, *104*
    handwriting, 20
    payment to Abel Rooker for half a year's contract, for Darlaston Workhouse, Staffordshire, 1822, *193*
    pre-printed, 20–1
    Pre-printed bill for expenses at the Griffin Inn, Penrith, submitted to the overseers of Threlkeld, c.1800, *133*
    preservation, 20, 223
    settlement, 29, 102
    survival rates, 18, 58, 113
    textiles, 53–79
    vagrants, 84–5, 94, 98–9, 101

Paine, Nathaniel, surgeon, Sussex, 50
pamphlets, 172–4

Index

A brief sketch of the state of the poor, 167–93
A brief statement of facts … in the treatment of the poor, 167–93
Papcastle, Cumb.
    provision of textiles, 65, 77, 79
Parkes, Mary, Sussex, 41
Parkes, Richard, Sussex, 39–41
parliamentary papers, *Abstract of the Poor* (1803–4), cost of poor relief in Brampton, Cumb., and Lichfield St Mary, Staffs., 111
parliamentary papers, *'Rural Queries'* (1832), 70, 150, 169
participatory,
    archival practice, 201, 211
    archives, 199, 210–11
    transcription, 200
    web, 199
Parton, Hannah, 46
Pearson, George, assistant overseer applicant, 153
pedlars, 86
Penrith, Cumb., 143
    pre-printed bill for expenses at the Griffin Inn, Penrith, submitted to the overseers of Threlkeld, *c*.1800, *133*
    Wilkinsons and the Griffin Inn, 133–5
phone app, 207
Pointon, William, vagrant, 101
Poole, William, 31
Poor Law Commission (1832–34), 47, 138, 145, 151, 160, 163
poor rate, 9, 29, 38, 42–3, 152, 171, 177–8. *See also individual parishes*
poor relief,
    and charity, 8–9, 178
    expenditure per capita, 5–6
    Christian views on, 175
    expenditure in Dorset, 172
    expenditure in Wiltshire, 172
    mismanagement, 174–84, 188
    national expenditure on, 171
    parochial wage subsidy, 48
    pensions, 2, 13, 18, 42, 86, 94, 104
    rent, paid for by the parish, 2, 8, 12, 13, 18, 88, 101
    tailored nature of, 13
    See also individual parishes
population, 26, 84
Porter, Rev., Thomas, East Hoathly, Sussex, 35, 39
potash, 125
Price, Henry, 101
Pringle, George, assistant overseer applicant, 154
Proctor, Robert, assistant overseer applicant, 152
Proud, Elizabeth, woollen cloth manufacturer, Hayton, Cumb., 61
public engagement, 197, 210, 212–13
public houses, 11, 33–5, 44, 112, 124
public history, 198–200, 211, 214–16, 224

Quakers (Society of Friends), 169, 175–6

Rabson, James, headborough, Laughton, Sussex, 32–3
ratepayers, 7, 9, 26, 29, 39, 44, 49, 138, 171, 172, 220
records management, 205
Research Excellence Framework, (REF), 210, 214
Revisiting Archive Collections, 210
Reynolds, Joseph, assistant overseer, Aldridge, Staffs., 156, 159
Ridge, Hertfordshire, 94
Ringmer, Sussex, 148, 155, 156
Robinson, Joseph, assistant overseer applicant, 154
Rock, William, 101

Rooker, Abel (1787–1867), surgeon, Darlaston, Staffs., 192–4
- Payment to Abel Rooker for half a year's contract, for Darlaston Workhouse Staffordshire, 1822, *193*

Routledge, John, workhouse master, Carlisle, Cumb., 143–4

Routledge, Ann (1807–81), grocer, Brampton, Cumb., 119–20

Routledge, Margaret (1799–1880), grocer, Brampton, Cumb., 119–20, 130

Routledge, Mary, grocer, Brampton, Cumb., 118, 119, 122

Routledge, Robert (d.1815), grocer, Brampton, Cumb., 119

Russel, Anne, pauper, 181

Rutter, John, Quaker and printer, Shaftesbury, Dorset, 167–93
- visits to workhouses, 183–4

Saint, John, overseer, Wednesbury, Staffs., 142

Saxby, Mary, 88

servant, 44

settlement
- examination, 28, 32, 39–40, 80, 90, 103, 217
- illegitimacy, 26, 28–30, 32–3, 36–7, 47, 90
- legal costs, 29, 91
- out-parish, 55–6
- policing, 33, 39, 41–2, 44, 47, 101
- removal, 29, 32, 37–8, 88, 96, 102
- system, 1–2, 102, 183
- vagrants, 84, 88–94, 98

Sewell, Elizabeth, grocer, Brampton, Cumb., 118, 123

Sewell, Jane, pauper, Skelton, Cumb., 2, 9, 15, 213

sexual reputation, 27

Shaftesbury, Dorset, 170, 174, 193, 179, 183
- John Rutter's observations of two poorhouses in Shaftesbury, 1819, *180*

Shenton, Rev. Paul, 35

shoemakers and dealers, *see* Anne Keen

shopkeepers, 8, 11, 22, 30, 43–5, 112, 114, 197

Skelton, Cumb.
- charity, 177
- provision of pauper clothing, 70, 73, 74
- See also, Preface

Slaney, J. P., John, 103

Small Bills project, 10–11, 15, 83–5, 91, 93, 97,101, 138, 140, 146, 150, 157, 163, 197–205, 207–9, 212–15, 217, 221–3

Smith, Samuel, 101

Smith, Sophia, 97

snuff, 122, 125

soap, 51, 122, 123

Sowerby, Sarah, pauper, Kendal Workhouse, 78

South Damerham, Wilts., 170, 179
- population, 179
- plight of poor, 179–80
- size of parish, 179

Sparrow, Thomas, 101

Staffordshire,
- clothing, 58, 70, 72, 78–9
- income from charitable bequests, 9
- industry, 14
- legal fees for poor law administration, 91
- overseers' vouchers, 53, 59, 62, 64–6, 75, 77
- percentage of assistant overseers, 141
- poor relief, 6, 9, 91. *See also individual parishes*
- population, 84–5
- removal expenditure, 91

Index

textiles, 62, 64, 66–8, 71
vagrants, 91–2, 94, 96, 101
Staffordshire Record Office, 201–3, 205, 212
Staples, John, J.P., Middlesex, 93
starch, 71, 122, 123, 125
statutes
    Bastard Children Act (1733), 28
    Data Protection Act (2018), 208
    Gilbert's Act (1782), 4, 19, 47, 162, 177
    Local Government (Records) Act (1962), 17
    Local Government Act (1894), 17
    Poor Relief Act (1744), 39
    Settlement Act (1662), 1
    Sturges Bourne Acts (1818–19), 127, 139, 141, 177
    Vagrancy Act (1744), 29, 90
    Vagrancy Act (1819), 96
    Vagrancy Act (1822), 96
    Workhouse Test Act (1723), 3, 177
Stevenson, Anne, 39–41
surgeons, 20, 50–1, 135, 140, 165, 192–4
surveyors of highways, 145, 156
Sussex,
    archival research volunteers, 203–4, 208, 212
    assistant overseers, 139, 141, 143, 145, 147–8, 150, 155–6, 160
    clothing, 54, 66, 79
    illegitimacy, 48–9
    income from charitable bequests, 9
    legal fees for poor law administration, 49, 91
    parishes, 47, 80
    percentage of assistant overseers in, 141
    poor relief expenditure, 88, 138
    removal expenditure, 91
    vagrants, 91–2, 96–9, 101
    workhouses, 47

See also East Hoathly
Swift, Susan, 25
Swing Riots, 148, 150

taxonomy, 206
Teaching Excellence and Student Outcomes Framework (TEF), 214
tenders for workhouse contracts, 129
Tester, Edward, assistant overseer, East Hoathly, Sussex, 156
textiles
    calico, 61, 64, 65, 66, 79
    check, 61, 62, 63, 68
    cloth, 55, 59, 60, 61, 62, 63, 64, 65, 66, 67, 69, 71, 72, 218, 219
    Coarse linen stays, 176–80, *74*
    corduroy, 66
    cotton, 61, 62, 64, 65, 66, 67, 75, 79, 219
    duffel, 61, 62, 63, 67, 68, 73, 77, 219
    flannel, 61, 63, 64, 65, 74, 77
    gingham, 64, 66
    harden, 60, 62, 67, 72
    hemp, 64, 65
    linen, 60, 61, 62, 63, 64, 65, 66, 67, 70, 71, 72, 74, 78, 79, 219
    plaid, 61, 62, 63, 68
    serge, 61, 63, 64, 65
    shrouds, 77
    stuff, 61, 62, 63, 64
    woollens, 61, 62, 64, 65, 66, 73, 79
    worsted, 61, 62, 75
Thatcham, Berkshire, 39
The National Archives (TNA), 211
Threlkeld, Cumb.
    clothing the poor, 75
    pre-printed bill for expenses at the Griffin Inn, Penrith, submitted to the overseers of Threlkeld, *c*.1800, *133*
    Sowerby, Sarah, pauper, 78

Thurnam, Charles, bookseller and printer, Carlisle, 21
Ticehurst, Sussex, 143
tobacco, 34, 113, 122, 123, 125
Tomkinson, William, vagrant, 101
travellers,
   drunken, 83
   Essex, 97
   Irish, 86, 91–2
   payments to, 18, 83, 92
   population size, 84–5
   Scottish, 92
   settlement, 84
   See also, vagrants
Trindle, Catherine, vagrant, 101
Trindle, Mary, vagrant, Mary, 101
Tull (formerly Vinal), Mary, 39
Tull, William, absent father, 38–9, 41
Turner, Thomas, diarist, shopkeeper and parochial officer, Sussex,
   business relationships, 43–4
   diarist, 11, 29, 37, 45, 47, 83,
   hop-picking, 38, 88
   legal fees, 31
   parish officer, 17, 19, 25, 30–5, 37–8, 40, 88
   unmarried motherhood, 25, 30–5, 44–5
   settlement, 36–7, 44
   shopkeeper, 11, 44, 50–1
   vestrymen, 42–3

Uckfield, Sussex, 32, 34, 37, 40
undeserving poor, 143, 148, 185
Uttoxeter, Staffs.,
   Gilbert's Act, 162
   Norris, Thomas, assistant overseer, 156, 162
   overseers' vouchers, 20
   pauper letters, 53, 76
   Wetton, Elizabeth, stationer and printer, 21

vagrants,
   contractor, 84, 90, 92
   distribution, 99–100
   expenditure, 91, 98
   gender balance, 98
   Irish, 93.96
   pass, 83
   policing, 94, 96–7
   punishment, 90–2, 96
   prosecution, 84
   removal, 88, 91, 94
   returns 1824, 98
   Scottish, 93, 96
   soldiers, 93
Verral, Edward, solicitors' clerk, 37
vestries,
   accountability, 17, 143, 144
   applications for relief, 152, 188
   Bolton, Lancs., 8
   businessmen, 43
   clergy, 169
   duties, 147, 177
   expenses, 19, 204
   Madeley, Staffs., 142
   meetings, 30, 44, 188–9
   minutes, 17, 46
   payments by, 41
   settlement system, 49
   vestrymen, 33, 42–3
   Wimborne Minster, Dorset, 178
Wharton, William, vagrant, 101
Vinal, Mary, 39–40, 45
Vinal, Richard, 39–40
Vinal, Sarah, 38, 41, 45
Vinal, William, 38
volunteers, archival research
   biographies, research and writing, 121, 200–1, 204, 212
   collaborative working, 197, 200–2, 209–12, 215
   consultation, 201, 205
   data collection, 205–9
   diversity, 203, 208

Index

groups, 203
intellectual property rights, 208
recruitment, 203, 214
specialist knowledge, 203–4, 212, 214
upskilling, 204, 212
well-being, 204, 214
workshops, 204

Waldron, Sussex, 36–8, 41–2
Walker, Anne (1772–1832), grocer, Lichfield, Staffs., 123, 125–6
Waltham, John, Abbots Bromley, Staffs., 18
Wannup, John, overseer, Greystoke, Cumb., 142, 156
Warrington (later Malbon), Elizabeth, pauper, 103–4
Watford, John, 33, 35, 43
Wednesbury
  cost of poor relief, 14
  Malbon, Elizabeth, pauper, 92, 103–4
  numbers in receipt of outdoor relief, 14
  population, 14
  provision of pauper clothing, 69
  provision of textiles, 64, 65, 67, 72
  workhouse, 14
Wetton, Elizabeth, stationer and printer, Uttoxeter, Staffs., 21
Wetton, John, assistant overseer, Colwich, Staffs., 156
Whitechapel, Middlesex, 93
Whitehaven, Cumb., population, 12
WiFi connectivity, 208
Wigton, Cumb.
  Buttery, William, assistant overseer, 155, 162
  Lancaster, Joseph, assistant overseer, 156
  provision of pauper clothing, 74, 75
  provision of textiles in, 62, 63, 72

Wilkinson, Julia (1768–1824), innkeeper, Griffin Inn, Penrith, Cumb., 133–4
Wilkinson, Thomas, assistant overseer applicant, 153
Wilson, John, assistant overseer, Brampton, Cumb., 156, 159
Wimborne Minster, Dorset, select vestry, 178
Winlaton, County Durham, 152
Wolstanton, Staffordshire, 104
women
  business owners, 107–32
  pregnancy, 27, 40, 44, 47
  unmarried motherhood, 25–8, 30, 38, 42, 46, 48–9
  widows, 30, 103
Woodward, Thomas, grocer, Lichfield, Staffs., 125, 126
Woolgar, Thomas, pauper, 43, 50
workhouses
  abscond from, 87
  accommodation, 3, 4, 177
  Advertisement for a Master and Mistress of St Mary's Workhouse, Carlisle, 1785, *149*
  discharged paupers, 87
  governors, 145, 156, 161–2, 164
  illegitimate children, 48
  matrons, 164
  resident of, 101
  scandal, 176
  unmarried mothers, 47
  See also, individual parishes
Workington, Cumb., population, 12
Worrall, Richard, 46
Wren, William, 152
Wrotham St George, Kent, 143, 144

Yoxall, Staffs., 53, 75

Zooniverse, 199

Lightning Source UK Ltd.
Milton Keynes UK
UKHW022313220922
409280UK00001B/3